REDNECK BOY in the PROMISED LAND

REDNECK BOY in the

THE CONFESSIONS

PROMISED LAND

OF "CRAZY COOTER"

BEN JONES

Harmony Books
NEW YORK

Published in the United States by Harmony Books, an imprint of the Crown Publishing Group, a division of Random House, Inc., New York.
www.crownpublishing.com

Harmony Books is a registered trademark and the Harmony Books colophon is a trademark of Random House, Inc.

Grateful acknowledgment is made to Scribner and the Estate of Thomas Wolfe for permission to reprint an excerpt from *Look Homeward Angel,* copyright © 1929 by Charles Scribner's Sons, copyright renewed 1957 by Edward C. Aswell, Administrator C.T.A. Estate of Thomas Wolfe and/or Fred W. Wolfe. All rights reserved. Reprinted by permission of Scribner, an imprint of Simon & Schuster Adult Publishing Group, and the Estate of Thomas Wolfe, Eugene H. Winick, Administrator C.T.A.

Second photo insert, page 7: (bottom) Sherryl Lockett.
All photos unless otherwise noted: Courtesy of Jones & Viator Inc.

Library of Congress Cataloging-in-Publication Data

Jones, Ben, 1941 Aug. 30–
Redneck boy in the promised land : the confessions of "Crazy Cooter" / Ben Jones.—1st ed.
1. Jones, Ben, 1941 Aug. 30– 2. Legislators—United States—Biography. 3. United States. Congress. House—Biography. 4. Southern States—Biography. 5. Television actors and actresses—United States—Biography. 6. Alcoholics—United States—Biography. 7. Recovering alcoholics—United States—Biography. 8. Southern States—Social conditions—1945– I. Title.
E840.8.J614A3 2008
328.092—dc22 2007041046

ISBN 978-0-307-39527-6

Printed in the United States of America

Design by Lynne Amft

10 9 8 7 6 5 4 3 2 1

First Edition

To Alma

You are all that
There is of life
For me.
All that I want.
All that I need.

You are the light of dawn and
The endless night of the silent stars.
Each day with you is a dazzle
Of waterfalls and rainbows, of
Silver moonbeams on the Blue Ridge.

Nature's royalty bows to your grace.
You, my little country girl.
All that there is of life for me.

Contents

Part Two

WAY DOWN DRUNK IN DIXIE

Part Three

OUT OF THE HORRIBLE PIT, OUT OF THE MIRY CLAY

Part Four
THE MOST UNLIKELY CANDIDATE

Part Five
PARADISE FOUND

Prologue: Miracle on the Mall

It was winter for certain in Washington, D.C., on January 20, 1989. Though the temperature was up in the mid-thirties, a brisk river wind slid off the Potomac, whirled down the National Mall, and hammered on the doors of the United States Capitol. It was partly cloudy, but there was no snow in the forecast, so it was a fine day for a presidential inauguration. In the chambers of the House of Representatives, the members of the 101st Congress, given to the great matters of the world, were attempting to form a simple line in order to proceed to the inaugural ceremony of George H.W. Bush, soon to be the forty-first president of the United States of America.

By tradition, the procession was to be formed by seniority. The longest-serving member of the House at that time was Representative James Whitten of Mississippi. Mr. Whitten had won a special election in the fall of 1941, and had been in the chambers on December 8 of that year to hear Franklin Roosevelt's "Day of Infamy" speech. So Jamie went first.

Representative Claude Pepper of Florida was near the front. Claude had been elected to the U.S. Senate in 1936, had lost his seat in 1950 to George Smathers in the infamous "Red Pepper campaign," but then had been elected to the House in 1963. He had told off Adolf Hitler in Germany in the thirties and was a good friend of Orville Wright, who flew the first airplane. Now eighty-eight years old, he was still the best orator in the body.

A few other members stood on ceremony and claimed their correct chronological place, but in the best American tradition the rest of us said "to hell with it" and just fell in with friends wherever we felt like it.

And there I was, freshman congressman Ben Jones, Democrat of Georgia, taking my place near the back of the line for the ceremonial walk to the West Front of the Capitol. We looked like a bunch of schoolkids heading out for a snowball fight at recess, covered with earmuffs, stocking caps, mittens, scarves, and overcoats.

We slowly made our way down the ornate hallways of marble, under the crystal chandeliers, past stained-glass windows and the bronze and granite statues of the storied men and women who had walked these same hallways before us.

As we stepped outside and took our seats in the temporary bleachers behind the podium, I was immediately struck by the size of the crowd. More than 150,000 people filled the Mall in front of us. Behind us, the Capitol was covered with red, white, and blue bunting and draped with American flags fifty feet high.

I had campaigned for two and a half years to win Georgia's Fourth District Congressional seat, and it had been an uphill fight all the way. It had gotten a lot of press attention, mostly for the wrong reasons. Dan Rather of CBS had called it "by far the meanest and nastiest race in America" and the *Washington Post* agreed. After what I had been through, I figured ol' Dan had understated the case. Politics down in Georgia is a full-contact sport.

Winning had been a very heady experience, and being sworn in was an exciting time. But it was all dreamlike, as if I were in a movie and none of this was quite real. Between the hard work, the pressure, and the excitement, it seemed I had somehow gotten out of touch with my emotions. Weeks had passed, but I still felt like I was in an extraordinary world that was not quite attached to reality. The full emotional impact of what had gone down in my life had not come home to me yet.

Then the U.S. Senate filed out and took their places next to us. The Supreme Court came out and took seats down front. Looking west down the Mall, I could see the Washington Monument and the Lincoln Memorial. I thought of my friends whose names were memorialized just by there on the Vietnam Wall. A choir somewhere above us sang the haunting "Shenandoah." President Elect and Mrs. Bush came out. President and Mrs. Reagan came out. Then the U.S. Marine Band played a stirring rendition of "America the Beautiful."

Right along in there, I started to get back in touch with my feelings. I remembered a line my mama quoted so often: "Breathes there the man with a soul so dead, who never to himself has said, 'This is my own, my native land!' "

And I thought of how far removed this moment was from my days growing up, a barefoot boy in a primitive railroad shack down on the docks of Tidewater Virginia.

The Reverend Billy Graham said a prayer. Then George Bush the Elder took the oath and Ronald Reagan took his leave, and America celebrated another peaceful transition of government, the quiet passing of power that has marked our nation's 230 years of trial and triumph.

As the giant crowd dispersed to Pennsylvania Avenue for the traditional Inaugural Parade, I stayed on in the emptying grandstand to savor the moment a bit longer. I felt like the most fortunate son of a gun who ever drew breath. I was filled at that moment with a feeling of deliverance, a sense of enormous blessing, and the firm belief that I stood there as a walking, talking miracle of the Grace of God.

You see, my road to the halls of Congress was an unlikely one. In fact, most folks who had known me twelve years before wouldn't have bet on me living much longer. I was just about dead then: physically, mentally, and spiritually. I was a rough and rowdy redneck who loved living on the edge of the cliff. Unlike my "Distinguished Colleagues," I had spent a whole lot of my time in jails and on the street.

I had been arrested for drunkenness, disorderly conduct, drinking in public, resisting arrest, criminal trespass, assault, and assaulting an officer. Many times I had "come to" in jail not having the faintest idea of how I had gotten there. And there was the more serious stuff that I didn't get busted for. Stuff that could have put me away for a long, long time.

Then came the morning of September 26, 1977, when I was dying of acute alcohol poisoning and delirium tremens on a filthy floor down in Atlanta. At the end of a five-week drunken blackout bender I was in horrible agony, in a terrifying place down below the darkest, hottest pits of hell.

But here I was just eleven years later, internationally famous as "Cooter" on the hit TV show *The Dukes of Hazzard,* and now the "Honorable" Mr. Jones of Georgia. Being there that day was evidence of a personal transformation that only a loving God could shape.

I felt it to my bones. And then this barefoot boy from the railroad shack stood on the Capitol steps in my tailored pinstriped suit and cried.

Part One

The SINGING COWBOY of SUGAR HILL

Everything Is Purple and Gray and Covered with Soot

Hey, what the hell kinda deal is this?! Everything is painted purple and gray, there is soot and cinders all over everything, and overhead gigantic silver dirigibles are flying around. There are freight trains clanging and banging in the front yard, and ships the size of skyscrapers are cruising by. Most folks I see have darker skin than mine. It smells like collards and sweat and cigars, and what's that I hear? Off somewhere, across the water that is all around me, a bugler is playing "Taps." I live in the country in the middle of cotton and peanuts and corn, but this is all surrounded by a city of eighty thousand people. I'm two years old and I'm asking you: What the hell kinda deal is this?!

Well, it really was that way for us. We lived in a railroad section house that looked out to a busy freight yard on the docks of Portsmouth, Virginia. But where we lived there was no neighborhood, no sidewalks, and no busy city streets; instead there were scrubby woods and plowed fields and marsh grass. You see, my father was the cigar smokin', tobacco chewin', whiskey drinkin' section foreman there for the Atlantic Coast Line Railroad, and my mama raised four boys in that big ol' shack.

Large railroads are divided into sections. The section foreman is responsible for the maintenance of a particular section of track. In those days, most railroads provided company houses on company land by the tracks for their employees. These were called "section houses." Most were well constructed, though many were quite old. But all of them lacked "conveniences."

Well, if it was primitive, my brothers and I didn't know it. You don't miss what you never had.

The one-lane road that ran along the tracks was called Harper Street. It was made of burnt cinders from the coal-fired steam locomotives around the rail yard. The engines produced clouds of thick black smoke all day long, and that soot settled everywhere: in the yard, on the house, and on Mama's wash out on the clothesline.

The house seemed to have been plopped from above into a field between the freight yard and Scott's Creek, a tidal inlet off of Hampton Roads, down where the James River meets the Chesapeake Bay and the Atlantic. The place was perched atop ten stacks of bricks about two feet off the ground. When Atlantic storms came on their howling visits, the old shack would sway and creak like a boat at sea, but would always settle back soft and easy on the brick piles. At one time, there were two scraggly Chinaberry trees in the yard. After a hurricane came through once, there was only one very scraggly Chinaberry tree in the yard. The rusting tin roof always hung on tight.

The only plumbing in the house was a cold-water spigot in the kitchen. Our bathroom was a "double-seater" outhouse over the creek, reached by a short bridge, and flushed by the outgoing tide. Two seats hardly did the job for my parents and me and my two older brothers, "Buck" and "Bubba." They called me "Buster."

We had no electricity then. Our world was lit by kerosene, and our entertainment was provided by battery-powered radios, windup Victrolas, and above all by Mama's beautiful singing voice. Royal Purple and Silver Gray were the official colors of the Atlantic Coast

Line Railroad. The section houses were all painted purple and gray, as were the depots, station houses, yard towers, toolsheds, roundhouses, shops, and as I could daily verify, so were the outhouses.

The paint crew appeared every five years or so to slap on another coat of gray over the sooty outer walls, trim it with purple, and seal the whole deal with a large black stencil next to the front porch marking the date of their work: **8/44.**

Across the tracks, on the north side of the train yard, was the now vanished dockside community of Pinners Point. But our nearest neighbors lived in Sugar Hill, a black neighborhood just up the road on "our side of the tracks." The men who made up my father's "section gang" lived in Sugar Hill.

The world I came into was at war, and Hampton Roads was crucially vital to the Allied effort. After Pearl Harbor, tens of thousands of Americans poured into Norfolk and Portsmouth to work at the Naval Shipyard in Portsmouth, the Norfolk Naval Base, and the Oceana Naval Air Station. The Atlantic Fleet was stationed at the Naval Base, and the world's largest warships cruised past Pinners Point on their way to the Shipyard. The streets of Norfolk and Portsmouth were filled with young sailors in their bell bottom whites, raising a little hell before their next deployment into the North Atlantic.

German U-Boats posed a constant threat off the Virginia coast, and mammoth U.S. Navy blimps floated overhead on a constant lookout for the Nazi submarines.

Troop trains shuttled through the freight yards as military personnel shipped out of Hampton Roads for the European front. P-38 fighters, B-25 bombers, and enormous cargo planes called "flying boxcars" crisscrossed the Tidewater skies.

"Us boys" studied silhouettes of all the aircraft and considered it our duty to identify and report any suspicious shapes in the sky. I was a four-year-old plane spotter.

And on quiet evenings, just at dusk, the sound of "Taps" would waft on the salt breezes of Scott's Creek as the bugler on the Naval Hospital grounds across the way sounded the sunset call. Then, at nine P.M. every night, the whole town would shake to the sound of the "Nine O'Clock Gun," a traditional cannon firing by the Marines at the Shipyard.

I have a vivid early memory of a Sears and Roebuck truck delivering a new Silvertone Console Battery Radio to our place. When I mentioned that to my mama in the 1970s she seemed surprised because I was not quite three years old when that happened. But she knew the exact date of the delivery. How could she have forgotten June 6, 1944? That was D-Day.

I also have memories of the coastal blackouts. With the German subs off the coast silently watching the movement of Allied shipping, every few weeks the Civil Defense whistles would call for "all lights out!" My father would go out into the dark with his best flashlight in hand and report to his railroad position. With the shades pulled down and the lamps blown out, we would wait in the orange glow of the round dial on that Silvertone Radio for the "all clear" signal.

Mama an' 'Nim

There is an expression that you will hear in the American South and nowhere else on the planet. A person will tell you that they are going to see "Mama an' 'Nim." The translation for Yankees and others is that they are going home to visit family; they are going to see "Mama and them." It comes out as one word, *mama-annim.* This is about mama-annim.

I took my first train ride at the age of three weeks, away from Tarboro, North Carolina, where I was born, up to Sugar Hill, which was to be home for nineteen years. Railroading is a family tradition with us. My father started working on his father's track gang when he was thirteen, carrying water and kegs of spikes to the crew. My mother's father, Daniel Stephens, was also an Atlantic Coast Line track man, as was one of her older brothers.

By the time my father was fifteen, he was the size of a bear and damn near as strong, and he was working on the railroad full-time, putting down crossties, swinging a twelve-pound sledge-hammer, driving spikes, laying in the rail, and building a reputation as one of the toughest steel-driving men on the Coast Line. They called him "Big Buck." In the South, the track gangs were made up almost entirely of black men, but among those giants of strength and fortitude, my father was a legend in his time. He also started drinking cheap whiskey when he was thirteen, and I heard tales from some of the old railroad men that after the evening whistle blew, he won many a drink by wagering that he could lift a pair of boxcar wheels up off the track by himself. My old man loved his whiskey so much that he never lost that bet. Within a few years he was made foreman, and the section gang that he supervised called him "Cap'n." They knew that he had come up the hard way, as they had, and for that he always had their loyalty.

He was old school. His father had been born in rural North Carolina before the Civil War, and when my dad was born in Nansemond County, Virginia, in 1909, little had changed since 1860. The South had reacted to its bitter defeat and the Reconstruction period by passing Jim Crow laws, establishing a strict code of "white supremacy," and resisting any sort of social progress. Yes, slavery had been abolished, but most blacks and many whites lived in a kind of economic slavery, where the ceiling of aspiration was set very low. The war had devastated the South, and when it was over there was no Marshall Plan for rebuilding the defeated nation. As my Uncle Hamp Stephens told me, "Nobody had nothing back then."

Daddy's rules were simple. He was the boss, he was never wrong, when he wanted something it should be brought to him, and if he were displeased there could be psychic hell to pay. Around the house, he was King Baby, ruling with scowls and grunts. None of us dared cross him and risk his wrath. Like a lot of men of his generation, he thought the expression of tender emotions to be a great sign of weakness, and he had great difficulty communicating any sensitivity. The funny thing was we could sense his kinder feelings, even as we could sense him simultaneously trying to stifle them.

His past was a great mystery to me. And so was most of his

present. He never spoke of his childhood, his parents, his schooling, his early years on the railroad, and certainly never of his feelings toward his wife and children. There were no old letters from family. There were no stories that began "One time me and a friend of mine . . ."

He did have an old tattoo on his left forearm that simply said "M.T." I asked him once what that meant. "Like your head," he said. "EMM-TEE."

He could be funny like that. He had a sense of irony and a brittle dry wit, but Daddy had a "NO TRESPASSING" sign in his head. He was the least forthcoming man I've ever known.

That was the sober father. The drunk father was another story. Booze was daddy's greatest pleasure, and his favorite pastime. My father was what is called a "weekend" alcoholic. His drinking habits changed over the years, but back in the 1940s and the early 1950s the pattern was consistent. He wouldn't touch a drop during the week, and made sure that everyone knew that. But we could tell that he couldn't wait for that whistle to blow on Friday afternoon so he could catch up for lost time. He then drank pint after pint of Four Roses blended whiskey, and chased it down with High Rock Ginger Ale. And right before us his personality would change as inevitably as Dr. Jekyll would become Mr. Hyde.

Then, as night fell, he would often throw a temper tantrum and storm out to do some serious drinking with friends. We never knew where he was going, but we were all relieved to see him go. A brief silence would settle in while we recovered from his verbal assaults, but soon the house would hum with the sounds of the Silvertone bringing us the world. We were big on Jack Benny, Amos and Andy, Fibber McGee and Molly, The Great Gildersleeve, and Spike Jones.

Saturday morning Daddy was up and at it early. By the time us younguns were up, he was already schnockered, Mama was already completely stressed out, and we all went into the automatic bunker mentality of our survival instincts. Saturdays were the worst.

A flashback: It is a Saturday morning in 1945, maybe 1946. I am four or five years old. I follow my father to the back porch, where there is an icebox. The iceman comes by once or twice a week and checks the ice sign in our kitchen window. It is a square placard with a number on each of the square's four sides: 10, 25, 50, 100. The number turned to the top is the amount he leaves. In summer a block of at least 50 pounds sits in the bottom of the icebox.

I cannot remember a time when my father did not chase his whiskey with High Rock Ginger Ale. But on this particular morning, after he pulls a slug from the pint of Four Roses, he lifts a large clear bottle of golden liquid and chases the whiskey with that. It is bubbly, it is foamy, it is beautiful. There is a picture of a lovely girl on the bottle; she sits in a swing. I am fascinated by this new thing. My father sees my interest and jokingly says, "You want a sip?" "Yessir!" I take the quart bottle of Miller High Life Beer and drink. My father expects me to spit it out as bitter, or at least to make a disgusted frown. I do neither. I smile and say, "That was good. Thank you, Daddy!"

That was sixty years ago, and I remember the moment and the taste with great clarity. I think I understood even then that it might have something to do with destiny.

On Sunday mornings us boys had our weekly bath. Mama would heat up some water on the woodstove and pour it in a galvanized washtub and we would take turns. Buck was the oldest, so he went first. Bubba went next and he was usually the dirtiest. Being the youngest, I went last and by the time it was my turn the water was a muddy brown. I dreaded Mama scrubbing out my filthy ears with a washrag. But that was a regular part of the drill.

Once we were relatively clean, we put on our best clothes and walked the mile or so up the tracks to the Port Norfolk Baptist Church for Sunday School. I liked it there. And one time, walking back on a sweet spring morning, my older brothers just ahead of me, I felt a great presence beside me. I had never felt so good before and would not feel that good again for many years. I thought it was Jesus. And I still do.

Mama sometimes went to church, but mostly she read her Bible and tried to live by the instructions in it. She succeeded at that far more than most of those folks who wear their religion on their sleeve.

Daddy's idea of church was to listen to about a half-hour of gospel music on the radio before his first slug of Four Roses. After a big Sunday dinner in the afternoon he would taper off, and then hit the sack early for another week of work. It was like another war was over.

Daddy and Mama both came from big Southern families, and both sides were farmers and railroaders. My father's family was English and Welsh, but Mama's family was a little bit of everything. She had American Indian blood on both sides of her family, plus Irish, Scots-Irish, French Huguenot, and one branch that the U.S. Census just referred to as "nonwhite" for several decades. It was like they couldn't exactly figure out what breed of cats we were, but they were damn sure we weren't "white folks." One of Mama's grandmothers was a full-blood Tuscarora, so Mama was a "quarter-blood," and I am one-eighth Native American. Actually, it's a bit higher than that, because there was another Indian stream in there, too. But I really don't much care. I identify myself as a Southerner. Other folks identify me as a "redneck." Fine with me. It is also very possible that the "nonwhite" folks were descendants of Matthew Jacobs, a "free black" from that neck of woods.

Mama had a hard life in a lot of ways. She was the youngest girl in a family of thirteen. Her name was Ila Virginia Stephens, but everyone called her "Ila V." Her father had worked his way up to a very good job on the railroad by 1931. He was a Roadmaster, overseeing the work of a number of "sections." Then, just as the Depression was beginning to hit the hardest, he died suddenly of a heart attack after giving a speech in Rocky Mount, North Carolina.

The family savings were lost in a bank that suddenly closed. There was no Federal Deposit Insurance in those days. Neither was there Social Security nor any other emergency benefits. So Mama and her family, like millions of other Americans, went from relative comfort to abject poverty in a matter of months. Then her older sister Lessie, a popular local singer, died suddenly and tragically. The bank foreclosed on the mortgage to their home. After shuttling around to different relatives and friends, the railroad let them stay in an empty section house in Tarboro. Mama often talked of the shame she felt when she had to start high school there without any shoes.

Shortly after that my father showed up to become the section foreman in Tarboro. By right, the section house was his. But he just took a small room in the house and let Mama's folks stay on.

Daddy's railroad reputation preceded him. He was a man's man and a lady's man, and when he wasn't drunk, he was a gentleman. It wasn't long before he and Ila V. were a couple.

In 1935 Mama's mother took ill. One night, Mama noticed that her mother's favorite rocking chair in the living room seemed to be rocking by itself. She went in to her bedroom to see her and found that she had passed away.

When they got hitched, Daddy was twenty-six and Mama was seventeen. For the next fifty-six years, Mama held the whole deal together.

The Geography of the Boxcars

I could learn a lot just walking to school. I had just turned six when I started at the two-room schoolhouse across the tracks in Pinners Point.

Actually, there were four rooms, but the two upstairs were never used, and we were forbidden to go near them. Of course, we went up there at every opportunity, but with cowardly caution, for if we were caught, we would be punished by Miss Mattie Wooster. Miss Wooster taught third and fourth grades, and we were all afraid of her, even the "big boys," those twelve-year-old fourth-graders who had been held back a time or two. My older brothers had come through her class for two years, and the stories they told made my blood run cold. Now, Mattie Wooster was probably a sweet old spinster with a sad past, but to this day I don't care what traumas she had endured. We hadn't done anything to her and she treated us like prisoners of war. She had only one punishment and she loved to administer it. She would take the offender into the hallway between the rooms, grab him up by an ear, and wash his mouth out with Boraxo Soap. I became the best-behaved boy in the history of the school.

Even attending the school had its hazards. In the first grade I was running at recess, tripped, and cut myself on a rusty tin can. I had to get stitches and a tetanus shot. In the second grade, I was running again when Big Pete Jackson came around the corner of the building going full tilt on his bike. I collided with the bolt in the center of his handlebars and was knocked dizzy. The reason Pete was going so fast was that he was being pursued by a swarm of mad hornets. The hornets descended on me. Another shot. In third grade, we were waiting to go downtown to see "The Train of Tomorrow," an event I had waited for all year. At that moment I got bit by a dachshund and had to go to the doctor again. By the time fourth grade rolled around, I was shell-shocked.

To get to school I had to go by the Pinners Point Colored School, then I had to cross the busy freight yard and walk through the Pinners Point neighborhood, past Yelverton's Grocery and Shack's Dry Goods and Sundries. I soon found out that in this case "sundries" meant "Miller High Life Beer."

I would pass the rowdy Daniels house and Hank Lauterbach's Hydroplane Shop, past Marty Brennaman's house and on up Hill Avenue to school. Miss Louise Clayton taught first and second grades and she was as benign as Mattie Wooster was not.

One day after school as I started to cross the rail yard back over to the Sugar Hill side, a couple of kids started teasing me and calling me a "nigger." "Sugar Hill nigger, Sugar Hill nigger!" they chanted. When I got home I asked Mama what a "nigger" was.

"That's a bad word," she said. "Don't ever use that word."

"What's it mean?"

"That's what stupid people call colored people."

"Am I a nigger?"

"No," she said. "And I told you not to use that word!"

But I felt different every time I started across those tracks for home. All the other houses I had been in had electric lights and bathrooms and even telephones. They had backyards with flower gardens and they had sidewalks that led down to playgrounds that had ball fields with backstops.

Yep, I was different. Those poor chumps just had backyards, but I had whole fields to play in, woods to explore, marsh reeds and cattails to muck about in, wrecked boats, washed up bottles with notes in them, a crabbing pier out back on the water, a chicken yard, dogs running free, and plenty of room to play ball and shoot BB guns and fly kites. Other kids had little pissant electric trains, but in my front yard was the real deal, real locomotives with real engineers, and coal cars and tank cars and gondolas and a gazillion boxcars and red cabooses everywhere. I was different alright. Why was I the lucky one?

I learned a lot about railroading just by always being in the middle of it. How switches work, what brakeman did, and the difference between a freight conductor and a passenger conductor. I was told how local trains were "made up," what the whistle signs were, what was meant by "deadheading," what the flagman's signals meant, and how to hop a train. The boxcars were how I learned American geography. Walking along beside the trains I would read: "Louisville and Nashville," "Lackawanna Valley," "The Rock Island Line," "The Atchison, Topeka, and Santa Fe." So I kept my nose in the big Railroad Directory, which had maps and timetables for all the lines. For what it was worth, I was the only kid in the Pinners Point School who knew where Atchison, Kansas, was. When I saw a rail line I hadn't seen before, say "Aberdeen and Rockfish," before dark I would know the names of all the towns between those faraway places.

When I was about eight years old, I figured I could hop a train and ride the rails to any place in the forty-eight states for free. And I could have, too. Only problem was, what does an eight-year-old boy with no money do when he gets there?

Where Rail Meets Sail by the City Jail

I want to go back home to Portsmouth
In the Old Dominion State
Where rail meets sail by the city jail
And High Street runs into the ferry gate
I want to stroll with my sweetie
In the springtime
And when that Navy Yard Gun goes 'Boom'!
I'll know I'm right back home
Where I belong
In Portsmouth, Vee-A

—ERNEST K. EMURIAN

Then there were those memorable Saturday mornings when us Jones boys, Buck, Bubba, and Buster, would go to downtown Portsmouth on our own. In the late 1940s that trip was the height of cultural experience for us runny-nosed younguns. We would walk up the cinder road to Lee Avenue, the first paved road we would come to. There by the railroad crossing, next to the "Colored" barbershop, was the Sugar Hill bus stop. The bus ride took us past the Pinners Point Colored School, past a large trash dump by the Belt Line Railroad Yard, through the little neighborhood of Shea Terrace, and on toward High Street, the main drag in Portsmouth. We would pass Woodrow Wilson High School and see Portsmouth Stadium, the home of the Portsmouth Cubs of the Class B Piedmont League. Then we would go through a black neighborhood on High Street, and along the thriving black business district we called "Uptown," centered around the Lyric Theatre, which featured "Negro Westerns" for their Saturday matinees. One that played there was called *The Bronze Buckaroo.*

When we crossed Effingham Street, everything turned a shade whiter. It always seemed to me that folks overlooked the fact that segregation was, in many ways, very integrated. As much as the white power structure tried to separate the races, the fact remained that we were all around one another just about all the time: on the street, at work, and in the stores. Blacks shopped at the white-run downtown stores, and we could certainly shop at the "Uptown" stores if we wished to. But custom and law denigrated the black folks by making them sit in the back of the bus, by denying them service in "white" restaurants and hotels, and by sending them to so-called "separate but equal" schools. (Even as a little kid I wondered, "Hey, if they are so equal, why are they separate?")

But in those days, though the race issue was all around us, we rarely thought about it. It just *was.* Besides, we had more pressing matters on our minds. Our aim was to get to the Virginia Theatre for the Saturday matinee and get a good seat for the previews, the newsreel, the cartoons, the serial, and the double-feature Westerns. All that for a quarter, and they threw in a U.S. Army patch as a door gift. "Co-colas" were a nickel, and a bag of buttered popcorn big enough for all three of us was a dime.

The Virginia was dank and dim but always packed on Saturdays.

As kids pelted one another with spitballs and wads of candy wrappers, an occasional rat would scurry across the foot of the stage in front of the screen to great applause.

The previews were generally sappy, grown-ups doing grown-up stuff, most of which was incomprehensible to me. The newsreel seemed dramatic and serious and important, and most of that was incomprehensible to me also. At the end of the newsreel, though, would be a lighthearted piece about the Soap Box Derby or some guy jumping off a building with homemade wings and busting his can.

The serials were usually exciting and if you had missed the week before they would catch you up and show you how Batman or whoever had ended up hanging from that limb on that cliff. The top cartoons at the Virginia Theatre were Woody Woodpecker and Mighty Mouse. If you wanted Disney stuff, Mickey or Donald, you had to go to the Commodore Theatre or to the Gates. Not only could we not afford that, but what five-year-old wants to see John Agar or Veronica Lake in some thing where all they do is talk for two hours??

Then the first Western would start, almost always out of focus, and we would all holler and hiss until the projectionist got it right. It happened so often I thought it was part of the show, a ritual that couldn't be missed.

The first film was usually half-baked, with some second-tier cowboy like Sunset Carson or Whip Wilson on a cheesy back lot riding a horse like he was half in the bag. Whip would win the day with his bullwhip, snapping the villain's gun away in a heartbeat, then coldcocking him with a roundhouse right that clearly missed by a foot and a half. Now the screen became the target for the spitballs and candy wrappers.

The next feature, however, was big-time stuff. A "real" movie. There were a lot of cinema cowpokes that made "real movies" in those days, with plenty of horses and extras, big brawls, and an actual musical score. Johnny Mack Brown, The Durango Kid, Lash LaRue,

Red Ryder, and Hopalong Cassidy were all fine if you just wanted to pass the time.

But none of them was in a league with the two giants of the Saturday screens, Roy Rogers and Gene Autry, both of whom laid claim to the title "The King of the Cowboys."

I was an Autry man myself, and my loyalty was pure and is undiminished even today. He was a deceptively talented guy who just seemed to be standing around being himself. But Gene's persona projected earnestness, compassion, and a humble nature that made him seem like a guy you could know.

I felt like I knew him. One time Mama had taken me to Norfolk, across the river on a big orange ferry, and we had walked a long way to the Norfolk Arena. I was maybe four years old and there I was in the same place as Gene, looking at him real. He came riding out on Champion, right out onstage, and as the Wonder Horse reared up, Gene waved his white hat as us kids went wild.

He could sing, too, and what we didn't know at the time was that he probably wrote those songs, owned the music publishing company, had produced the films, had in fact cast Gabby or Curly or Smiley or whoever the comic sidekick was, and had already cut deals with the theater chains for personal appearances. Gene Autry was one smart ol' cowpuncher.

Something else was at work in those stuffy, smelly movie houses. The reason we loved Gene and Roy and the others was for their heroism. They always made the right moral choice no matter what the circumstances. Yup, podnuh, they were willing to sacrifice it all in order to take what was clearly the right action. They were willing to risk their lives to save the rancher's daughter from the evil banker and his henchmen. Those Saturday Westerns were like medieval morality plays in that way. Now, even though the good guys always won and nobody really got hurt or even bled, and Gene always ended up with the girl, we knew, of course, that it didn't really happen that way out in the world. But when we went back out into the blinding light of High Street, some little bit of the way Gene behaved had rubbed off on us. And we were better for it. To me, Gene Autry was a lot like Jesus, except Gene would whip your ass if he had to.

We would swing right out of the Virginia Theatre and walk up past the Port Theatre. The Port was down by Crawford Street and the block that was Portsmouth's red light district. It wasn't much, just a few foul-smelling bars, a flophouse, and a pawnshop. The city jail was conveniently located right next door. The Port showed "sailor movies," the raunchiest stuff allowed in public back then. Today you can see more skin on an afternoon network soap opera, and those old "sailor movies" would probably get a G rating.

A short block east of Crawford Street was the main office of the Seaboard Railroad, and it looked out on the legendary Norfolk-Portsmouth Ferry docks.

Even though Norfolk and Portsmouth were two good-sized cities separated only by a half-mile of water, until the late 1950s there were no bridges or tunnels connecting them, and the great orange ferries ran constantly. At the foot of High Street you could drive right onto the ferry for the ten-minute crossing, and drive off onto Market Street in downtown Norfolk. And it was a great trip. There being no other way to cross, it was a boat load of bankers and beggars, plus hookers, lookers, and society matrons, all packed in together. There were blind vendors selling newspapers, peanuts, and candy bars.

For the sailors on leave, taking a gal on a ferry ride was as close to a romantic outing as they were likely to get around that town. There would even be music for the occasion, for as often as not, some old-timer would draw a clump of folks around for a bit of harmonica or accordion playing. The world's largest warships shared that harbor, and fishing boats, sailboats, and tugboats all plied the choppy waters of the Elizabeth River.

We'd cross over High Street to catch the bus for the ride back to Sugar Hill. When we got back to the house, I'd take off by myself down by Scott's Creek, where I would re-create the Gene Autry movie. Soon I'd be improvising a plot in which I became the hero, Gene's best friend who would always help him out of trouble, and I would overcome all odds and become beloved and honored as the singing cowboy sensation of the nation, Buster Jones.

I was a king in that backyard, a cowboy, sure, but also a pirate, a knight errant, a great baseball player, and a soldier in the Pacific, killing "Japs" with a broomstick rifle and bringing world peace to a grateful planet.

We Few, We Precious Few, We Band of Brothers, Us Boys

Hubert C. (H.C.) Jones, Jr., was born in 1937, and James Stephen (Steve) Jones was born in 1938. My oldest brother got the nickname "Buck" after my father. When Buck started calling Steve "brother," it came out "Bubba," and that stuck. So when I came along, my ever-creative mama gave me the handle "Buster" for the sake of consistency. Buck, Bubba, Buster. It worked. At least until I got another nickname.

But though Buck and Bubba certainly did favor each other, that is where the similarity ended. Buck was manic, hyperactive, mercurial, melodramatic, and brilliant. Bubba was steady, industrious, practical, unpretentious, and easygoing with a laconic wit. They were so different, they even had trouble having conversations with each other.

When Buck was five, he contracted rheumatic fever, and the damage to his heart meant he had to have bed rest for a year. I have a clear memory of him in that room, drawing pictures of everything outside the window. He hated the confinement, felt imprisoned, raged against it, and never got over it. The fever was complicated by St. Vitus Dance, and frankly he was forever after a bit insane. Buck and Bubba started first grade together and were always three years ahead of me in school.

Once, when Buck was eight, we three brothers were down at the pier behind our house at low tide when he suddenly announced that he was going to Germany, and with that he hopped down off the pier into the thick black mud and began trudging to the east, in the general direction of Frankfort, Berlin, and the Pinners Point Piers. This created a lot of excitement around the section house. Bubba and I reported to Mama that Buck had headed off toward the Rhineland, and when he didn't answer her repeated calls, she got worried.

Daddy and his track gang happened to be working nearby. As soon as they found out what was up, the whole crew spread out in the search. We always called them "the Men." And men they were: Monk, Geech, Red, Daily, and the others. (One of them, a man hardly five feet tall with cartoonlike bowlegs was called, of course, "Shorty." Red said of Shorty, "He so bowlegged he can't hem up a hog in a ditch!" But Shorty was the strongest man I ever saw.)

They looked all over, through Sugar Hill, up and down through the freight yard, checking out boxcars, gondolas, and old cabooses. They looked through the cornfields, down at the piers, and through the marsh reeds.

Mama feared he had drowned. Bubba and I were wondering if he could speak German and if we would ever see him again. The men finally found him in some woods, at the water's edge, realizing that a boy cannot walk to Germany from America by going east.

The Water Is Wide

Scott's Creek, the tidal inlet behind our house, had a lot of personalities. On a warm Sunday afternoon in late spring it could be festive with pleasure craft, powerboats pulling water-skiers, small silent sailboats breezing by, and folks just puttering around with their outboards jerryrigged onto their old rowboats. Seagulls swooped about, cackling about the proceedings.

On a Saturday night, under a full moon with a big high tide and a sweet soft breeze, it became a lovely lake, as enchanting as Loch Lomond, as romantic as any sleepy Southern lagoon.

And on a muggy hot August afternoon when the tide was all the way out, there was nothing there at all but the blackest mud emitting the foul stench of long-rotten death. The drained soggy flats revealed years of detritus, rusted old engine parts, tires, chains, greasy oil barrels, sunken rowboats, and some objects that were no longer identifiable, but you really didn't want to know what they were anyway. It looked and smelled like flush. And a lot of it was flush.

On our side of the creek was nothing but woods along the water, broken by a few crabbing piers and the railroad outhouses. Several neighborhoods bordered it across from us: Park View, Shea Terrace, and an area just called Scott's Creek. Over there were docks, a small boatyard, a restaurant, and a sailboat marina. Directly across from us, no more than five hundred feet away, was a street whose name I did not know. It was a short street with maybe ten houses, mostly brick, mostly Tudor style. They were fine, solid-looking places, with driveways and garages and tiled porches with swings and neatly cut shrubbery. In front they had boat docks with sailboats, and one had a sleek-looking Chris-Craft cabin cruiser with mahogany railings and polished brass fittings.

I lived on that creek for nineteen years and I looked at those homes and dreamed that maybe someday I could live in a place that nice, that comfortable and civilized. I could see these distant strangers across the water come and go from their houses, park their cars, put out their cats, take in the milk in the morning, get their papers, turn out their lights at bedtime, and drive off to work the next day. I watched as their children grew and as they themselves slowed with age. And in all those years I never knew any of them, never met a soul who lived on that street. I never even set foot on that street in all those years. I guess I just didn't feel worthy enough to go there. I just looked across, like Jay Gatsby dreaming of Daisy Buchanan across the water. And I imagined a different life than the one I had.

And ten years on, twenty years on, and even now I still wonder about that street and those people. In my mind, they may as well have lived ten thousand miles away.

Just a few years ago, at a reunion of the Wilson High School class of 1959, I was chatting with a girl I had known slightly in those days.

"What part of town did you live in?" I asked her.

"We lived in Park View," she said. "On Bradford Terrace."

"Was that near Leckie Street?"

"No, it was right on Scott's Creek. Right on the water."

"Is that the little street with the pretty brick houses?"

"Yes, did you know that street? Where did you live?"

"I lived across the creek. On the Pinners Point side. Near Sugar Hill. In an old railroad house."

"That was you?! Oh, you were so lucky! That was so beautiful-looking across there. We all envied you so much! We called that over there Paradise Island," she said.

The Boys Who Came Home from the War

In August of 1945, when I was almost four, the section house came alive one day with much talk of what I understood to be the greatest event in any of our lifetimes. "The War" was over because "we" had dropped a secret weapon called something like a "tomic bum" on the "Japs." And then another. "The War" had been a presence in all of my memory. It was the ominous cloud that had seemed to infect everything. And just two "bums" had ended it.

The best that I could make of it at that age was that the "Japs," who didn't look like us and were little crazy people, had sneaked up on us and attacked us and then they had joined up with the Germans so they could take over the world and split it up between them. And my mama's brothers were fighting the "Japs" and before we went to sleep we prayed that they didn't get killed.

The war was what all those big gray ships were about and the planes and the dirigibles and the trains full of soldiers. I had it figured out pretty good for a four-year-old, and my dog, Prissy, had it figured out, too. She would go with me to look for Japanese soldiers in the chicken yard.

The end of the war was the first time I had seen everybody

happy at one time. Not just my family, but everybody. Daddy was feeling great and he wasn't even drinking yet. And Mama got a purple satin banner with gold fringe on it that said "VICTORY" and under that: "WE WELCOME HOME OUR BOYS FROM THE WAR." And she hung it in the window by the front door. Because of where we lived, nobody really saw it but us. And my uncles, Hubert and D.C., the boys who came home from the war.

Li'l Hubert came down the road in his Army Air Force uniform and I saw him first. Mama cried when she hugged him. Hubert Stephens was the baby of the family and they had all been through a lot together already. He had been only ten years old when their father died; they had lost their sister Lessie right after that; and when their mother passed away he was just fourteen. Mama and Daddy had just gotten married and she was expecting, but they took in Hubert and his fifteen-year-old brother, "D.C."

Because my daddy's name was Hubert, too, they started calling my uncle Li'l Hubert. Well, he *was* on the slight side. In his dress shoes he was a shade under five-foot-seven. D.C. was a big fellow, round-faced, broad-shouldered, and bighearted. Before long both boys got work with the Civilian Conservation Corps, the famed CCC that put so many unemployed kids to work during the Great Depression.

A year or so after that, they enlisted in the Army. Li'l Hubert went into the Army Air Force and was a ball turret gunner on B-25 bombers, and then in the larger B-29s. D.C. was regular Army. A machine gunner, he fought up in the Aleutians and then went down and across the Pacific Islands. They both fought all the way through the war, they were both badly wounded and returned to service, and they both came home with the "thousand-yard stare," that look that men have when they have seen too much.

And D.C. came home looking for the morphine to which he had become addicted for his war pains. Both of the boys loved their beer, but D.C. also loved the wine, the whiskey, the drugs, and anything else he could get hold of that could ease his memories. A lot of guys came back from the war less than whole. It always seemed to me that the part of D.C. that had gone missing somewhere on those Pacific Islands was a big piece of his soul.

Both of the boys met and fell in love with North Carolina girls. Hubert married Mabel, just as sweet a woman as the Lord ever made. And D.C. married Annie Laurie, who was sweet except when she wasn't. She had her wild side, too.

D.C.'s devils plagued him. He would sober up, clean up, get a job, and do as well as he could at it. As soon as things began to go well, they would fall apart. He could self-destruct any kind of success that came. And for awhile, Annie Laurie went along for the ride. The illegal drug business was buried much further underground in the late 1940s. But around Norfolk and Portsmouth, for that matter around any large port in the world, anything was available for a price. Anything.

For a few months they lived in a shack behind our house while he was "in between jobs" and looking for work and a living situation. There was just about enough room in there for a double bed, and all their belongings were stacked to the ceiling around it. I was about seven years old when I discovered there his pack of pornographic playing cards, fifty-two positions. For me, it was an immediate and certain loss of innocence. Understand, I wasn't quite sure what I was looking at, but I was damn sure I'd better keep it to myself.

Daddy once got D.C. a job at Stump Rountree's Garage. Stump said he was the best mechanic he'd had there in twenty years. But after two weeks, when D.C. got his first paycheck, nobody saw him around for quite awhile.

Li'l Hubert was reliable, and things began to go very well for him. He was living down in North Carolina, but he would come visiting once in awhile to do some crabbing off our pier. He would catch a city bus to Pinners Point, stop at the grocery and buy some beer and pick up some scrap meat for bait, then walk the mile or so down to the section house. He'd tie the scrap meat on some string along with a couple of sinkers, toss out a few lines, and then enjoy some quiet time to himself, crabbing, thinking, and drinking.

Once he brought a guitar with him and after a few beers launched into "Old Shep," a sad old song about a boy and his dog. And when the dog died in the last verse, Uncle Hubert choked up from the sentiment and started crying real tears. To say the least, I was impressed, and everytime I saw him after that, I'd ask him to do "Old Shep."

Another time he stopped in Pinners Point, bought his beer and got the bait, and bought himself a brand-new crab net. He was in a fine mood as I helped him put his lines out. I headed back up to the house to catch up on my Classic Illustrated comic books. Mama was downstairs writing letters when we heard him screaming a stream of profanities. I ran out just as he stormed past the house and headed back up the cinder road toward Pinners Point. Mama looked very concerned. Li'l Hubert was not a bad-tempered man. In fact, in that family he was the quiet one.

We went down to the crabbing pier to see what we could. He had left all his lines in the water and there was a half-bushel of crabs and four unopened beers on the dock. Leaving the beer was not like a Stephens at all.

"What do you think happened?" I asked Mama.

"Beats the tar out of me!" she said.

The next day we found out what had gotten into him. He had been having a fine old time, pulling in big blue crabs left and right. But then, just as he was dropping a crab from the net into the basket, he saw something that made him snap. On the handle of his net was the label "Made in Japan." He had thrown it as far as he could out into the middle of Scott's Creek.

But things went well for Hubert and Mabel. They had a little baby boy and then he got a good new job on the paint line at the Ford plant in Norfolk. And then another baby was on the way. Uncle Hubert came by one Saturday to show off his new used car, an old Dodge sedan that was clean and sharp.

"Brakes are lockin' on me, though. I'm goin' over to Harold's to fix 'em."

That night, after he "fixed" the brakes, they locked on him on a country road out in Norfolk County. He left the road at sixty mph. He was killed on impact. He was thirty-three years old.

When D.C. was a few sheets to the wind, he would tell his war stories.

"We was moppin' up on Saipan," he said. "And the Japs were all up in caves. They were really dug in, so what we did was just put a lot of grenades and flame in there and when they come out on fire or all fucked up we'd let 'em have it with the machine guns. And they'd be a pile of 'em outside there, and we'd come up on 'em careful 'cause some of them sonofbitches might get up and shoot. So we'd wait awhile and let 'em suffer and die off, and we'd hear these real loud 'pops' ever once in awhile, and what it was, was they was slidin' their rifles in their mouths and blowin' their own heads off. That's the way the Japs was."

He and Annie Laurie and their pals careened their way through postwar America with all the adventure, fierce passion, and self-destruction of the "Beat Generation," but without the Buddhism and the literary pretense. They were hardasses, good ol' boy rednecks running liquor, running dope, and if they had to knock off a roadhouse, they knew how. But it ran out. The drugs created a self-administered nightmare on the fringes of the American dream. He slowly but surely lost his struggle with his demons. There were a few happy periods when he cleaned up off booze and drugs, but those times grew shorter and shorter. His stays at VA treatment centers would be followed by even more desperate binges. Then Annie Laurie left him. For good.

In 1963 I had a summer job working on the railroad in Georgia when I got the news. It had ended for D.C. on a bed in a tiny room in a cheap apartment house in Norfolk. A self-inflicted gunshot wound to the head.

My Uncle Harold had found him, and after the cops removed the body, he had cleaned up the blood and the bone and the tissue off the wall and floor. Then he pocketed D.C.'s .38-caliber pistol.

I headed up for the funeral and met up with my cousin Ty Stephens, one of Uncle Harold's boys and as good a friend as I ever had. In the family, we called him "Tronnie." We went over to D.C.'s to get his stuff. We stopped at a grocery store and each bought a six-pack of National Bohemian beer.

The wall and the floor by the bed were smeared the color of bleached blood where Uncle Harold had cleaned. There wasn't much to pick up. A khaki work shirt and a pair of white socks. A small metal pot and an old frying pan. In the pantry there was one small can of Chef Boyardee spaghetti.

We left the stuff for the next tenant and cracked open the beer. Tronnie and I talked about D.C. "He had a real good soul." "The salt of the earth." "He never caught a break." "The war fucked him up." "Annie Laurie broke his heart." "He never got over Lessie's dying."

And then the truth. "He just couldn't kick the habit." Then quiet. Then, "Yeh."

I sat on the edge of the bed and wrote out a piece of doggerel on a scrap of paper.

His pain, his strain, his songs in vain
His soft story's told in the floor's bloody stain

It tells of a day when roads were the way
Some road tomorrow, this road today
It tells of a nomad, the "tough luck," the "too bad"
From the men with the money that he should have had
But it fails to tell, for nothing can well
Of a man whose heart was too big for hell.

In the days before his death the only folks who had come by to see D.C. were the Jehovah's Witnesses missionaries who proselytize from door to door. They had become concerned about him, and took him to services. And so his funeral was at their church. It was all about the Rapture and Armageddon. And D.C.'s coffin was draped in the flag of the nation he had served. God and Country. He was forty-one years old.

On an afternoon back in 1932, my Aunt Lessie Stephens, whose singing was the talk of Portsmouth, went down to the Blue Moon Inn, where she had been performing in the evenings. She wrote two long notes, then with all the windows and doors closed, she opened the oven and turned on the gas. She was nineteen years old. The boy who discovered her lifeless body two hours later was her little eleven-year-old brother, D.C.

Me and Stan the Man

Every spring Daddy would lay out his garden and I would share in the work. We plowed a good acre of land and planted butterbeans, snap beans, black-eyed peas, cabbage, lettuce, squash, potatoes, tomatoes, watermelons, cantaloupes, bell peppers, and red peppers, and then we planted another acre of corn in an adjoining field.

Daddy was proud of his crops and it was one of the few things that he and I did together. I learned that I loved dirt and mud and dust. And I learned to love those tomatoes. As songwriter Guy Clark wrote, "Only two things that money can't buy, and that's true love and home-grown tomatoes." Amen.

My brother Buck was an electronics genius, although it didn't do him much good until we got electricity. Even so, he always had a pile of radio parts littered about, but finally gave up trying to explain the difference between a resistor and an oscillator to me. Bubba was a skilled woodworker, and when he wasn't busy with his carpentry tools, he was up to his elbows in grease, fiddling with old cars.

And I played one-man baseball. In 1946, I began a lifelong idolization of Stan "The Man" Musial. It had started with a cover photo of Musial in his unorthodox batting crouch, wearing the beautiful St. Louis Cardinals uniform, then and now the best-looking outfit in baseball. And he looked to me like a guy who would get along really well with Gene Autry.

From then until he retired in 1962, the first thing I did in the morning was to check the Cardinals' box score of the previous day. My most important priority was to learn how Red Schoendienst, "Country" Slaughter, Marty Marion, and the great Musial had played the day before. It might read:

	AB	H	R	RBI
Marion	4	1	1	0
Schoendienst	4	2	2	1
Slaughter	3	1	2	0
Musial	4	3	2	4

And then I mentally added:

Jones	4	4	2	3

In the field by the house, I'd hit fungoes while I improvised the situation: First I'm Musial in the classic pose, curled up in a left-handed knot, ready to uncoil and lash a line drive. I'd toss the ball straight up, and then miss it completely. The umpire in my head says, "That didn't count." Then the fungo toss again and a dribbler foul. "That didn't count neither. Not warmed up yet." Then good wood, a ground ball all the way out to the first row of string beans. I fetch the ball, whack it back toward my imaginary home plate, and trudge back. I'm up next with Stan on second with a double and Red Schoendienst on third. The fungo toss. A whiff. "Didn't count. That was batting practice." The toss, another foul tip. "A good change-up. He fooled you." The toss again and real good contact! Now the Harry Caray in my head would scream, "There's a long drive, it's going, it's going, it is gone! That ball is completely out of the stadium, across the street and on top of an apartment house. It must have traveled seven hundred fifty feet! Buster Jones has done it again. His fifty-second home run of the season and it's only August third! The crowd is going berserk!"

My years with the Cardinals were good ones. They retired my number when I was ten years old.

The summer I was ten, I was in J.C. Harrell's Sporting Goods downtown on High Street when I saw the Holy Grail of baseball bats. It was a twenty-nine-inch Little League–sized two-toned Stan Musial autographed Hillerich and Bradsby! I went home and begged and pleaded for the $7.99 it would take to liberate the bat from Mr. Harrell. Mama understood about my thing with Musial and she went into her hidden stash of dough. The next day I went downtown by myself on the bus, praying all the way that the bat was still there.

It was. Walking out of Harrell's with the bat was a spiritual experience. My cousin Tronnie came to see me that weekend. He was a year older than me and could hit and throw a year better. We went out into the field by the house and hit fungoes to each other, shagging the ball and tossing it back in. We took turns, ten hits at a time. He hit first, with my old bat that had been nailed back together in several places and had black electrician's tape wrapped around it all the way up the barrel. When my turn came up, I went in the house and got the Musial wonder stick. Tronnie thought he was playing me deep, but the new bat gave me a mysterious power that surprised even me. The first fungo jumped off the bat as Tronnie turned and gave chase, but it rose ever higher and landed at least thirty feet beyond any of our previous Ruthian blasts. In fact, it landed on the windshield of Mr. Frank Netherley's 1932 Chevrolet, which he had left parked by the three rows of vegetables he tended after work. When he clocked out in the afternoon from his job as an engineer in the freight yard he would come over and work for an hour or so with his crop, and then drive home from there. Even Buck and Bubba had never hit one that far from "home plate."

But there was that sound that every kid dreads, as the ball broke his windshield and landed on the front seat of the old Chevy. Why is it that baseballs hit by kids find automobile windshields the way that tornadoes always head straight for trailer parks? Tronnie and I reacted instinctively, as kids have since ball first met bat. We ran like hell. We figured nobody could finger us.

This strategy really didn't make a lot of sense, since there were only two kids playing baseball within a mile and that was us, and there was my baseball in Frank Netherley's front seat.

When Daddy got home from work, he called me into his "office." He got right to the point.

"Did you boys break the window of Mr. Netherley's car?"

"Yuh yuh yuh yuh yess, uh, sir."

"Why didn't you come in here and tell me when I got home?"

"I was uh, uh, uh skeered to."

"That's an old car. It's gonna be hard to find a new windshield for it."

"Yessir."

"Who hit the ball?"

"I did."

"Where did you hit it from?"

"The rabbit house." There was a hutch connected to our woodshed where we had once had rabbits. Now Daddy was intrigued. He knew baseball; he had been a catcher.

"You got ahold of that one pretty good."

"Yessir. But it wasn't my fault."

"Well, whose was it then?"

"It was Stan Musial's."

I explained about the new bat. I really think my old man was very proud at that point, but would never show it. It was one of the highlights of my athletic career. He found a windshield in a junkyard in South Norfolk. I walked off the distance the next day. It was 251 feet. And I was ten years old and I weighed 82 pounds. The way I figured it, when I was grown and weighed 260 pounds like my daddy and had muscles and was hitting pitched balls rather than fungoes, 750-foot blasts were clearly within my possibilities. The speed of the pitch would greatly increase the power of the contact and the length of my drives.

Unfortunately, it was the pitched ball that ended my baseball prospects. The next year a Little League was started in Port Norfolk and I was picked for the Kiwanis Club squad. In my first at bat, Warren Madry of the Kilby Florist's nine put a fastball right upside my head, cracking the little batting helmet that went over our caps. For the next two years, as soon as the pitcher released the ball, I ducked. In my second season, however, I did raise my batting average up to .171. Good field, no hit.

In 1951 I saw my first Big League ball, an exhibition game played at Portsmouth Stadium between the National League Champion Philadelphia Phillies, and their crosstown American League counterparts, the Philadelphia Athletics. In those days as spring training wound down, clubs would travel northward by train and play exhibitions on the way up from Florida to pay for the trip.

The stadium was overflowing to see the Phillies, the "Whiz Kids" of 1950: Robin Roberts and Curt Simmons on the mound, Richie Ashburn in centerfield, and my favorite on that squad, Willie "Puddinhead" Jones at third. The A's were mediocre as usual, but they had little Bobby Shantz pitching for them, and slick-fielding Eddie Joost at shortstop.

Down the right-field line were the "Colored Bleachers." Although Jackie Robinson had broken the Big League color barrier four years earlier, not much had changed in Portsmouth.

The Phillies won that game, but the afternoon was memorable for another moment. Connie Mack stepped out of the Athletics' dugout that day and waved his scorecard as the assembled roared in tribute. He was lean and handsome in his dark suit with a starched collar, a black bow tie, and a vest with a watch fob. He stood as straight as a hickory pole, and he carried himself with a dignity that commanded respect. He was a nineteenth-century gentleman of the old school, and he had dressed that way and walked that way through all the years he had managed the Athletics. If someone had taken a color picture of Connie Mack it probably would have come out in black and white.

Mr. Mack was eighty-nine years old and had ended his managerial career after the previous season, but they couldn't keep him away from the ballpark. Born during the Civil War, he broke into the big leagues in 1886 as a first-rate catcher, was owner of the Philadelphia club when Ty Cobb broke in with the Tigers, and was in his fifties when Babe Ruth came up to the Red Sox. He had managed against Shoeless Joe Jackson and against Jackie Robinson.

When he was born, there were people alive who had lived during the American Revolution. I saw Connie Mack, and Connie Mack had seen people who might have seen George Washington. Either America is very young or I am getting very old.

But Most of All, I Remember Mama

Mama carried sadness and secrets and a sense of entrapment despite her best efforts to put on the smile of a showgirl.

Her singing voice had a shy, sweet quality, a hesitancy balanced by perfect pitch, and a bone-deep honesty which could bring a lifetime of joy and pain into a lyric as plain as "I'm looking over a four-leaf clover." Even the endless daily grind of cooking, washing, nursing, sewing, and cleaning couldn't stymie the creative force that was Ila V. Jones. Mama was a constant carnival of homemade entertainment.

She sang naturally. Tunes would spring out of her when she was feeling good, or when she was feeling blue. There was nothing preconceived or slick about it. To her, it was just like talking. She memorized songs off the radio by writing the lyrics in composition books, scribbling as fast as she could in black ink as Vaughn Monroe sang "Racing with the Moon" or Ella Logan warbled "How Are Things in Glocca Morra?" That way she really learned the songs, while saving the price of the lyric magazines.

When we were all in the house at the same time, the joint was a cacophony of racket. The old man's radio would blare out Guy

Lombardo and the Royal Canadians or "Swing and Sway" with Sammy Kaye. Mama would be singing along to Peggy Lee or Dick Haymes or Helen Forrest, while Bubba would have Hank Williams or Ernest Tubb wailing away upstairs. I would be spinning old 78 rpm platters on the windup Victrola, a stack that included George M. Cohan singing "Over There," Gene Austin crooning "My Blue Heaven," and "The Wreck of the Old 97" by Vernon Dalhart. And Buck would go about re-creating all the sounds of Spike Jones and His City Slickers. The dogs would howl. As long as there was music, Mama was okay.

And this country girl, an artist trapped in a railroad shack far from the stages of Broadway, went about washing work clothes by hand, all the while quoting Shakespeare and Shelley, Longfellow and Tennyson, Robert Service and Ogden Nash.

Then there was the timely dramatic use of great lines of poetry. When she had scrubbed the kitchen walls clean of a year of soot, she would look at her handiwork and declaim, "In Xanadu did Kubla Khan a stately pleasure dome decree!" If we came in from playing outside and said, "I'm thirsty, Mama," the response was "Water, water everywhere and all the boards did shrink, water, water everywhere and not a drop to drink."

If somebody mentioned a family with fifteen children, she would smile and say, "Abou Ben Adhem, may his tribe increase!" I remember one time she grabbed up a chicken to whack off its head for supper as she said, "It is a far, far better thing I do, than I have ever done before, a far better rest I go to than I have ever known before!" Has any ol' roastin' hen ever had a better send-off?

In a roundabout way it was Mama's penchant for lyrics that led to great progress coming to Sugar Hill. In the late 1940s, television appeared like an all-out invasion from another planet. In High Street show windows, TV sets with seven-inch screens drew crowds that stared by the hour at the faint images of old vaudevillians like Ed Wynn and Milton Berle doing live shtick, or John Cameron Swayze on *Camel News Caravan.* "It's the movies and the radio put together," said the salesman at Sears and Roebuck, "and now you can afford to put one right in front of your settee."

Well, we had to wait a few years before we could afford it, and it wouldn't have done us much good as we had no settee. Not only that, we didn't have any electricity.

But we prospered from the advent of "the tube." Local radio stations, sensing a crisis as their ratings began to slide, went into full promotion mode. Every station had ongoing contests, "Name the Mystery Voice" or finishing a line like "I love Grumbach's Sausage because . . ." in twenty-five words or less. Mama was born to write jingles, mail in box tops, be the first to call, or answer "The Ten-Dollar Jackpot Question." Mama was the quintessential "lucky listener." Among other prizes, she won money, she won tickets to shows, she won a sewing machine, a year's supply of BVDS, a new bicycle, a portable vacuum cleaner, and a three-month supply of Dr Pepper. One time she won an electric washing machine, but sold it immediately for thirty-five dollars because we had no electricity. But her coup de grace, in 1950, was an all-expenses-paid trip to Hollywood, California, to appear on *Double or Nothing,* a national hit radio show on NBC starring Walter O'Keefe.

Mama was the first in our family to fly, and the first to make it to Hollywood. And she didn't let the opportunity go to waste. When O'Keefe asked her about what she would do if she won the jackpot, she replied that she sure would love to have electricity in her house. Well, she didn't win the jackpot, but by the time she got home the railroad was running an electric line from the switchyard to the section house. On national radio, she had embarrassed the powers that be in the division office of the Coast Line into improving the living standards of the workers. The juice was put into all the section houses on Sugar Hill.

Electricity day was a memorable event. We all gathered around the white enamel receptacle in the center of the living room ceiling.

The living room was small, dark, and extremely cluttered. When Buck screwed in the seventy-five-watt bulb and Mama pulled the string, the place lit up in a shocking, blinding glare. Seventy years of section house life were suddenly excavated and exposed. The refuse of generations was revealed in the unforgiving harshness of a simple bare bulb. The walls were water-damaged slabs of grime, soot, and grease. Along the floorboards behind the couch were layers of dog hair, cobwebs, and assorted mousetraps, hair curlers, ancient Tootsie Rolls, and an assortment that could only be labeled "unidentifiable." We solved the problem by replacing the seventy-five-watt bulb with a more agreeable forty-watter.

Electricity meant the gradual banishment of the kerosene lamps, the battery radios, and the windup Victrola to the back porch. The arrival over time of each new electrical appliance was a cause célèbre around the section house. We fought over who could use the big Hoover vacuum cleaner. We watched the electric clothes washer with the same fascination as we watched *The Cisco Kid* or *Kukla, Fran and Ollie.*

King Arthur and the Knights of the Double Holer

It was not long afterward that an indoor bathroom was jerry-rigged into an old closet space upstairs. A commode! A bathtub! A sink! No hot water yet, but out went the piss pots.

The well-worn path down to the outhouse bridge began to grow over. Weeds and briar bushes soon covered the trail. The toilet house sat abandoned for four years, a sad emblem of faded glory. Then in 1956, after my cousin Tronnie and I had discovered how to surreptitiously buy and consume large amounts of cheap beer, we were inspired to give the outhouse a royal send-off. Under a big moon at a high tide, we wrenched and pried the house from its moorings and gave it a shove into the water. As it started to move out with the tide, we fired up the Sears and Roebuck catalog with a cigarette lighter and tossed it in through the door.

It was beautiful. We watched as our plan worked. The tide shifted quickly, pulling the blazing johnny out to the channel of Scott's Creek, then into the Elizabeth River and on toward the Chesapeake Bay. Under the moon, in the quiet of the summer night, it was a sight to behold. Tronnie waxed eloquent.

"Looks like King Arthur going out to the Misty Isle of Avalon," he said.

I didn't have a clue what he was talking about.

"Do what??"

"King Arthur. You know, the Knights of the Round Table and all that. When he kicked the bucket, they put him in a barge and he floated off to Avalon. The barge was his funeral bier."

"Oh yeah. I kinda remember that. Speaking of beer, let's go get some more."

Orville and Wilbur and Sir Walter Raleigh

Just after the war, Daddy bought a '39 Buick, and in 1947 we went down to Kitty Hawk, North Carolina, for our first family vacation. Down past the Great Dismal Swamp and across the Carolina line at Moyock, then through the low country to a bridge spanning the Currituck Sound and across to the Outer Banks, the long string of barrier islands that have forever been a part of American history.

We had rented a cottage for a week, just a mile or so from the Wright Brothers Memorial, the site of the first manned flight in 1903. There were still people around Kitty Hawk then who claimed they were there that day when Orville soared along the dunes. Over the years, our family would return to Kitty Hawk and Nag's Head many more times, and I found it thoroughly enchanting. I loved the ocean, the salt breeze, and the shouting of gulls. And I looked forward to the fishing on the surf, on the piers, and on the Albemarle Sound. I could hardly wait to climb the great dune at Jockey's Ridge. I loved the sun, the smell of Coppertone, and I even loved the sunburn and the smell of Noxzema. I was fascinated by the shipwrecks along the beach, the lighthouses, the stories of pirates, and the wonderful mystery of the "Lost Colony" of Roanoke Island.

We went to the island, site of Sir Walter Raleigh's settlement in 1585, whose citizens disappeared in the years of the Spanish Armada, before England could resupply them. And it was there that I saw my first live theater.

Pulitzer Prize–winning playwright Paul Green of North Carolina wrote *The Lost Colony* in 1937. It is still playing on Roanoke Island today, on the very site of the vanished community. Green called his work a "symphonic drama," a blend of choral music, dance, rich costumes, and broad "outdoor" theatrics. I was entranced with every bit of it, especially the stealthy Indians creeping through the sand just next to my seat, intent on taking the scalps of the unaware colonists. Unlike the movies, it was real, these guys were right next to me, and I was thrilled.

Sir Walter Raleigh was played by a young music student from the University of North Carolina named Andy Griffith, who has become one of America's most beloved character actors in the years since. When I got back to our backyard, I reenacted *The Lost Colony* myself, taking all the parts. I even found an old Sir Walter Raleigh pipe tobacco tin and made it part of my permanent collection of valuable things, not to be thrown out by Mama.

The Kitty Hawk trips had only one serious problem. For my father, who would spend his weeks at home on a dry drunk waiting for Friday afternoon to come, an entire week off meant no holds barred. At the beach he would drink from dawn until he passed out after supper, knocking down a quart or more of whiskey a day, and becoming obnoxious and incoherent by two in the afternoon. We all went into kind of a "prevent defense," cutting ourselves as much slack as we could get away with. We felt as if we were trapped in an insane asylum when we were around him, and we searched for excuses to go off, anywhere. It wasn't until a few years later, when Mama got her driver's license, that escape became easier. As for Daddy, well, he felt like he had earned his pleasure and that he certainly deserved it, and besides, it was going to be another whole year before he could again get so royally wasted for an entire week. Made sense to him.

High Tide

As the twentieth century came to its midway point, the Joneses were finally keeping up with everybody else. An automobile, electricity, indoor plumbing, even a telephone.

Buck, at fourteen, was technologically way ahead of the rest of us. He had taken over the shed behind the house and turned it into a haven of wires and gadgets, antennas and transistors. The "radio shack" emitted the constant click of the telegraph. That was "ham" radio station W4GRX, to become simply WGRX when he got his first-class license and went to the microphone for his cryptic conversations with similar radio nuts all over the planet. His walls were covered with QSL cards, the postcards ham operators send to one another after they have made contact.

Bubba was always working at part-time jobs. For a time, he worked at the boatyard in Shea Terrace, across from us on the other side of Scott's Creek. During the summers, when school was out and the tide was in, he would go down to our pier, untie the rowboat, and shove off, pulling the oars with steady strokes until he was at his job. He would return at suppertime, to vie with the rest of us for the last piece of fried chicken on a hot Southern night.

Daddy's routine didn't vary. On weeknights after supper, he would sit in his "office," which consisted of a desk and a company calendar, and play an endless game of solitaire. It was an odd form of meditation. By the hour, he would deal the cards, stopping only to refill his pipe with Prince Albert smoking tobacco. During the workday, he took his nicotine in the form of King Edward cigars, or a "chaw" of hardcut Beechnut chewing tobacco. But nighttime was pipe time. To my knowledge, he never lit a cigarette in his life. He considered cigarettes unmanly. And unlike his constant intake of whiskey, cigars, pipe smoke, and "chaws," he thought smoking cigarettes was a "bad habit."

One Saturday morning, he did something out of character. I do not know how much Four Roses he had knocked back beforehand, but he went down to Sears and Roebuck on High Street and came back with a brand-new automobile, a 1951 Allstate, bought on Sears' classic fifty dollars down and twenty-five dollars a month credit plan. The Allstate was a stripped-down Henry J, a compact car made by the Kaiser-Frazer Company. It listed for about $895 new and was immediately the rage of Sugar Hill. We rode around in it just to be riding around, although since at that time Daddy was the only one who could drive, we had to catch him during the week when he was sober for a cruise. It was the first new car anyone in our family had ever owned, and all the relatives came over to take an admiring look and a ride also.

Mama's routine changed dramatically in March of 1951, when she returned home from King's Daughters Hospital with baby Bryan Lane Jones, a healthy lad with his father's heft and his mother's dark brown eyes. So now there were four of "us boys" and it was my nickname for Bryan that stuck. It had to start with the letters *B* and *U,* of course. We voted down "Buddy" and "Buzzy." "Bugs" got no support at all. But "Butch" was a keeper. And to me, he is still "Butch," whether he likes it or not. Because now I was a big brother rather than a baby brother.

My other big deal in 1951 was finishing the fourth grade at Pinners Point School and graduating to fifth grade at Port Norfolk School. The big highlight of fourth grade was when the Battleship U.S.S. *Missouri,* coming back from maneuvers, ran aground on a sand bar off Pinners Point, only about fifteen minutes from port. The world's largest battleship sat there for almost a month, with every tugboat in Hampton Roads pushing and pulling.

I started having trouble "paying attention" in Miss Wooster's third and fourth grade. If the subject was arithmetic, I would be about halfway through the multiplication table up to twelve, around about "six times seven is forty-two," when my mind would drift to Long John Silver counting forty-two doubloons, and then to a mock naval battle between Long John Silver and John Paul Jones. They would become friends and come to Portsmouth in the old days and invent baseball and Stan Musial's grandfather would be playing and the English soldiers would take off their red coats and become rebels because they loved baseball so much, and about that time a plane would fly over and I would pretend I was on the plane looking down at Pinners Point School just as I would hear Miss Wooster say, "Ben Lewis Jones, read your multiplication table to the class!"

Nowadays, I suppose, Miss Wooster would stick a tab of Ritalin in me and there would be no pirates, no baseball, no airplanes.

But then there was no more Mattie Wooster. The fourth grade was going "up" to Port Norfolk School, the Big Time compared to Pinners Point. It was in a neighborhood with bigger houses, nicer yards, five stores, two beer joints, and an A&P. There was some culture shock every time we crossed the Belt Line tracks from dingy ol' Pinners Point to spiffy Port Norfolk. But after a bit of intimidation from the Port Norfolk bullies, we settled down for some good years of growing and learning. But for me, it was not to be.

The Story I Don't Want to Tell

Everybody has that story they don't want to tell. It is too painful, too embarrassing, too hurtful, and too shameful. And, according to the healers, that is the story that we must tell. In my life there are many such stories. There are those who would argue that a public setting is not the place to reveal such secrets, that no good purpose is served. They would argue that such confessions are merely self-serving and should remain private. I thought about that a lot when I decided to tell my tales, and realized that I have respected that opinion for over fifty years. But in trying to figure out why I went from being a sweet, loving child to a raging and often violent man, I had to consider the impact of events that had overwhelmed me at a time of innocence.

I understand now that when I was twelve years old, I had not even begun to enter puberty. I felt then as if my entire mind and body were being wrapped inside me tighter and tighter, that something was smothering not my breath, but my very essence. As the other boys in my class were starting to become men, I felt like I was becoming an eternal eight-year-old, and it was for some reason physically excruciating. I could not begin to describe it, for I had nothing with which to compare it. But it hurt in every way. And what self-confidence I might have had vanished, to be replaced by a disabling shyness.

I suppose that one of the worst things that could happen to a sensitive kid like I was at that point is to be sexually molested by an older male. That is what happened to me, and although there is no way to fully measure the effect that it had on me, I can tell you that the shame and guilt I felt was such that this is the first time I have ever talked about it.

Our family didn't seem to have a way to deal with such things, or for that matter, a way of dealing with much of anything. But from what I have come to learn, most families don't have a way of dealing with it, either. My school grades suddenly went from straight A's to an inconsistent mess. Nobody said anything. I quit going to Sunday School. Nobody said anything. I stayed in my room a lot, just day-dreaming. Nobody said anything. The molestation continued for two years. The shame of all ages was upon me and I felt it was somehow my fault and though I dreaded it, I felt trapped. I began to accept it, to expect it, and to try to separate it from my real life, as if it were all a dream of no consequence. It ended when I was fourteen, just as I finally entered my long-delayed puberty.

There is a saying about that goes, "You are only as sick as your secrets." No doubt about it, y'all, it is the stuff that gets lodged up in your head and stays there that causes the problems. That is the end of the story I didn't want to tell.

Lost in the Fifties

One Slightly Damaged Redneck Boy

Nowadays there are common terms to describe what was going on with me back in the 1950s. These days our family would be called *dysfunctional.* Nice to have a fine label like that. Better to be called "dysfunctional" than something like "a bunch of crazy rednecks." And attention deficit disorder had yet to be given its proper place on the bookshelf. Kids like me were thought to be at best "distracted" or "dreamy" and at worst, "dumb as a box of rocks." Delayed puberty was not a physical or psychological problem then, but a social one. It was no fun to be the only kid whose balls hadn't "dropped." The only part of puberty that wanted anything to do with me was a serious case of acne. I still carry those scars, too.

My athletic dreams became just that, fantasies. Compared to the other kids I was suddenly squat and fat and very slow. My coordination seemed fine until I was in any sort of competition. Then I thought too much. By worrying about making a fool of myself, I inevitably made a fool of myself. In the field by the section house, I could hit like Musial, run down a fly ball like Joe DiMaggio, and throw like Willie Mays, but at Port Norfolk Park I was less active than the statue to the Confederate Dead on Court Street downtown.

In football I was useful on the line, but played hesitantly, not really wanting to hurt anybody. As a result, I was a mass of contusions. Basketball was over my head, literally and figuratively. I figured that I had peaked as an athlete at age seven. Yet underneath all the ineptitude and angst was a very gifted athlete who was simply yet to be. As it was, I gave up on being a jock several years before I could have become a very, very good one.

Of all the kids in Portsmouth who headed to Woodrow Wilson High School in 1955, I was the least ready. When I was twelve years old, I had the maturity of a nine-year-old. When I was fourteen, I had the maturity of a twelve-year-old. I was closing the gap, but not quickly enough. High school terrified me. In fact, practically everything terrified me. It must have been in those years that I developed my natural acting skills. I acted smart, I acted cool, I acted tough, I acted as if I were sexually experienced, I acted as if I knew things about which I was totally clueless. I acted as if everything was just fine and dandy. My acting may have convinced some folks. But it sure didn't convince me.

The movies provided one handy escape from reality. For a few months in 1955, my brother Buck was the doorman at the Colony Theatre, which meant my cousin Tronnie and I could get in free. The Colony was across the street from the classy Commodore Theatre, which was the only one of Portsmouth's movie houses to survive the advent of television. The Colony was a "second run" house, and during that summer showed a double feature with *From Here to Eternity,* a terrific film, and *The Wild One,* starring Marlon Brando. Tronnie and I thought *From Here to Eternity* was okay, but we thought *The Wild One* was clearly the greatest piece of cinema ever conceived, and we saw it at least fifteen times during its run at the Colony. In it, Brando plays an alienated, misunderstood, rebellious biker. Even though that was totally unlike our feckless fourteen-year-old lives, we identified completely. We memorized the entire dialogue, and for months afterwards spoke to each other only in our Brando impersonations.

The only thing I didn't have to fake at school was talking. I was compulsive about it. Maybe it was because there were no kids my age around the section house to chat with, but every one of my teachers in grade school had written on my report card something like "Ben is a very sweet and smart boy, but he talks too much and is very messy." Those comments were true then, and they are true now. I can still talk the chicken off the bone.

I did have an unusual sexual encounter in those years, and though I didn't initiate it, I was a willing participant. For a year or so I was the Pinners Point delivery boy for the *Portsmouth Star,* the town's afternoon newspaper. On Saturday mornings, I would go door to door to collect the weekly payment and I would occasionally get a tip from a generous customer.

Pinners Point was on the docks, and a lot of U.S. Navy and merchant seamen lived there. In a garage apartment behind a home on Hill Avenue, there was a young woman, maybe thirty years old, whose husband was always "out at sea." I never saw the guy and she always claimed she couldn't pay me until he got home. "Sorry, honey, I'm just plain broke," she would smile.

Then one day she invited me in and told me to sit on the couch while she tried to find a couple of dollars. She came back into the tiny living room, sat down very close to me, and said, "Honey, have you got a girlfriend?" I stuttered that I didn't have a steady girl, and she allowed that she wanted to show me how to treat a girl just right. I was too petrified to move, and I'm glad I was. Since I was totally clueless as to what to do, she made all the moves. Her payment worked out just fine. I left that place a very different boy. The next Saturday when I went to collect I was sweating with a week's anticipation, but she wasn't home. The week after that, the folks in the front house told me she had moved to Norfolk. The journalism trade sort of lost its luster for me after that. And if only getting a girl at Wilson High would have been that easy.

Buck and Bubba were three years ahead of me in school, and they graduated from Wilson about the time that I arrived. Buck disappeared right after that. It turned out that he had joined the Air Force and gone off to Lackland Air Force Base in Texas for basic training. The only problem with that was that he had lied about his health to get in. He had omitted the part about having a rheumatic heart and living under doctor's orders not to engage in any physical activity. Here was a kid who was forbidden to take gym class working under a drill instructor in sunny Texas. He fessed up after two weeks and came back home with an honorable discharge. Other disappearances were never explained. Once he vanished along with Daddy's pistol. A few weeks later we got a postcard from him in Roanoke. When he returned, he denied any knowledge of the gun and acted surprised that anyone was concerned about his whereabouts.

Then Buck got a job at a small UHF TV station in Portsmouth and was the on-air talent until he converted to Catholicism. Buck insisted on wearing his forehead ash during airtime on Ash Wednesday, and the owner gave him his walking papers. Shortly afterwards, a young evangelist who had preached revival at Pinners Point Church bought the station. His name was Pat Robertson.

Bubba started working full-time on the Atlantic and Danville Railroad as a brakeman. He married his high-school sweetheart, Beverly Baker, in 1957, and started a long career on the railroad and as a solid family man.

One Drink Is Too Many, a Thousand Isn't Enough

When I was fifteen, my buddy Bruce Laughon started going on about the wonders of Country Club Malt Lager. Country Club, he said, was no ordinary beer. It came in eight-ounce cans, and according to Bruce, four of these mighty mites were the equivalent to drinking six twelve-ounce cans of regular beer. Bruce seemed to me to be quite an expert on these matters, but having seen the effects of my father's drunkenness, I was willful about not drinking. That shaky determination, and the fact that I had no money, enabled me to resist the peer pressure. Until the night that I didn't.

Bruce had use of his family's 1952 Plymouth, and he knew a food market that didn't check ID cards for beer purchases. In Virginia, twenty-one was the legal age to purchase booze, but perhaps because it was a Navy town, the rules were lax in a lot of stores. Bruce bought two six-packs of Country Club, and we rode around with nothing to do except drink and lie about our nonexistent exploits with girls. My first beer was like magic. It was as if I was Billy Batson, the crippled newsboy, and I said "Shazam!" and instantly become Captain Marvel.

By the time I had finished the second beer my inferiority complex had vanished. The pain and shame I had been carrying seemed to be lifted. I was suddenly witty, urbane, ballsy, musical, talented, and ready to rumble. I was also ready for the third beer, and the fourth. I finished the six-pack and drank two of Bruce's. Between us we had about a dollar left, which in 1956 would buy a six-pack of National Bohemian. By now I was filled with bravado, and I made the stealthy purchase. I was fifteen and I didn't look a day over thirteen, and the clerk rang up the purchase without a second thought. By the time we finished that six-pack, I was knee-walkin', toilet-huggin' drunk.

I was the dynamite and booze was the match. And I was exploding with excitement. I was no longer a boy and afraid. I was a man who had found the missing elixir. After Bruce dropped me off at the section house, I staggered down to the pier, lay down, and watched the world spin out of control. I felt like I needed to throw an anchor off the pier to hold it steady. Things were different now and even as I threw up into Scott's Creek, I felt that beer had just become my new best friend. The next morning the feelings of being worthless reappeared. But now I knew how to make them disappear, if only temporarily.

I could not wait to get drunk again. I did not want to just have a beer or two. I did not want to get high. I wanted to get drunk again. As drunk as I could possibly get, the sooner the better, the more the merrier. I wanted to be the drunkest man in the world.

And often in the next twenty years I probably was.

Rebel Without a Clue

When I was a senior at Wilson, I got a job at Parker's Open Air Market, bagging groceries and doing stock work. At night, when I was back in the stockroom, I would ease out the back door with a bag of beer and hide it behind the trash dumpster. Over time I worked up quite a stash, which I hid behind the old woodhouse at home. I had never stolen anything in my life, but my new love affair with alcohol had instantly turned me into a thief with nerves of iron. The man who ran Parker's was a terrific person, and good to me, and I repaid him by shoplifting without any conscience about it. After all, I reasoned, beer oughta be free. As, of course, should cigarettes. By now I was smoking a pack of Old Golds a day.

I spent a lot of time over at my buddy Steve Lasting's house, where he had easy access to his father's liquor cabinet. Steve had the same attitude as I did about booze, that one simply could not drink enough. He was deep into jazz, which was unusual in those rock-and-roll days. One Sunday he came by, honked the horn, and said, "Let's go to Virginia Beach!" But Steve wasn't into checking out some teenage beach scene. We went to a club where Dizzy Gillespie was playing and spent the evening digging his great combo. Mr.

Gillespie would come and sit with us during his breaks, and he was very kind to a couple of plastered white kids from Portsmouth.

I did manage to graduate from high school, but it wasn't pretty. After the drinking started, I bailed out on my last two years there. My procrastination became worse, and I could not seem to concentrate for more than a few seconds at a time. I had then and still have what I call "pinball brain." If you have it, you know what I mean. I paid little attention in class and rarely cracked a book. I ranked something like 147th out of 219 graduates. Now, we had some very bright kids back at dear ol' Wilson High, but with all humility I don't think that 146 of them were smarter than I was. But I was a teenage alcoholic and nobody was mentioning it around our house or at the school, much less trying to deal with it. And that is because I lived in an alcoholic household where all of us lived in denial as a way of life. And that is the hand they were dealt and it was the hand I was dealt and it was the hand I dealt myself.

After graduation, I took a job in Norfolk driving a delivery truck for the Norfolk News Agency. In the morning I would load up for my route, and then make the rounds of the drugstores, the newsstands, and the markets, bringing the world new copies of *Look, Life, True Detective,* and *Ladies' Home Journal,* and picking up the remainders. When I got back to the warehouse, I was put to work sweeping. The warehouse manager there was a man named Aaron, who was a Holocaust survivor. This was in 1959, and I realize now that his life in the concentration camp was to him a very recent experience. Occasionally I would see him deep in thought, seeming to stare into space and forget his surroundings. Once, he noticed me looking at him at such a time. He smiled sadly, pulled up his sleeve, and pointed at the tattoo of his concentration camp number.

I learned from him that as we pass strangers on the street every day, we should show respect, for they might be people who have struggled and suffered in ways unimaginable to us.

There was a girl from Portsmouth who had moved to Richmond,

taking my huge crush with her. In a moment of inebriated inspiration, I decided to move to Richmond, find a job, and win her heart. I caught a bus up there, got a room at the YMCA, and found a job selling encyclopedias the first day I was there. But the girl was no more interested in my advances than she had been for the last two years. So I blew off the encyclopedia gig, the YMCA, the golden girl of Richmond, and hitchhiked on back to Sugar Hill.

Then I went to work for Stump Rountree. My Uncle D.C. had worked for Stump years before, and my brother Bubba had worked there for a year or so when he was in high school. But they were practical, handy guys with mechanical skills. I didn't know the difference between a brake shoe and a float valve. I did go at it earnestly, though, and after a few weeks, Stump called me into the garage for an assessment.

"Buster," he drawled, "you're doing a mighty fine job in the front, pumpin' gas. I really like the way you talk to the customers, cleanin' them windshields, checkin' that oil and water, and checkin' them tires. And you done got the handle on the grease jobs, and changin' folks' oil. And I believe you're as good as anybody I've had at fixin' flats. You're real good. But Buster, far as being a mechanic is concerned, I just want you to stay the hell away from my tools!"

Stump needed a mechanic and I wasn't going to be it. But he got his money's worth. At a time when the minimum wage was eighty-five cents an hour, I was working twelve hours a day, six days a week, for thirty dollars. I think that's about forty-one cents an hour. With that I bought a 1950 Plymouth sedan with a leaking block for $125. The car had an enormous 1946 Chevrolet radio bolted to the front floor. It had great reception and could pick up stations in New York and Chicago. My buddies said I had bought a radio and gotten a car attached to it.

One day a couple of guys came by looking for help on a house-painting job for a dollar an hour. Stump wished me well and that was the end of my career under a car hood.

There are a lot of enormous wooden houses around Norfolk and Portsmouth. Built in the late nineteenth century for the large extended families of that era, many of these houses are three stories tall, and some are even bigger. The first work of the painter's morning is to mix the day's buckets, and then to rig the scaffolding. On an early afternoon in spring of 1960 I was up on the scaffold, painting the trim on the outside of a third-floor window. My partner, Bob, had ducked through the window earlier to take a break for a smoke and the john. As I stretched to reach a place with my brush, the other end of the scaffold lifted up because ol' Bob hadn't nailed it down. I was suddenly sliding off into space forty feet above the ground. I instinctively grabbed ropes, walls, windows, and boards as I scrambled for survival. As a British officer said of Waterloo, "It was a near run thing!"

As I sat on the scaffold, gratefully getting my bearings, some of the kids I knew from high school happened to cruise by on Mt. Vernon Avenue in a 1957 Chevy convertible. I figured they were home from college on spring break and were heading to the beach. At that moment I had a minor epiphany. I realized that I had better figure out a way to get into college, because my other option seemed to be hanging on to my life on some scaffold at some minimum-wage, dead-end job. And I wasn't even any good at those jobs. That night I went down to the Portsmouth Public Library and started looking through college catalogs.

While I pondered my future, I took a job plastering ceilings in the tiny Filipino community down by the Navy Yard. I really liked the guy I was working with, a black guy named Shag. He was an evangelical preacher who said he had been converted by looking at his reflection in a store window on High Street while he was dancing backwards by himself under the influence of a great deal of Thunderbird Wine. It stopped him cold, and he told me that in Jesus he had found everything he was looking for in Thunderbird. Thinking myself more sophisticated, I thought he was naïve. I didn't seem to understand that he had something I wanted. Shag was a happy man.

Just down the street from the work site was a Mexican restaurant, the only one around that area in those days before Taco Bell. It was run by a fellow named Ralph, a Boston "Yankee" who had retired out of the Navy and stayed around town. Shag said we should get lunch there, and I was thinking that it might be the last lunch we ever ate, because if Portsmouth was known for anything in those days, it was strict segregation. The idea of eating with a black friend indoors in a public place was unthinkable in Virginia in 1960. But Shag seemed to be very cool about it.

Ralph's was a small, dark, smoky joint about a block from the Main Gate of the Navy Yard.

We took a table and Ralph welcomed us with a couple of menus. There was a table full of sailors in uniform, a Hispanic guy and his lady, two Filipinos from the neighborhood, and a Mexican cook. The only time I had eaten "Mexican" food was when Mama's supper featured canned chili con carne. To me, Ralph's chow was exotic and amazing. And so was the idea of eating with Shag. I felt like we were in another country or another time.

But the word had gotten around about Ralph's open-door policy. Shag said that the only color that mattered to Ralph was green, and that he would serve anybody who could reach the counter with a dollar bill. I left that lunch feeling like a man of the world. And it left me with a question: If Shag and I had been working next to each other all day long, and I was giving him a lift home after work, what was the big deal about having an enchilada?

My drinking buddy Bruce told me that it wasn't hard to get into East Carolina College down in tobacco country. They didn't require SATs in those days, just a decent score on their entrance exam. I hitchhiked down to Greenville for the test, did well enough to pass, and was accepted as a student for the fall of 1960. Now I had to raise a little more dough.

When the job with Shag ran out, I accepted an official position with the U.S. Federal Government. In fact, it was so official they gave me a badge and a briefcase. I was hired to be an official Census enumerator. You know, a Census taker. A people counter. They work only about three weeks every ten years. Talk about seasonal work!

We were to be paid a base fee plus a rate for each person counted. I was assigned to the neighborhoods within a few miles of my house: Sugar Hill, Pinners Point, Port Norfolk, and Mount Hermon, plus some other blocks that were tucked in around some industrial areas. The other "enumerators" were almost entirely housewives looking for part-time work. Since I was now a hefty kid, I volunteered to go into some of the "tougher streets" that were considered too dangerous for the ladies.

For the most part things went easily. But along the Belt Line switching yard near High Street and in several other pockets of mystery, were many houses generally labeled "nonresponsive." Now, I can certainly understand the tendency of a poor person of color to be reluctant when a white person in a coat and tie wearing a government badge and carrying a briefcase approaches the front door.

"Good afternoon, ma'am! Is the head of the household here?"

"Naw, he ain't here."

"Do you expect him back in the near future?"

"Naw, I ain't got no idea when he comin' back."

"Well, is there a way I could possibly get in touch with him?"

"Naw, he out in Utah or some place like that."

She yelled back into the house. "Hey, Sylvia, you know where Uncle Pike is?"

A voice from within. "Ain't he gone to Chicago?" Then another voice from within. "Naw, shit! He ain't in Chicago. He in Alabama. Milwaukee, yeah, that's it. Milwaukee, Alabama!"

One "nonresponsive" dwelling was a vast ramshackle place that appeared to have been a hotel in better days. From inside I could hear music, laughter, and many voices. My knock on the door would bring immediate silence and a slight crack in a window blind while somebody peeked out. After about a week of trying, I persisted until finally an unseen voice was heard from behind the front door.

"What you want?"

"Excuse me, ma'am, I'm with the United States Census. Are you the head of the household?"

The voice told me that only she and her invalid husband resided there. They had no children.

A few doors up the street, I sat with a genial old man on his front porch.

"Do you know the folks in the big house on the corner?" I asked.

"Hmmmm. Well, some of them I know. Some of the time."

"How many folks would you say live there?"

"Hard to say. Maybe ten, maybe twelve lives there all the time. But folks come and go, you see."

"Is it like a boardinghouse?"

The old man laughed and laughed. "Lord no, son. That house is the biggest whorehouse in the city of Portsmouth!"

It slowly began to dawn on me that there were a lot of citizens in our city who did not consider it their patriotic duty to be enumerated by their government. And since I was being paid by the number of people I counted, I faced a dilemma that required a creative solution.

Not counting vacant houses, there were twenty-six "nonresponsive households" in the area I was assigned to. I sat down the next night and created twenty-one households, complete with full names, birthdates and birthplaces, races, occupations, and marital status. The other five households I left unfinished, so as not to raise suspicion. I gave birth to a total of 122 "real" Americans in one room of the section house on a night in 1960. At fifty cents a soul, I made sixty-one extra dollars that evening. So ended my first brief stint with the federal bureaucracy.

Creating fictional citizens was, and still is, quite felonious, of course. And here's hoping the statute of limitations has passed on "fraudulent people counting."

The next census-taking job wasn't coming around for another ten years, but I got hired at the Virginia Ice Cream Company, a small factory near downtown Portsmouth. My job was to stick sticks in Popsicles. Somebody in this world has to do that, you know. The ice cream mixture was poured into a rack of twenty-four molds. As they were placed in a vat of freezing chemicals, I would quickly stick the sticks into the mold and push the rack along when it was ready. Other than the old Greek man who ran the plant, I was the only white person there.

We took our lunch every day in a small coatroom, sitting on the floor with our sandwich bags from home, a piece of fruit, maybe a candy bar. Often someone would pass around a bottle of cheap wine. We drank after one another like family. I was only at the ice cream plant for about five weeks, but I made good friends with everyone there, and I figure I stuck sticks in maybe fifty thousand Popsicles. I quit just before July 4, because I got a better job over at the StarBand Company making Halloween masks on an assembly line. Definitely another seasonal gig, but it paid a dollar and a dime an hour and there was the chance for a lot of overtime.

On my last day at Virginia Ice Cream, as we sat around on the coatroom floor, Charley Buck gave me a farewell toast. Charley had worked there since he was a young man, and had become sort of an ex officio manager. In the shop, he always dressed like an Eskimo, because part of his job was taking the newly made Popsicles and ice cream sandwiches into the freezer right away. Once, years before, Charley had been trapped in the freezer when the exit plunger had broken. He had spent hours in there, banging on the door in desperation before someone checked on him and got him out. So every time Charley took a load into the freezer he would give us a look of

"Don't forget I'm in there," and every time he pushed the plunger and came out, he would have a look of divine deliverance.

As the old-timer, Charley was the spokesman for the crew as we shared the cheap wine and ate our baloney sandwiches. "Ben," he said with great portent, "we gone miss you around here at the Virginia Ice Cream Company. You a good boy, and we don't care what color you are, you can go fishin' with us any ol' time. And Ben, you don't know where you gone go in life, ain't no tellin' where you might end up, only the Good Lord knows. You might end up being a preacher in the Panama Canal, or you might be sellin' used tires in England or France. But Ben, as you travel down the highways and the byways of life, cross the rivers, and down the valleys and up the mountains and cross the deserts, there is one thing I wants you always to remember: Ben, bullshit rules the world!!"

Everyone agreed, and although it wasn't the message I was expecting, as time goes by it seems like Ol' Charley Buck gets more and more right every day.

Rob Crenshaw was a Navy brat whose father was stationed at the Navy Yard. Rob had just gotten back from Coronado, California, where his family had been stationed earlier, and he had brought back with him several gallons of tequila and rum he had smuggled across from Tijuana. On July 4, 1960, he and I drank a lot of beer, then consumed a gallon of the tequila. We decided to head down to Virginia Beach, and as Rob drove my Plymouth, I rode shotgun and nipped away at the present he had brought back for me from Tijuana. It was a bottle of 192-proof grain alcohol, the Mother Lode of Booze, the purest strain of hooch known to man. It was a clear bottle of clear liquid, and the label said simply, "192." Beneath that was a picture of a skull and crossbones.

Rob pulled up to a girl's house near the beach, and I decided to head for the bars. He asked me if I was okay to drive, and I said, "Sure," then headed across a golf course toward the main drag. I remember being on Virginia Beach Boulevard and thinking I had to get off, that I was passing out, and then pulling onto the service road and driving straight into a telephone pole. I knocked out the windshield with my head. I don't remember the ambulance ride to the hospital.

I got off lucky. I told the cops I had been run off the road by some crazy drunk. There were no charges against me. Apparently they thought my drunken incoherence was due to the head injury. I was covered with blood, and the doctors shaved my head to get a good look at the damage. But other than a concussion and a few stitches, I was good to go. My folks came down and drove me back, and apparently they also thought my incoherence was from the lick I took. Because not a word was ever said about drinking. Not one word. Ever. Nada.

For weeks after that when I ran a brush across my head, little bits of glass would come off my scalp. But I was at my new job the next week. For six weeks I worked on a silkscreen assembly line at StarBand, making Halloween masks. Devils, witches, pirates, ghosts, gypsies, and monsters. I started having weird dreams. It was a colorful job, though. Every night when we punched out we were all covered with bright primary colors.

After making a few dollars and thousands of Halloween masks, I got ready for college. In my case that was easy. Mama bought me a cheap suitcase and I put in two shirts, a pair of pants, some socks, some underwear, and a shaving kit. Then I stuck out my thumb for Greenville, North Carolina. I left the section house at Sugar Hill to become the first in my family to go to college. I could tell that my mama was very proud. I could tell that she was worried, too. For never was a person more ill prepared for the groves of academia than was her boy Buster.

Part Two

WAY DOWN DRUNK

in

DIXIE

Camelot Comin' in the Tobacco Fields

By the time I got to the crossroads village of Beargrass, North Carolina, the aroma was unmistakable. The familiar fragrance all about meant it was tobacco auction time, and everything that goes with it. Farmers were loading up their pickups with their wives and young'uns and their cash crop of cured "brightleaf bacca" and heading for the markets. The pungent sweet smell of the leaf was thick in the air of "downeast" Carolina, bringing a palpable sense of anticipation and celebration along the back roads and the two-lane blacktops leading to the auction towns.

My last ride dropped me off a mile or so outside of Greenville and I hoofed it the rest of the way. The enormous auction barns were jam-stacked and -packed with the leaf, and so was every empty house in town with a good roof. The streets were lined with pickups and flatbed trucks waiting to unload. Both sides of my family had grown tobacco in North Carolina, and I knew how important the auctions were, particularly to the small farmers. It was an exciting time, since getting a good price meant having food on the table, shoes on the feet, and a full stocking come Christmas.

I have long since kicked the habit of the evil weed, but in those days in North Carolina tobacco was king and folks who didn't smoke were as rare as Republicans. I had been chain-smoking since high school and by now was going through at least two packs a day, maybe three when I was out drinking, which was more often than not. I started on Old Golds and Pall Malls. In Greenville in 1960 I could buy a carton of them for a buck fifty.

But there was so much tobacco in Greenville at auction time that all you had to do to get your nicotine fix was to take a big whiff of the town, piled to the housetops with that golden leaf.

East Carolina College had long been East Carolina Teacher's College, and was still called ECTC by most folks around there. Therefore it was jokingly referred to as "EZ-TC." The campus was in a cozy grove of longleaf pines and oak trees, just a short walk from the downtown section of Greenville. I was referred by the student housing department to a rooming house at 1111 Forbes Street, the home of the Widow Hawkins. Worn out from a hot day of hitchhiking and walking, I crashed out early in a small upstairs room with two beds.

Somewhere around midnight I was awakened by my new roommate, a hefty, boozy, happy, fast-talking country boy from the Blue Ridge Mountains of Virginia named "Bubba" Hazel. We hit it off immediately. We talked for hours, but it didn't take that long for me to realize that I had been serendipitously hooked up with one of the wiliest and most mischievous characters of the Southland.

He was already a wizard at wheeling and dealing, something for which he was to become legendary. Not only could he sell iceboxes to Eskimos, he could throw in an air conditioner and some old ceiling fans for just a little bit extra.

In his senior year of high school he had been lined up for a football scholarship at the University of Virginia, but while pushing a stalled pickup truck on a mountain road he had been struck by an automobile and suffered a serious back injury.

So instead of a football career, he had headed for ECTC in an old Renault Dauphine, a car which the French had introduced in America as a competitor to the Volkswagen Bug. That strategy was to be another case of Germany overwhelming France, but Bubba Hazel and I had a hell of a good time in that Renault before it came apart. Regular gas in those days ran about 25 cents a gallon and the Renault got over forty miles to the gallon. At one point, there was a "gas war" in Greenville, and one station was pumping at 9.9 cents a gallon. We filled up for less than two bucks, drove to Washington, D.C., and back and still had plenty left in the tank for a trip to the beach.

Bubba managed to get one more last gasp out of that car when he sold it to a couple of ol' boys up in the mountains for twice what he had paid for it. He said they were able to drive it only about a half-mile up a hill before it completely gave out. Then it became Southern yard art.

I had been at East Carolina for only about a week when I went to cover a political event one Saturday morning for a journalism course I was taking. The campus football stadium was packed, awaiting the arrival of the Democratic candidate for the presidency, John F. Kennedy. Kennedy was running late, caught up in the action down at the tobacco auctions. The college band tried to keep the crowd entertained, but the only song these old wool-hatted FDR Democrats wanted to hear was "Happy Days Are Here Again!" The band played it over and over. And they played it when Jack Kennedy finally arrived, in a convertible. It was a grand entrance. I was maybe a hundred feet away and JFK's charisma shone like a great actor taking the stage. His presence seemed to draw all the available attention from this crowd of college kids and gallused, sun-wrinkled farmers.

"That smile!" I thought. I had never seen a man who seemed to genuinely enjoy every second of what he was up to like he did. Kennedy was having fun. He took the podium to another chorus of "Happy Days Are Here Again!" and launched into his stump speech.

"I am proud to be here in North Carolina!" he began. "Of you Tar Heels it was said, 'First at Bethel, farthest at Gettysburg, and last at Appomattox'!" The crowd roared, JFK soared, the band hit "Happy Days," and Jack Kennedy had the vote of everyone there. On Election Day, North Carolina went for Kennedy and that gave him his victory over Richard Nixon. In that clipped Boston accent he had praised the Old South in a way that was neither condescending nor patronizing, and that gesture was downright uplifting.

And I was uplifted. North Carolina was one of the few states then that had the eighteen-year-old vote, on the belief that if one is old enough to die for one's country, one is old enough to decide who is going to make the decisions about war. And so I cast my very first vote for John F. Kennedy, Democrat of Massachusetts.

Just as I had arrived at East Carolina, my folks moved from the section house at Sugar Hill to Wilmington, North Carolina. My father had taken a promotion from being a section foreman and became the Roadmaster of the Wilmington division, a big step up and one that he had resisted for years. It also meant going from a union job to a management job. As he had always put it, "I don't want a job where I have to wear a damn hat."

So he bought his first hat, and suddenly he and Mama and my kid brother Bryan were living on a city street in a neighborhood. This was some serious culture shock for the old man, but Mama finally had the dignity of a real home.

Daddy also quit drinking the cheap Four Roses Blended Whiskey and upgraded to the cheap Seagram's 7 Blended Whiskey. It cost a dime more for a fifth. Far as I could tell, nothing else changed. Money was still tight, because he was usually about half-tight.

I made one trip back to Portsmouth that fall. Having nothing better to do, Bruce Laughon and I were sitting in his car at a local hangout sharing a few beers when we were arrested for "drinking in public" and taken to the downtown jail for the night. It was the first of many nights I would spend behind bars in the next seventeen years.

Somehow I managed to feel victimized by that cop that night. He made us pour our beer out in the parking lot, while a lot of our friends watched, and he seemed to get a kick out of his power. He was playing the role, while the role I assumed was that of a misunderstood innocent citizen, minding my own business, being hassled by the Man. It was the first time my deeply rooted resentment toward authority surfaced. It was to become a habit.

I was also becoming a skillful liar, a guy who could bullshit you with the best of them. This was great training for the actor's trade, but the big problem was that I was even better at bullshitting myself. Nothing was ever my fault. I was always the victim of some imagined injustice.

I spent the year at East Carolina drinking, shooting pool, and trying to get laid. I was only successful at drinking. I was usually too drunk to win at pool, and that year I couldn't have gotten laid in a women's prison. I picked up a part-time job at a golf driving range, collecting the balls, keeping the clubs clean, and showing folks how to handle a driver. Of course, I had never played a round of golf in my life, but that didn't mean I couldn't fake it. At that point in life, I was faking everything else.

After a day of classes I would head right for Happy's pool hall and beer joint, where I would hang out, eat a cheeseburger, drink a few beers, and do all I could to put off what work I had to do. Then I would stop off at a bar called the Varsity, and sit drinking and listening to the jukebox for an hour or two, usually by myself. I must've played Sam Cooke singing "You Send Me" on the big Wurlitzer until it was about worn out. Then I would stumble on back to the rooming house to do the class assignments. I was not the first to discover that it is very hard to read world history when you are drunk and seeing double. And I was often seeing triple.

I was lucky to have some very good professors, though, who could penetrate my most pounding hangovers and my mind's thickest fogs. Because of encouragement from a man named David Whichard, who edited the local newspaper and taught a journalism course at the college, I determined to become a writer.

One day I was browsing without purpose in the library when I came across a booklet about the Department of Radio, Television, and Motion Pictures at the University of North Carolina. The brochure pictured smiling students studying scripts, pushing cameras, and sitting behind big microphones like John Cameron Swayze. On a long-shot chance, I wrote a letter to the University, applying for admission. Miraculously, I was accepted despite my mediocre academic record. When I visited Chapel Hill, I was told my admittance was based entirely on the quality of that application letter. Suddenly, the angry alcoholic redneck railroad boy was going to be a student at one of America's finest universities. Well, I guess I'd rather be lucky than good. That's how I felt at the time, lucky but unworthy. Looking back now, I know that going to that school at that place at that time was one of the great blessings and fortunes of my life. That experience shaped everything I was, into everything I was to become.

That spring, while visiting the folks in Wilmington, I was arrested with a bunch of other drunks at the Azalea Festival in Carolina Beach. I only have vague memories of that night, including driving home in the family car with one eye closed so I could see the white line in the middle of the highway. Over my drunken years I must've driven thousands of miles with one eye closed. And most of my brain was closed, too.

But somehow I muddled through East Carolina College with a B average and a new dream. I said good-bye to Greenville and my buddy Bubba Hazel. I didn't see ol' Bubba again for thirty-eight years.

That summer of 1961 I got a job at Corbett's Basket Factory in Wilmington, working on an assembly line. The factory was a major producer of peach baskets. My job was to "catch" the basket bottoms as they came through a stapling machine that stamped three pieces of heavy plywood together. A finished bottom would come through the machine almost every second, about 50 a minute, about 3,000 an hour. Working six ten-hour days with two half-hour daily breaks meant that I would handle about 27,000 pieces a day, over 140,000 a week. After the first day or so, the work was so monotonous and automatic that there was no challenge. So I lived in my stream of consciousness. And the rhythm of the stories in my head.

I read Jack Kerouac's *On the Road* during that summer, and in my fantasies on the assembly line I became Dean Moriarty, *hipster angel at the basket factory, planning visionjourneys on blacktop horizons of endless dharma nights with fireblown Mexican princesses singing bop rhapsodies to the lovesick moons and the green dawns of hallelujahville.* And the machines continued to throb. "Another one, another one, another one . . ."

Once again, I was the only "white boy" on the job. After twelve weeks of catching basket bottoms, I figured I had handled over a million of them, and that was enough for any lifetime. Besides, it was about time to go off to Chapel Hill. Melvin, the black foreman for my section of the factory, gave me a lift home on my last day. And he also gave me one of the great compliments of my life. "Ben," he said, "you 'bout the best basket bottom catcher that Corbett's has ever had." That was my Oscar, my Emmy, my Pulitzer, my Nobel Prize.

My departure coincided with my father's "vacation," which for him still meant at least two solid weeks of uninterrupted whiskey drinking. And for some reason, this time he decided to turn his demons directly on me. After three days of his ceaseless verbal abuse, I finally told him off and hit the road hitchhiking. I left there with the feeling that I was never going to take any shit off of anybody ever again. The old man hadn't intended to, but he had taught me a great lesson.

Redneck Boy in the Promised Land

My last ride to the University was with a grizzled old farmer in his ancient pickup truck, up through the red clay Piedmont hills, through the unchanging tobacco towns, and into Chapel Hill, the fabled "Southern Part of Heaven," and home to the nation's oldest public institution of higher learning.

I knew a little bit about the school's liberal academic tradition and political reputation. But I knew a lot about Carolina's excellence in sports, the football teams of Charlie "Choo Choo" Justice, who ran, passed, and kicked UNC into the Cotton Bowl after World War II, and the undefeated basketball team of 1957, which had beaten Wilt Chamberlain and Kansas in triple overtime for the national championship. This was a big-time place, and I felt like a redneck boy in the promised land.

The farmer dropped me off with some words of hope. "You gonna like it up here," he said. "My grandbaby went here and she's teaching school now in Chatham County. You work hard and it ain't no tellin' where your road's gonna take you!"

As I walked down along Franklin Street toward the campus, I

window-shopped the college town's business district. There were two movie houses, the Varsity and the Carolina, several restaurants, a beer joint, a post office, and three men's clothing stores. The show windows of the men's stores left me immediately intimidated. They featured upscale "ivy" threads, tweed jackets, button-down shirts, paisley ties, London Fog rainwear, and expensive loafers. These stores catered to the fraternity crowd, whom, I assumed, had parents who could afford them. The best my wardrobe could show was a new pair of Sears and Roebuck slacks, along with two old white shirts with matching white socks. I had a debilitating surge of self-consciousness before I even reached my dorm room. As I walked, toting my cheap suitcase, I felt like everyone who passed was looking at my worn-out work shoes and my ragged jeans that were at least two inches too short.

When I reached the entrance to the campus, I asked a lady if she knew the whereabouts of Battle Hall, the dormitory to which I had been assigned. "If it was a snake, it'd bite you," she laughed. We were standing in front of it.

Battle was the only men's residence hall which faced Franklin Street. It was directly across the street from a watering hole called "Harry's." This was an odd fate.

After a shower I put on my cleanest pair of socks and headed out to see the campus. My first stop was across the street to check out Harry's for lunch. The place was a New York–style delicatessen, with foods I had not only never eaten, but had barely heard of. I passed on the lox and the pastrami and ordered a cheeseburger and a beer. The burger was thirty cents and a National Bohemian beer was twenty cents. My tour of the town and the school didn't really get past Harry's for the next several days.

To my surprise and delight, Harry's was the bohemian capital of the Southeast, a legendary hangout for artists of all stripes: musicians, painters, actors, dancers, writers, poets, and (mostly) drunkards.

Since I was already something of a professional drunkard myself, I soaked up the atmosphere and the information with unabashed glee. Brer Rabbit was finally in the Briar patch.

The legendary folksinger Ramblin' Jack Elliott rambled through Chapel Hill for a show on the first Friday night I was there. Afterwards, we all took off for a party. Ramblin' Jack put on an even better show there. He was a Jewish kid from Brooklyn whose real name was Adnopoz, but he could yodel and flatpick as good as any Southern picker I had ever heard. And he's still at it.

Before that first weekend was over I had established myself as a first-rate drunken madman. I had consumed the most likker, sang the loudest, told the most dirty jokes, broken a banjo, smoked some rare marijuana, fallen for two girls, gotten in one and a half fistfights, and spent the night with a strange gypsy woman in a hayloft somewhere in the woods. I had not only fallen into bad company, I was bad company. I had set a personal standard for reprobation that would be hard to match, but I tried, lawdy, I tried.

I immediately took a part-time job at Harry's, waiting tables at lunchtime so I could pay for the beer I drank there at night.

A small local newspaper in the county was rumored to keep a secret "beatnik list"—don't ask me why. I was told that the editor was a paranoid sort who thought our early manifestation of the "counterculture" was somehow inspired by the KGB. What he didn't get was that we represented everything America's enemies hated. We were modern Thoreaus, or at least we thought we were. Yep, individualistic to the core, that was us. We were free as the birds. Uh huh, we were some kinda birds, alright.

A piece of dialogue from "The Wild One."

A girl admires Johnny's (Marlon Brando's) black motorcycle jacket with the emblem "BRMC"

GIRL: BRMC . . . What's that stand for?

BRANDO: Black Rebels Motorcycle Club.

GIRL: What you rebelling against?

BRANDO: Whaddya got?

I soon figured out that I had something of a natural synergy with this ragged, offbeat bunch of misfits. The way I grew up, in a dirt shack filled with liquor, music, and madness, well, we had always been "beatniks," according to society's definition. My mama was a poet and my daddy was a man who turned down promotions because he would have to wear a new hat. Some of these cats wanted to be like I already was.

By the thinking of the frat boys I was a "redneck," a rural roughneck with no culture and not much chance of any culture rubbing off on me. That was a "class" thing, as in "You ain't as good as me."

But the artists and the hipsters seemed to welcome me in as a "culture" thing, something that had nothing to do with where you lived or who your parents were. So we could practice our own prejudice now. We were on the outside. The insiders were "squares," losers who were never going to be liberated like us. So, as it so often is, just about everybody was wrong about one another.

Besides my newfound cronies, I also loved everything about the school itself. It turned out that my dorm room, number 8 Battle, had once been home to North Carolina's greatest novelist, Thomas Wolfe. Wolfe, a lanky mountain boy who put his memories of Chapel Hill into his finest work, *Look Homeward, Angel,* was eaten up with talent and alcohol. He was dead at thirty-eight.

Like him, I would take long, feverish, chain-smoking walks at any time of the day or night, soaking up the sights of the old campus and town. Eight Battle looked out onto McCorkle Place, the lower quad, and from my window I could see the statue of a Confederate Soldier, facing north, erected in symbolic memory of those students who'd served in the War Between the States. This soldier, armed and at the ready, is called Silent Sam by the student body. It is said that he fires his rifle every time a virgin walks by. I never heard it go off.

The sidewalks led southward through dogwoods, poplars, and elms to the Old Well, on the spot of the original well of 1790. Just across from the Well was the Playmakers Theatre, where thousands of young actors and playwrights had paid their first dues. Back during the Civil War, Union General Sherman had used it as a stable.

Further along, the upper quad was lined with classroom buildings on either side and terminated at the grand Wilson Library. Beyond there was old Woolen Gym, where the brand-new basketball coach in 1961 was a twenty-nine-year-old from Kansas named Dean Smith. After a tough loss the following season, Coach Smith was hanged in effigy on the campus. Good thing he didn't take it personally and decided to stay around for awhile.

The campus had a lovely arboretum, a glorious old football stadium in a forest of pines, and a forty-five-acre park area called Battle Woods. I felt as if I was going to school in a forest. In those days Chapel Hill had the feel of a quaint European village, unsullied by thoughtless trends or needless development.

It also was considered to be an oasis for political progressivism. In 1961, almost everything in the Southland was segregated, but in Chapel Hill the Merchants Association claimed that 95 percent of the town's public businesses were integrated. The campus certainly had a long tradition of tolerance and liberalism when it came to civil rights and academic freedom. Men like Paul Green and Frank Porter Graham were outspoken social crusaders at a time when progressive positions on race matters could lead to serious personal danger. It was easy to stir up the lynch mob mentality of the Klan and others of their ilk. Segregationist politicians played to those baser instincts as they preached the gospel of white supremacy. The so-called South-

Scenes of Portsmouth, Virginia, just before World War II, about the time I got there.

My Mama, Ila Virginia Stephens, at age 16.

Daddy in 1930 had been working on the railroad for eight years and was assistant section foreman (second from right).

The Section House by the freight yard on the Sugar Hill side of the tracks. By this time, we had electricity.

McNair's Crossing, Edgecombe, North Carolina, where I was born.

Me and two other puppies, 1945.

Doing our part on the home front, 1944.

Clearly headed for trouble.

The Singing Cowboy of Sugar Hill, 1944.

Getting back from work at Stump's Garage.

On the work train in Alabama, August 1962.

Me and Mary Alice. Everything they say about the sixties is true.

On the coast of Maine, early 1970s.

Mama was the only acting teacher I ever needed.

Hard to get any work done at the garage with all these distractions (with Catherine Bach).

The first picture of our entire cast taken in January 1979. Nearly 30 years later the show is still a hit.

"Two good ol' boys." Cooter with the King of the gas pedal, Richard Petty.

What a cast!

ern moderates went along complacently, not wanting to rock the boat and literally risk their necks. But despite the prevailing climate, the University of North Carolina had earned respect and a national reputation as a bastion for equality. That was soon to be tested.

John F. Kennedy spoke in Chapel Hill that fall. He had won that job he was trying to get when I met him the year before at East Carolina. And he once again used the line about the Tar Heels who were "First at Bethel, farthest at Gettysburg, and last at Appomattox." I guess if it works, don't fix it. He looked ten years older and twenty pounds heavier to me. But he still had that magnetism and that appeal to "the better angels of our nature." To me, he was the man.

The Radio, Television, and Motion Pictures Department was located in Swain Hall, which once had been the school cafeteria and was therefore called "Swine Hall." It had been started in 1948 to provide North Carolina with homegrown communications talent—the producers, directors, writers, and on-air talents to build an indigenous industry within the state. We learned the rudiments of radio and television production in a real studio, and cranked out eight-millimeter silent films just to learn the editing process. We wrote and produced radio plays at a time when that was quickly becoming a dying art. We studied the language of film by watching and breaking down the work of pioneers like D.W. Griffith, Sergei Eisenstein, and Buster Keaton. We watched many hours of the great television dramas from the golden era, like *Playhouse 90, Kraft Television Theatre,* and *Studio One.* We studied Edward R. Murrow, boned up on FCC regulations, argued about cinema verité, and learned the difference between a tilt down, a dolly in, a pan right, and a boom up.

It was the writing that pulled me. I met Paul Green, the Pulitzer Prize–winning playwright and campus contemporary of Thomas Wolfe, and the man who had written *The Lost Colony,* that drama on

Roanoke Island which had so captured my fancy when I was five. He sounded just like the farm boy he was, with an accent as thick as the tar in the Downeast pineywoods. One of the first times I met him he asked me, "What do you think life is, Ben?" "I don't guess I rightly know, Mr. Green," I said. He shrugged his shoulders and smiled. "I don't either." He was my kinda guy.

I got a job pushing a television camera for the local news at the campus station, WUNC-TV. The student sportscaster there was a fellow named Woody Durham, who remains until this day the "Voice of the Tar Heels." I envied his job then, and I envy it now.

One thing I found I had a knack for was "voice work," not only sounding like an announcer, but taking various character parts in the student-written radio plays. In radio you could do anything. It was, as Archibald MacLeish said, "the theatre of the imagination." I wrote a radio drama about Christ returning to earth as a greatly misunderstood green bear. Thereafter I felt like a greatly misunderstood green writer.

Still, the biggest problem I had was concentrating for more than a few minutes at a time. I don't really know if what I suffered from was what is now called "attention deficit disorder," but I do know that what I suffered from exactly fits the description of ADD. Yet I also know that alcohol was a constant distraction. It called to me relentlessly. I wanted it from the moment I woke up. I would kick the thought back, tell myself I might have a few beers later, and within a few minutes the urge would return. I would shuck it off again and try to get on with the day, but no matter what activity I was involved in, I was more involved in trying not to think about wanting a drink. When I would go for a day or so without booze, I would allow that brief abstinence to become the evidence that I had no problem, that my love of drinking was natural and right, and then I would play "catch-up ball" by drinking as much as possible as soon as possible. It was the old "I can take it or leave it" that I heard from my old man so many times. Yeah, leave it for two days and take it for a week.

It is easy to live the drinking life in a college town. Getting drunk is a rite of passage for most college kids, and the serious alcoholics in their midst often won't be revealed for a few years on. Chapel Hill seemed downright proud of its reputation for being a hard-partying, hard-drinking school, and I felt like I was certainly doing my part. But the voices in my head were running my ass ragged.

Railroad Days

Although at this point in time my father and I really didn't have much of a relationship, he did me one of the great favors of my life when he lined me up for a summer job on a work train, killing weeds along railroad right-of-ways throughout the Eastern United States. I hopped aboard as soon as the spring semester at Chapel Hill was over.

It was a great adventure. I was a compulsive rambler to begin with, always ready to stick out my thumb and go somewhere I had never been. I must have inherited an old gypsy traveling bone in there somewhere. I worked that summer for a company out of Virginia that contracted to various rail lines to battle the growth of weeds, which are a summertime hazard in several ways. They hamper the work of trainmen along the tracks, can get into crossties and cause erosion, and they are an eyesore, of course. Some lines had their own solutions, dumping a light coat of oil, for example. I'm certain the stuff we were using has been long since banned by the Environmental Protection Agency, which didn't exist back then. Or if it did, we paid them absolutely no attention.

I liked the other fellows on the crew, hardworking country boys for the most part. We were all young guys, except for the foreman, a colorful character we called Bill from Jacksonville who was to become a regular drinking companion. Bill was in his forties, and he had the first credit card I had ever seen.

Buddy Baird was from Memphis, a couple of years older than me, and wonderfully bad company. One night after work in Baltimore on the Baltimore and Ohio Railroad, we headed down to "the Block," the old red light district in that northernmost of Southern cities. We ended up in a tavern which featured "B girls," hookers who were hired to sit with lonely guys and ask the fellows to buy them a drink. The "drinks" were usually colored water, so the house really cleaned up on the operation. And if you had more dough, the girls would go to your room and earn that, too. But we hadn't made it to payday, so we settled for talk.

"What kind of work do you guys do?" asked a sweet little black-haired Italian girl. I figured she was just starting out in the trade, because she didn't have the hard look or the street savvy of her older redheaded companion.

"We don't really like to talk about it," Buddy said.

"How come?" said the redhead.

"It bothers some people."

"Why?" asked the little black-haired girl.

"Well," said Buddy. "Cause we're hired killers. We go from town to town, mostly on the trains, taking care of business."

"Oh my goodness," said Blackhair. Redhead didn't blink.

"Well, it's just a way to make a living," said Buddy.

He was right. Our job was to go from town to town, mostly on trains, killing off things.

"Doesn't it make you feel terrible when you do that?" said Blackhair.

"Well, yeah, sometimes. I have bad dreams and I get a guilty conscience about it. But Spike there," Buddy said, indicating me, "he really enjoys it. He gets off on it."

I gave her my best Charles Bronson "You're gonna die" look.

The girl was shocked. She stared at her drink. "Well, I could never do that. Nuh-uh!"

"You probably could," said Buddy, "if you needed the dough real bad."

"No, I never would," she said.

"Why?" asked the big redhead.

"Because I'm a Catholic," said the hooker.

Right away I had learned something about Baltimore.

Something else happened on that Baltimore stop. On a Sunday afternoon after a visit to the Edgar Allen Poe House, I stopped in a ramshackle old bookshop and came across a first edition of *You Can't Go Home Again,* Thomas Wolfe's posthumous novel, roughly rewritten by an editor named Asbell. At the time I didn't know about the severe editing, only that Wolfe had lived in my dorm room, that he was a "big ol' boy" from the mountains, that he drank too much, and that he died young. And that he wrote one of my favorite pieces of prose/poetry:

. . . a stone, a leaf, an unfound door . . . and of all the forgotten faces . . .
Naked and alone we came into exile. . . .
Which of us has known his brother?
Which of us has looked into his father's heart?
Which of us is not forever a stranger and alone? . . .
Remembering speechlessly we seek the great forgotten language, the lost lane-end into heaven, a stone, a leaf, an unfound door. Where? When?
O lost, and by the wind grieved, ghost, come back again. . . .

Why, I don't know, but I really related to that kind of thing. I suppose it was because I was really, really lost. But now that I am found, I still like it.

The next morning we were deadheading out on the work train. "Deadheading" is just hauling ass on the train to the starting point of the work, or heading back in after the work is done. As we rolled out of the city I was kicked back with my feet up on a tool chest, reading *You Can't Go Home Again.* Wolfe's narrator, George Webber, is on a train heading home to North Carolina from New York City. His train is in Baltimore, and as it entered a tunnel in Baltimore, so did the train I was riding in Baltimore. Mine entered the tunnel at the same moment I read of his train entering the same tunnel. The "ghost came back again."

⊰⊱

We pulled into Nashville, Tennessee, on the old Louisville and Nashville Railroad, better known as the L&N, coming from Memphis and feeling frisky because it was Friday and we had the weekend off.

While the other guys would go to the hotel and sit around the television, I would go exploring. I had an alcoholic's second sense, a kind of radar which would quickly lead me to my favorite kind of hangout. It was always a few blocks past the nicer, cleaner joints, down by the bus station and the pawnshops. It just felt like my side of the tracks.

It would be a place called something like The Bluebird Grill or Joe's and Jean's or The Cedarwood Lounge. To me it was Neon Nirvana. These joints had the smell of decline, of warmhearted losers, of bartenders who are past cynical. In the afternoon light there would be a couple of regulars at the barstools watching a black-and-white TV which inevitably had a problem with the vertical hold. One guy might be loud and stupidly opinionated and the other guy was a grunter. A lady with problems always sat in a cracked Naugahyde booth. The big Wurlitzer jukebox was there to reinforce your broken heart.

I would find a little place there, like a dog curling up in the thick dust under a porch. There I would sit, alone with me, listening to the long-playing album in my head. And I would observe. And as the booze would take hold, the hours would lead to strange places, to one-night friends, and one thing would lead to another, and many was the time I should have been shot.

In Nashville, on the down side of town, I hooked up with a woman whose boyfriend was too drunk to take her to the Grand Ole Opry. I watched them fight and I watched her leave, and I slid out a few minutes behind her. About three blocks from the Ryman Auditorium, as I caught up with her, I asked as innocently as I could muster, "Is this the way to the Grand Ole Opry?"

"Yeah, it's right up here," she said. We had eyed each other back at the bar. "Why don't you just walk with me?"

"I ain't never been," I said. It was the last true thing I said that night.

We stood in line and I paid for two. I was always a big spender when drinking. More often than not, I woke up with empty pockets wondering if whatever had happened had been worth it.

The girl saw some people she knew, thanked me for my generosity, and went off to sit with them. I sat close to the stage, in the middle of a row of wild characters from Kentucky who were passing bottles of "white lightning" back and forth, through either side of me. I got a slug coming and going.

Hank Snow, "The Singing Ranger," came out and sang his recent hit, "I've Been Everywhere." I was amazed. The song amazed me. And that moonshine likker really amazed me.

After the show, as I was lighting a cigarette, I saw her right outside, by herself, looking at me. My liquid courage went to work. She went with me to my room and she welcomed me to Music City.

She was gone when the phone rang at two in the morning. It was Bill, the foreman. "Hey," he said, "I'm down here in a place called Printer's Alley. Come on down, this place is wide open!"

"I ain't got much money left."

"That don't matter. I'm buyin'. I got a credit card."

Somebody was paying somebody off around Printer's Alley in those days. This was some serious after-hours jukin'. The downstairs club in which Bill had ensconced himself was a rug joint, the rug a bit worn and tattered, but still a step up for me. It was segregated, of course, except for the black bartender and the fabulous black pianist who sang as well as he played. Bill and I lost track of time. When the place finally closed and we climbed the stairs to the alley we were greeted by blinding daylight and the excruciating gonging of church bells. It was Sunday morning, 9 A.M.

Half asleep at noon, I heard something on the TV about a show at the Parthenon. Nashville is, after all, the "Athens of the South." I caught the bus to Centennial Park and there before me stood the glory that was Greece. I "laid out" on the grass while Roy Acuff and the Smoky Mountain Boys performed on the Parthenon steps. I think I dozed off right about the time Bashful Brother Oswald launched into a Dobro riff during Roy's hit "Night Train to Memphis."

I've had a deep affection for that town since that very moment. But it would be a long time before I would see it sober.

And so went the hot railroad days and nights of my searching, misspent youth. I had that compulsion to explore the dark side of town and the other side of the tracks. And the rusty clank and the squeal and the scream of steel wheel on steel rail was my theme music, the background to my real compulsion, to drink every drop of liquor on the planet. I was lost out there but I didn't know it at the time.

So I just kept on keepin' on like that. For a long, long time.

That Was Not a Chip on My Shoulder, It Was a Crosstie

Whatever the source of the anger, it was there. In 1962, I don't recall anyone using terms like "repressed animosities" or "anger-management" difficulties. What you would hear is, "That hoss's got a bad temper," or, "Be careful not to piss that guy off."

Back in Chapel Hill in the fall, and hard as a rail from the summer of work, I was on my way to somewhere when I passed a fraternity house where a half-dozen drunk frat boys were sitting on the porch. They started mocking me. I assumed it was because of my long hair and my work clothes.

"Hey, Lizard!" one said. "Yeah, look at that lizard!" said another. They all laughed. I had never heard the expression "lizard" before, and I don't think I have heard it since, but I could tell they weren't throwing me any compliments. My anger thing kicked off. I started up the walkway toward them.

"C'mon you muthafuggahs, I'll take ever one of you sumbitches on!" I heard myself saying. They all went inside except one. He just smiled at me and said, "It's alright, buddy. They were just drunk and mouthin' off. You wanna beer?"

It was good to be back in Chapel Hill.

Back at Battle Dorm, I was a real pain in the ass for my studious roommates. I would come in late and loud at night, stumbling and singing, interrupting their serious work like a madman talking in tongues. They were cursed with a rapscallion in their midst and I was blessed by knowing the great group of guys who came through there. Charlie was into art. Stuart studied and played classical music all day. He turned me on to Bach and Wagner and my all-time favorite, Dvorak. Sonny was a good ol' boy and a baseball player, who chewed tobacco and would spit it out the second-story window. Lynn was very quiet and very hardworking. He became a Federal Judge. Next door, Curry Kirkpatrick was a freshman who was the only guy around who knew more about sports than I did. He became a senior editor of *Sports Illustrated.*

In that bunch, I was least likely to succeed.

What Is Wrong with "Buster"?

Alcoholism is a chronic disease. That means it doesn't go away. Alcoholism is also a progressive disease. That means it gets worse. And it is a fatal disease. That means if you don't overcome it and find abstinence, sooner or later it will kill you. And before it does, it will bring a lot of unhappiness to you and those around you.

You never see an obituary that says, "The cause of death was alcoholism." It will say that the deceased passed away from a liver ailment, or kidney failure, or a heart attack, or a stroke, or in an automobile accident, or took his or her own life.

Statistics consistently show that one out of every ten drinkers "drinks alcoholically." That means that one out of every ten drinkers has the disease, and despite every effort at controlling the addiction, alcohol takes over their life. And it seems that a consistent part of the addiction is the denial of the addiction. Weird, but true.

Another amazing but consistent statistic is that the 10 percent of drinkers who drink alcoholically consume over 50 percent of the booze that is manufactured. That is a statistic that the alcohol industry doesn't want known. But it is also true.

I know because I was one of the 10 percent.

One sure sign of the disease is the sudden change of the drinker's personality when boozing. When I was sober, or if I had just had a few beers, I was one jolly young soul, full of jokes and songs and stories. But at a certain point several hours into an evening of drinking, something could trigger a sudden rage, an explosion of senseless anger that seemed to come from nowhere. And like my father before me, kindly Dr. Jekyll changed into the diabolical Mr. Hyde. This did not always happen, but on those occasions when it did happen the eruption was always threatening and always tinged with violence. The folks who had always known me as the sweet little soft-hearted guy couldn't figure it out. "What in the world has gotten into Buster?" they wondered. And being totally clueless, all I could do was blame it on whatever had made me flare up. "Couldn't have been my fault." I was certain of that.

Acting Naturally, Naturally

Just off of Chapel Hill's Franklin Street, down the "Porthole Alley," was an all-night coffeehouse and restaurant called "Byron's," where our crowd of boozy beats would go after last call for beer at Harry's. What money that Harry didn't get now went to Byron for eggs and coffee. The coffee did not sober us up. It simply made us wide-awake drunks.

One night in the spring of 1963, a theater student named Dick King came into Byron's looking for a favor from me. He was directing a production of three one-acts by Edward Albee for a graduate course and he needed an actor.

"It's for a group called Petite Dramatique," he said.

"Say what?" I mumbled.

"That's French for 'Little Theater,' " he said.

I acted like I knew that. I wasn't much interested in doing the show until he played his hole card. It seemed that a gal I had the hots for was playing the female lead. Apparently I agreed to do the part, because Dick came by the next afternoon while I was sleeping off a hangover to tell me it was time for rehearsal. I didn't quite remember what he was talking about, but I went along to see what was up.

It worked out well. I did the shows, and I even got lucky with the actress for a few weeks. But it was really the genesis of a love affair with the theater and the beginning of a career I could not have imagined. Right away, I loved the sound of an audience laughing. And when I heard the applause at the first curtain call, I was flat hooked, y'all, happily and totally and forever on the old "roar of the greasepaint and the smell of the crowd."

One week I had never been onstage, and the next week I knew what I wanted to do with my entire life. It seems I was a natural ham. All of those years around Mama's Ongoing Poetry and Songfest Recitals (accompanied by the sounds of Spike Jones and His City Slickers) had developed my performance skills far past my experience level. And acting was a way to be somebody else, not the inept and insecure social dud I believed myself to be. Now I could be whoever the playwright imagined. Behind the door I had wandered through was my passion. It was something I just had to do. Whether or not I was any good at it starting off, I really don't know, but in my head I was the next Brando, and an immediate rival to Richard Burton.

Chapel Hill was a good place to be for a newly aspiring thespian. It had developed a reputation for excellent theater after Professor Fred Koch had created the Carolina Playmakers in 1919, encouraging his students to "Write about what you know, write those folk stories you've heard all your lives." Students like Paul Green and Thomas Wolfe and Andy Griffith "got it." They got it good. Before long the Carolina Playmakers was one of America's most esteemed theater environments.

By the time I first set my tentative, shaky feet on their stage, there were those who suggested that the theater folks were still living off that old reputation. But that didn't faze me. What did I know? Or care? To appear on the tiny Playmakers stage was as thrilling to me as a Broadway opening.

I took one acting class in the Drama Department. The professor didn't have a lot to profess. He told good stories when he showed up, which was irregularly. And since I showed up irregularly also, we passed each other like ships in the night. I don't recall him ever commenting on my work. I got a C in the course. I'm not sure when it came time for him to mark down my grade that he really remembered which one I was.

That was fine with me. I was learning by doing it. I would volunteer for every student project, every off-the-wall experimental play, and anything else around at which I could throw my inexperience and zeal. I played the Gravedigger in *Hamlet,* Mitch in *A Streetcar Named Desire,* Lenny in *Of Mice and Men,* and countless original plays by writing students that ranged from the merely mediocre to the unmentionably wretched. But I loved it. I learned something about the craft every day, and I thought about it constantly. I did Chekov, Strindberg, O'Neill, and Brecht. I played Christ in a W.B. Yeats one-act and I played the Mock Turtle in *Alice in Wonderland.*

I'd audition for everything. For musicals I would try to dance even though I didn't know how and I'd sing off-key at the top of my lungs. I built sets, painted drops, hung lights, and worked as a stage manager. If someone had asked me to play the part of a ham-and-cheese omelet for their scene class, I would start thinking like an egg.

I had found something I thought I was good at. Something besides drinking. I might not have been much, you see, but in those days I was all I thought about. I was totally full of myself, and totally full of bull.

The parties in town started getting bigger and wilder. After one bash, about a block from the police station, nine of us piled into a car to go to another party. We made it as far as the police station, where we were busted and charged with disorderly conduct and disturbing the peace. We should have been charged with "disturbing the police."

That spring I was quickly cast in a couple of other things, including the lead in a well-made student film. The quirky director insisted I dye my hair a bright blond. That was fine with me. With a new head of hair and makeup covering my pocky face, I felt like Troy Donahue in *A Summer Place.*

A day or so after the film ended, I showed up for a second summer of my job on the work train. The foreman took one look at my long blond curls and decided that the "new me" wasn't about to get on his train without a serious haircut. So I went from being Troy Donahue to being Telly Savalas in about twenty minutes. This, I figured, must've been how Samson felt.

A Sign of the Times Comes Down

Some big changes were beginning to take place in the Southland in those years. A hundred years after the Emancipation Proclamation, the descendants of slaves were standing up for equality after decades of third-class citizenship. The entrenched system of segregation and "white supremacy" which had always been a part of my surroundings was now being challenged by a generation of civil rights activists who were not going to be turned around. Most of the white folks I knew stood for the status quo, and some were violently passionate in their opposition to integration. Almost all of the black folks I knew were willing to go to jail for the cause, and some were ready to die for it. And then there were those of all colors who just chose not to "get involved."

I was much influenced by some of the black students I had befriended and by the extraordinary eloquence of Dr. Martin Luther King, Jr. It was time to take a stand. My friend Bob Brown had it right. "Not deciding," he said, "is a decision. Not choosing is a choice." And so I was an idealistic "white" Southern convert to the notion that the South, my South, must thoroughly integrate its public accommodations and begin finally to address the terrible legacy of Jim Crow.

In the spring of 1963, I "hit the streets," demonstrating, marching, and picketing for a new kind of South.

It was, as always, a splendid spring in Chapel Hill. The magnolia, the honeysuckle, and the wisteria perfumed the dogwoods, the azaleas, the lilacs, and the crabapple blossoms. The campus was in full bloom. But down on Franklin Street there was tension among the blossoms and the flowers.

As our civil rights march moved toward the business district, some angry hecklers shouted racial epithets and held placards that said things like "SEGREGATION NOW AND FOREVER!!" and "NO RACE MIXING!" Yet to come in that watershed year was the cowardly murder of Medgar Evers. Yet to come was the assassination of JFK. Yet to come were the murders of Viola Liuzzo and James Chaney, Michael Schwerner, and Andy Goodman. Yet to come was the church bombing in Birmingham that killed six little girls. Yet to come was the March on Washington and Dr. King's "I Have a Dream" speech. Already in the past few months there had been increasing violence around the sit-ins and marches throughout the South. The old ways die hard.

I understood the dangers better than most because I was no "wild-eyed outside agitator from up North" but a "redneck" Southern boy raised in the strict segregation of the times. But now I had come to believe that no American should be denied a hamburger in a public place because of the way that the Good Lord designed him. Nor should he or she be denied the vote, the most basic right. Or denied equal job opportunities. These seem like obvious notions now, but there was a wall of defiance to those ideas on that beautiful spring day in 1963.

This was our biggest demonstration yet, about three hundred fifty people. We were mostly white students and black townspeople, but there were a significant number of faculty members, clergymen, and even a few business folk among us. The tension eased as we sang and chanted slogans.

There were heroes in those days, and I saw two of them that day.

Our march route passed by several segregated businesses where we paused in silence, then marched on. At one, a tiny breakfast spot called the College Café, two men stood in the front window. One was black, one was white. In front of them was an old sign which read, "WHITE ONLY." I remember noting the irony to the lady next to me as we moved on.

Later I heard what happened. The white man was Max, the owner. The black man was Joe, the cook. They had worked side by side for many years, opening at five in the morning and closing at three in the afternoon. There had never been a cross word between them.

Our march passed on by, heading for a church in the black neighborhood for more singing and speechmaking. But back at the College Café, Joe the cook took off his apron and laid it on the counter.

"Max, I can't work here no more," he said.

Max was genuinely puzzled. "Why in the world not?"

Joe was quiet for a moment. Then he found the words.

"That was my preacher went by just now. My friends. And my grandchildren. They can't eat here. So I just can't work here."

They looked at each other for what seemed like a long time.

"Well, alright," said Max. He went over to the window. He took up the "WHITE ONLY" sign, tore it in half, and threw it in the trash can. "Well, I reckon now you can work here again."

Joe put his apron back on.

"Yessir," he said, "now I surely can."

They never spoke of it again. They didn't need to. It seems to me that in the vast sweep of history, the great revolutions are made one heart at a time.

My new roles of artiste and agitator didn't go over very well with some of my old railroad buddies that summer. And it sure didn't go over particularly well with my father, the old-school "Cap'n" of the section gang. He had been born and bred to a way of life that was long taught and deeply ingrained. We both knew, from our different paths, that change was not going to come easily. One side was saying, "Now!" The other side was saying, "Never!"

In the South, in the cabs of the great steam locomotives of the legendary trains, there usually sat two men, a white engineer and a black fireman. Most likely they were men who had partnered together for many years, and had formed a bond of friendship that transcended normal work relationships, a bond built on skill, on performance, on trust, and on the shared experiences of tens of thousands of miles of railroading. Yet always at the end of the day they went their separate ways. To me, the only thing that had to change was the sense that even though they might still go their separate ways, they did not have to. In that understanding would be the beginning of a respect for the individual, and just that little change of attitude would put reality into the notion that is basic to our great religions and to our great governing documents. That notion being that all of us are equal in the eyes, the mind, and the heart of our Creator. And with that understanding, with that acceptance would come a better life and a better world. And yes, I was a hopeless dreamer. And yes, I still am.

That train was pulling out and I was sure gonna be onboard.

One morning, working on the L&N, I was sitting in a diner in Etowah, Tennessee, eating grits and eggs and listening to Elvis sing "Follow That Dream" on the jukebox, when a story in the Knoxville paper caught my eye. There had been a large sit-in back in Chapel Hill with a lot of arrests, including my good friend, Bob Brown. Bob was a Korean War veteran, and he had cojones the size of cantaloupes. I was proud of him that day, and I felt like I was AWOL from something that really mattered.

She Talked a Lot About Texas

Her name was Vicki Andersen and she was the first girl who really liked me. She thought I was funny and smart and talented and good-hearted. To me, she was surely all of those things and more. She really believed in me and supported my dreams. She was my first steady girlfriend and she became my first wife.

Vicki came from a West Texas oil family and was a graduate student in Library Science. She had a slow Texas drawl, drove a brand-new Chrysler, and drank expensive Scotch whiskey straight from the jug. I had met her at a springtime party somewhere, in a crowded kitchen, and we had hit it off. But I didn't see her again until the fall, when I was back in town from the railroad. We walked smack into each other on Franklin Street, went to share a few beers, and just like that, became inseparable.

I had moved out of old Battle Dorm and found a room in a house out on Justice Street, north of town. Tom, my landlord, shared my interest in booze and music. Our place became known as a party house. The folk music craze was taking hold and there would always be a bunch of pickers around. One kid, just sixteen years old, really had a style. His name was James Taylor. Yep, Sweet Baby James.

I just took a couple of classes, and besides working at Harry's, I got a job running a slide projector in the art department, learning a lot about painters like Giotto and Hogarth. And I was cast in a production of *Little Mary Sunshine* at the Playmakers, playing a comic Indian chief. On top of that, I was marching and picketing for integration just about every day. Since Dr. King's speech at the March on Washington in August of that year, it seemed like the passion for change had really intensified. It wasn't a strong request anymore. It was a demand for justice.

In the years since, not much has been written about how very important music was to the movement. Folksingers like Odetta, Joan Baez, Josh White, Pete Seeger, and Bob Dylan came through town for concerts that lent support to the demonstrations, lifting our spirits and reassuring us that what we were doing was part of a great moral heritage. The first time Joan Baez came to the campus, a bunch of us took her down to a local pub after her concert. I have a great memory of Ms. Baez learning the second verse of *The Battle Hymn of the Republic* while sitting in a booth at the "Rathskellar." Her pure, ethereal singing somehow gave us courage.

My whole life has been threaded through with music, woven and held together by songs, a constant chorus of swing and bop and rock and bluegrass banjos. If you see me, there is a song going in my head. Oh, yeah, I hear voices like the crazy people do. I hear Billie Holiday moaning "Strange Fruit" and Sinatra talking out "Where or When" and Hank Williams, that desperate, dangerous whippoorwill, trying to break out of a prison that was only in his mind. I've been there, too. Do you hear it? "That midnight train is whining low . . ."

I was lying around in my room on Justice Street on a warm November afternoon when outside I heard a neighbor telling my buddy Tom to go in and turn on the television, something about an incident in

Dallas. And after much confusion and speculation, Walter Cronkite told us that young Jack Kennedy was dead.

In the shock of that day and night I made a vow to myself to try to make a difference, to put my sorry shoulder to the wheel, and as they say in sports, to leave it all on the field. For those of us dedicated to the Civil Rights Movement, that meant civil disobedience.

We Southerners had heard the virulent hardened voices of segregation and white supremacy all of our lives, often at dinner tables, and the nation had seen firsthand the terrible retribution that challenging that system could bring. All it took to get fourteen-year-old Emmett Till murdered was to look at a white woman. His lynching went unpunished, like hundreds of others. We were in a dangerous time, and no one knew it any better than I did. Everybody's blood was up. Things were about to hit the fan in Chapel Hill.

And Before I'll Be a Slave, I'll Be Buried in My Grave

It was a simple deal. Those of us who insisted on a public accommodation law in "liberal" Chapel Hill were willing to break the "white only" law and take the consequences. These were not private establishments, but publicly licensed businesses, ostensibly open to everyone. Since most of the town was already integrated, we felt that we could become the first fully integrated town in the South, and it would serve the South and the Nation as an example of the way it could be done.

But the leaders of Chapel Hill wouldn't lead. All it would have taken was a few phone calls and a couple of meetings making it clear that the University favored the law. All that was needed was one more vote on the town council. But the great, progressive University of North Carolina was suddenly silent, refusing to become involved. I suppose they feared the recriminations of the state government and the powerful "traditional" money, traditional in this case meaning "segregationist." With the advantage of forty-five years of hindsight, I can understand their concerns (as I did then), but I still feel that their failure to lead was an act of moral cowardice.

It wasn't until 2006 that the University acknowledged their silence during the sit-ins of 1963 in the *Carolina Alumni Review* magazine. Yet some of those old "moderates" who caved to the segregationists in 1963 still defend their actions and their votes. I reckon most folks, myself included, can occasionally convince themselves of just about anything.

And so it began when the board of aldermen rejected our proposal. It began with a sit-in at Brady's Restaurant on December 15, 1963. The students were treated very roughly by some of the Chapel Hill Police, which served only to increase our determination. On December 19, a group was arrested at The Tar Heel Sandwich Shop, and several were attacked by onlookers. One black kid was hospitalized after being kicked in the head repeatedly. This was directly across the street from the police station. The next night I joined in at the same place and was arrested for trespassing and resisting arrest. The resisting arrest charge was for "going limp" in the nonviolent way. This was not easy for me. I would have gladly gotten up and walked to the squad car or across the street to the slammer. But this was Gandhian nonviolence, and I had signed on. Going to jail was a new thing to some of the more innocent and naïve kids. But for me it was getting to be routine. What was different for me was that it was the first time I'd gone to jail sober.

The scene in the Chapel Hill jail was celebratory. In a cell with four bunks, there were twenty-two prisoners, singing and backslapping like it was a pep rally. Among the arrested there was Father Clarence Parker, an Episcopal priest. The kindly Father was eighty-two years old.

In the cell down the hall from us were the female prisoners. Around two A.M., when things became totally silent, I heard an angelic voice echo through the building. It was a black girl, Stella Farrar, singing from her cell.

She sang,

Oh freedom, oh freedom,
Oh freedom over me
And before I'll be a slave
I'll be buried in my grave
And go home to my Lord
And be free.

That night, in jail, I felt free. And for the first time in a long time, I felt the presence of my Lord, just as I had on those spring Sundays walking home to Sugar Hill from Sunday School.

A bunch of us decided to stay locked up through Christmas and we were moved to the Orange County Jail in Hillsborough. A large crowd gathered in our support when we were taken to the paddy wagon for the ride there. Across the street some fraternity boys were waving a Confederate Battle Flag. Officer Lindy Pendergrass walked over there, just gave them a look and waved his hand and the flag disappeared. Lindy was a good guy and like a lot of us Southerners, he didn't think the flag of our ancestors should be used in that manner. I really liked Lindy and Sgt. Jimmy Farrell. They were serious lawmen, strictly business. Whatever their personal feelings might have been, they didn't let it affect their work. If the South had had more officers like them, the Civil Rights Movement would have been much less violent.

Once we were out on bail after Christmas, I went to a demonstration at a "white only" grocery store. Now, I had spent my entire life in the South, and by that point had traveled the length and breadth of Dixie by thumb and by train, and I had never heard of a "white only" grocery store. But just down the hill from the campus was a place called The Rock Pile, run by a man named Carlton Mize. Mr. Mize's politics made the John Birch Society seem like liberals and the KKK seem like racial moderates. So we didn't expect a warm welcome. What happened was worse. Once our leaders, John Dunne and

Quentin Baker, were inside, Mr. Mize closed and locked the front door. The rest of us sat down outside. Then Mize started dousing John and Quentin with ammonia and bleach. He opened the door at one point and tossed a bit our way. I got a splash across the face.

That was a night when we were really happy to see the cops get there. Quentin had to be taken to the hospital, while the rest of us went back to the slammer, where we washed our eyes out and got back to singing those songs.

One night in the Hillsborough jail a group was brought in from a sit-in at Watts Restaurant, a "white only" joint south of town. Lou Calhoun was laughing and when I asked him what was so funny, he told me that while he was on the floor of the restaurant, that Mrs. Watts had squatted over him and urinated. I am not making this up.

As more national attention was focused on Chapel Hill, both sides hardened their positions. The Klan was beginning to make a little racket around, and the protesters raised the ante by blocking streets and intersections. That was something I didn't feel was right, either as a strategy or a nonviolent action. So I just watched as there were more arrests, and more violence, more silence from the University and more condemnation from the local press and politicians. Not a one of those few segregated establishments integrated.

In March we all went to trial in Hillsborough. The judge was an arrogant arch-segregationist and the prosecutor was an ambitious sort out to make a name for himself. We pled guilty, because we were guilty. Most of our cases were eventually "nol prossed," i.e., basically thrown out. But the powers that be in North Carolina intended to make an example of the movement's leadership and so John Dunne, Quentin Baker, Pat Cusick, and Lou Calhoun were sentenced to six months of hard labor at a State Prison Farm.

Those guys were examples, alright. To me, they were examples of the best and the brightest and the bravest of our generation, just like my friends who were serving in Vietnam. Because of people like them, America changed and the people of the South, black and especially white folks, were liberated into a better and freer future.

Three months later Congress passed and Lyndon Johnson signed the Civil Rights Act, which stated that all public accommodations would now become open to the public. Overnight the goal we had been fighting for became reality. One of the people who tested the acceptance of the new law was that new basketball coach, Dean Smith, who took an integrated group to the Pines Restaurant.

During the period after the sit-ins and before the trials, I was at a party at my friend Ed's house, just east of town in a neighborhood called University Heights. Ed was kind of a wild ol' boy from the Sandhills area of North Carolina. There were maybe thirty people at the get-together, and maybe five or six of them were black. A black fellow came up to me in the living room and said, "There's some kind of trouble on the front porch."

I stepped out the front door onto the small, dimly lit porch. There were two men on the steps, one stocky, the other rail thin.

"Do you live here?" the stocky one said.

"Naw, just stoppin' by. What's the problem?"

"Get all of these niggers out of here right now," he said.

The skinny guy never said a word.

"Hey now, that ain't no way to talk," I said.

"Are you a nigger lover?" said the talkative guy.

It was macho time down in Dixie.

"Hell yeah," I said. "What about it?"

"Well, you're a son of a bitch to admit it," he said.

"Well, you're a son of a bitch to say that," I replied.

He hit me quick and hard with a short right-hand sucker punch. I've got a pretty good chin, but it rocked me. As I instinctively swung back in his general direction he ducked, and as I grazed his head, his backward movement took him down the steps. I started toward him, but at this point the skinny quiet guy aimed a small-caliber pistol at my feet and started firing away.

"Get back in there, goddam you!" he said. I backed quickly through the door and into the crowd that had come toward the sound of the commotion.

"What's going on?!!" somebody hollered. I felt my jaw.

"It was the Welcome Wagon," I mumbled.

The punch had cracked a tooth, which fell out a week or so later. Even now, when I run my tongue over the filling, I think of the Welcome Wagon.

And that was just Round One with those guys.

Getting Paid to Show Off

Vicki's folks flew in from Texas to meet me. I thought I had cleaned up pretty good to meet them, but her mother's displeasure began with her first look at me. I had gotten a haircut, and had on a clean shirt, but she never took her eyes off of my shoes. I was wearing a pair of J.C. Penney basketball shoes with white socks. It was really the best I could do at that point. She did not approve of the shoes or of her daughter's fiancé. And looking back, I don't blame her. I was a mess and she knew it.

Vicki and I were both clueless about life for the long haul, about how to build a lasting relationship, and about the consequences of the boozy lifestyle we fully embraced. In my head I was still a scared kid trying to hide my demons and my fears while I was losing the struggle against them.

Vicki's folks were very conservative Republicans from Midland, Texas. They were close neighbors of George H.W. and Barbara Bush. Mr. Andersen had hit it big in the oilfields, discovering a sizable chunk of the Permian Basin, the biggest field in Texas. The Andersens were big at the bank and at the country club, and the only thing we had in common was that I was crazy about their daughter.

Unlike her parents, Vicki was crazy about me, too. Problem was, I was bona fide crazy, so she was crazy to be crazy about me.

I didn't go back to the railroad that summer. Vicki and I got married in May, and in June I started my professional acting career at the Triangle Theatre in nearby Durham. A fellow named Buck Roberts had created a summer stock season in the grand ballroom of the Jack Tar Hotel, long since demolished.

The first paying production I was in was *Showboat,* the great Jerome Kern musical. I played a character named Dirty Pete.

My first line was, "Hey Nigger!"

Is it just me, or was there some irony in that?

While *Showboat* was running at night, I began daily rehearsals for the next show, a bedroom comedy called *Under the Yum Yum Tree.* I played the male ingenue while the comic lead role of Hogan was played by Wayne Rogers, who later starred as Trapper John on the great television series *M*A*S*H.* Wayne was just a couple of years older than me, but he was a very savvy pro. He is now one of Hollywood's smartest businessmen, but even in those days he would run downstairs to the hotel lobby between scenes to check his stocks on the electronic ticker.

That was a good summer. Vicki and I had rented a little bungalow and gotten a German shepherd pup we named Casey. Vicki was a cat person and suddenly our place was full of them. You couldn't take a step without the danger of stepping on a cat. And then they started having kittens. That was our family. Casey and all those blessed cats.

Vicki got her master's degree and I was making good money as an actor. I felt like I was getting paid just to show off. I find it amusing when I hear actors complaining about how tough the life is. To me, it sure beats the hell out of picking cotton, or pulling tobacco, or working on a roof in the summer in the South. I've done all of those things and a whole lot more and believe me, acting isn't work. And if an actor acts like acting is work, well then, he's just acting.

The Return of the Welcome Wagon

It was September 19, a perfect fall Saturday afternoon in Carolina, with the hills around all dappled with the bright rust of autumn in the Southern Piedmont and a clean blue sky showing it all off. Vicki and I went to a cookout back out at Ed's place in University Heights. A good six months had passed since the night I had gotten slugged on his porch. This was an afternoon barbecue and a big crowd had gathered, as many as one hundred folks. Maybe ten of them were "negroes."

And as we were all standing around eating ribs and drinking beer and talking, we heard the very distinct sound of gunfire from the woods nearby.

"Deer hunters," somebody said. "They shouldn't be shooting this close to town."

"Deer season don't start for more'n a month," I said.

There were more shots from several rifles. They were coming from an area about a hundred yards down a dirt road near an old farmhouse. The firing was sporadic and after one burst I saw branches from a big oak tree right overhead being shot off. It was clear they were sending us a message. We started hollering down at them, they hollered back and fired off a few more rounds. That was enough to start an exodus from the party. Most of the guests, unaccustomed to gunfire from neighbors, just said, "Let's get the hell outta here!" and headed for their cars.

As it got dark there was more shooting and shouting, and more folks split. One guy leaving the party roared his car right at the gang which had gathered down the road, and that just riled them up more.

Finally there were just six of us left. We just weren't going to be run off by a bunch of dumbasses and we were also concerned about what might happen during the night to our friends who lived there. We could see cars and trucks with CB antennas rolling into the yard down at the other house. This was in the early days of CB radio, and the antennas were enormous affairs. We figured it was a gathering of the Klan.

One fellow who stayed with us was Big Hugh Wilson, a garrulous old dairy farmer who was a "yellow dog" Democrat and an avid beer drinker. He was also the constable of Bingham Township, whatever that meant. He called the County Sheriff's department. A couple of deputies showed up, talked to us and the neighbors, and a truce was declared.

That lasted until the deputies left and the Klan boys got more likkered up. Around two A.M. we could see them outside in the woods, surrounding the house. I was in a darkened front room with a single-shot .22 rifle. The bullet in the chamber was all of my ammo. Vicki was underneath the bed with a bottle of Haig and Haig Pinch Scotch Whiskey. My cousin Ty, who was staying with us, had Ed's .25-caliber pistol. Ed was by the front door with a .12-gauge pump shotgun. Hugh Wilson was back in the kitchen on the phone, desperately trying to get the cops to come back. Tom Brame, a gifted and eccentric artist who was staying at Ed's, was passed out on a couch.

Somebody in the thicket across the road yelled, "Nigger lovers!" and fired a shotgun. At that point Ed stepped out onto the front porch and shouted, "I will not have my colored friends intimidated!"

and let go with a blast of buckshot from his shotgun. From the window, I fired the remaining bullet up into the air. I sure didn't want to hit anybody, but they didn't know that, and they didn't know it was my last bullet.

And then there was a minute or so of silence. It got very quiet.

Suddenly the front door flew open and a fellow named Billy Earl came flying in, grabbing at Ed and the shotgun.

"You done shot me, you sumbitch!" he said.

I got to the living room just as Big Hugh Wilson emerged from the kitchen and began whacking Billy Earl over the head with a large table leg.

"You're under arrest, gawdammit!" bellowed Hugh. After all, he was the Constable of Bingham Township. Billy Earl flew out the door even faster than he had come in. It got quiet again. Hugh got back on the phone, again pleading for the Sheriff's department to come back. Outside we could see an even larger crowd gathering, maybe twenty-five people, men and women. None of us had any doubt that we were going to attacked by the whole bunch. Ed's shotgun blast had just "pinked" Billy Earl a little, but now this was a war between two stubborn groups of Southerners with redneck blood, and even though we didn't want to fight, we felt like we had to hold the fort. And at this point we were not exactly committed to Gandhian nonviolence.

The cavalry showed up at the last minute, just like John Wayne. The deputies implored us to leave the property, promising that they would watch the house all night. And so we drove out through a screaming bunch of bigots. But that wasn't the end of it. The next day Ed and Hugh filed charges against a couple of the Klan boys, especially Billy Earl. He was originally charged with first-degree burglary, which was defined as "entering an occupied house at night with the intent of committing a felony." And at that time in North Carolina, it was a capital offense. A person could go to the electric chair if found guilty. Of course, that charge was made just to scare the everlovin' dogshit out of Billy Earl and the rest of them. The County reduced it to criminal trespass, a misdemeanor. At the trial, the Klan boys were represented by attorney Dog Brogden, a legendary Durham "slopmouth" who said that we were "a bunch of pinks, punks, pimps, and perverts!" The objection was sustained. Billy Earl was fined twenty-five dollars and costs.

Meanwhile, even though all public accommodations were now nationally integrated, our civil rights leaders were still doing hard labor in prison for trying to buy a meal.

I never really disliked that bunch that fought us. I understood exactly where they were coming from. Their old way of thinking was being challenged, and it threatened them because they didn't believe they could handle that change. But when the change came, most of them changed with it.

About seven years later I was sitting in a well-integrated bar in Atlanta when a crowd came in after a Peach Bowl football game in which UNC had played. I knew a couple of them and invited them to sit with me. And I knew the guy they were with. It was Billy Earl. He turned out to be a pretty good guy, buckshot wound and all. The guy who had slugged me that time was his brother, Tommy. He wasn't such a bad guy, either. But I never did like that skinny little sumbitch who shot at my feet with the pistol.

The Ol' Die Had Been Cast and Had Done Come Up Snake Eyes

So I had a career and a lot of talent, and I had a really sweet, loving wife. I was in a great educational environment and I had a love of learning and a fiery ambition to become a success. But I also had a debilitating belief that I was unworthy of any of this. At a deep level I felt undeserving of love, undeserving of success, and that I was "less than" other people. I felt like I carried a huge well of nameless guilt and shame, and that I was a complete phony.

The desire for a drink was always there, a constant partner in my thinking, directing my every thought and movement, always with the goal of a drink and the satisfaction that would come with it. It motivated me and it controlled me. My mangy tail was wagging this old dog.

Normal people might have a drink or two. As an alky, I didn't understand that or relate to it. I didn't want some of it. I didn't want a lot of it. I didn't want most of it. I wanted all of it. And it wasn't just liquor. Once I got high I wanted all of the women, all of the dope, all of the grits and fried chicken, and every ounce of excitement and pleasure available. I wanted to be ever higher.

My friend Jeff Foxworthy, the Southern humorist, has a line that goes: "You might be a redneck if you have ever been too drunk to fish." I have been too drunk to fish. I have been too drunk to drive. I have been too drunk to make love, and too drunk to fight. I have been too drunk to walk, and I have been too drunk to get up off of the floor. But I was never, ever too drunk to drink.

It is a progressive disease, and for me it was getting much worse. My pal Vicki was the first one to suffer from my behavior. On my first trip to Texas, her folks showed me the oilfields and the country club, but they could tell it wasn't going to be a fit. The only thing I liked about Midland was their liquor cabinet.

And then there was the way my thoughts would bounce around as if I had a pinball machine for a brain. I had all sorts of resentments and jealousies working, but down deep it was Ben Jones whom I really didn't like. When I drank, the resentments grew, but I seemed to like myself better. Here's the deal: The alcoholic self-medicates negative feelings with booze. But the booze causes big problems and then the hungover drunk feels worse than ever, filled with remorse. And then he or she medicates *those* feelings with booze and that becomes a merry-go-round that goes faster and faster until it wrecks. It ain't the fun house no more. It is the chamber of horrors. The carousel becomes the scream machine.

Within a year of our marriage I was cheating on Vicki and living the life of lies that comes with infidelity. Once I thought I could get away with it, it became an exciting challenge to see how many successful seductions I could accomplish. In those days I had the libido of a young lion and the discretion of a tomcat in heat. And I was very easily seduced by any temptation, danger, or treason. Back at dear ol' Wilson High, I had been too shy and damaged to even ask a girl for a date. Now I thought I was making up for lost time. The cheating created another momentary euphoria, another addictive stimulant that removed me from reality. No, this was nothing good. The devil was on the loose. And he was my new best friend.

Another seduction was the mailbox. I had always lived hand to mouth, as they say, but now the mailbox contained money, residual checks that Vicki received from a number of oil wells out there in Texas. Although it seemed great at first, I soon knew it wasn't a good thing for me. There was no point in waiting tables down at Harry's when all I had to do was open the mailbox. I wasn't making any money, and Vicki was totally sharing with her dough. I was happy to spend it on the good times, but inside I felt like a worthless gigolo. I was living the Life of Riley, except Riley had to get up and go to work in the morning. I didn't.

These patterns continued, and even though I was the one who was the guilty party, out drinking and carousing, I was also the one who became verbally abusive toward Vicki. We had some good times and she was a great person, but the anger that boiled in my bones would spill out at her for absolutely no reason. Vicki was a humble lady and a class act, but I often treated her like I owned her. I don't know how she put up with it.

Hooray for Hollywood

One day in early 1966 a buddy of mine told me that the Trailways Bus line was selling a ticket that allowed a passenger to ride one hundred days for one hundred dollars. So I decided to use the deal to go to California and seek my fortune in Hollywood. Vicki was totally supportive of that, probably because she needed a break from the craziness.

So me and a couple of road buddies took off straight for Mexico. Hollywood would have to wait for a bit of cultural exchange. We crossed the border at Laredo, hitchhiked to Mexico City, hung around there for a couple of weeks, and then headed down to Acapulco. We slept in hammocks in empty cabanas at night and hung around the beach during the day, living large for about a dollar a day American. Finally I split from the other guys and headed for L.A. by way of Puerto Vallarta.

At one point the rides dried up for a couple of hours, so I hopped aboard an ancient bus that was packed to the ceiling with passengers. After a few miles we heard a loud "clunk" followed by an even louder "kerplunk," as the transmission fell off onto the highway. We all got off and waited on the roasting roadside for the next bus to come along. It arrived an hour and a half later. Even though it was already full, we clambered on, carrying suitcases, children, farm equipment, and bags of home-cooked burritos and enchiladas. I would reckon there were maybe eighty souls and their belongings on that little dusty, airless jerryrigged vehicle which was built for thirty. But we rattled merrily along, and the chatter of rural Mexican gossip became a mesmerizing melody of the road.

When we came to a village a few people got off and I spotted a small opening near a window where there appeared to be some sort of a seat. I settled down onto it as if I had my own stretch limo. This blissful state lasted only about thirty seconds. My "seat" suddenly became noisily animated, kicking and goosing me, squirming and squealing. I jumped up as if I had been shot from a cannon, banging my head on the bus ceiling. I had sat upon a large burlap bag containing a good-sized piglet.

My fellow passengers roared with laughter all the way to the next village. They shared food and drink with me and we talked in our best broken Spanish and English. When I got off near Guadalajara, there were great warm good-byes. I think I even heard that pig squealing "*adios*" as the bus rambled on.

When I eventually crossed back over into the States, the American border guard decided he didn't like my grungy looks and told me to follow him in to be searched. As I went into the guardhouse I put my straw cowboy hat on a metal table by the front door and went into a smaller room. He looked me over pretty good, finally said, "You can go," and I did, picking my hat up on the way out the door and thanking the gentleman. In the crown of that hat was a lid of fine Mexican grass. God let me off that time and I don't know why.

My time in Hollywood was pretty much a bust. I was getting hustled by every weirdo who ever claimed to be in showbiz, and I really didn't know where to start. Finally I went over to see Wayne Rogers and I asked for advice about getting an agent. Wayne pointed to their living room couch.

"Peter Falk came out here from New York trying to get an agent and he slept on that couch for two months," Wayne told me. "He couldn't get anybody interested in him because of that glass eye. And Peter had just been nominated for an Oscar for *The Balcony.*" It wasn't exactly what I wanted to hear.

I would take long walks just to get out of the cheap hotel room I was in. One day I came across the famed Warner Bros. studio. It had walls and gates like a military base. The walls seemed to say, "Don't even think about coming in here," and their formidable height added to the impression. Dreamland seemed to be off limits to this dreamer.

After two months of total frustration, Vicki phoned to say that *Unto These Hills,* an outdoor drama in Cherokee, North Carolina, had phoned and wanted me to play a lead. I still had plenty of time on my Trailways deal, so I went up to see some friends in San Francisco and Berkeley for a few days and then caught the bus east, happy to be heading home. It took awhile. I read the *Lord of the Rings* trilogy across the country. I remember changing buses in Chicago, the first time I had been to the Windy City. The wind they call "the hawk" was howling and there were snow flurries. This was in late May. Point me South.

I loved doing that show up in the Smoky Mountains and I especially loved the Cherokee Indians, who treated me like a brother and a friend from the first day I got there. The Eastern Band of Cherokee are the descendants of those who hid from the U.S. Army during the Indian Removal of the late 1830s. Of the fifteen thousand who were forced to march on the Trail of Tears, nearly five thousand died on the bitter trip to Oklahoma.

The Cherokee are generally shy mountain people. When whites began to come into the mountains, they were an advanced and literate nation. In 1966 there were still Cherokee up in the coves who spoke no English. Despite their venal treatment by the U.S. government, they are the most patriotic Americans I have ever met. One elderly gent named Sam Owl told me how he and a friend had walked the nearly three hundred miles to Raleigh in 1917 to enlist for World War I.

In the canteen there I directed and acted in a few shows on Saturday nights. Once I played the role of the poet Dylan Thomas in the play *Dylan.* I was captivated by Thomas, an astounding lyric poet and an even more astounding alcoholic. I memorized his poetry and learned to mimic his barrel-organ voice. I didn't understand his self-destructive compulsions any more than I acknowledged my own. I thought he was just a sensitive, misunderstood chap who loved his booze. I could relate to that. Later it occurred to me that many of my literary heroes were notorious drinkers. Thomas Wolfe died at thirty-eight and Scott Fitzgerald was a burnout at forty-four, when he dropped dead. Hemingway finally shot himself and the great Faulkner, arguably America's finest master of fiction, was the town drunk of Oxford, Mississippi. So even though I would never admit that I even had a drinking problem, I was still attracted to my fellow insufferable sufferers.

Finally, though, an obnoxious drunk is an obnoxious drunk, whether he has won a Nobel Prize for literature or cleans the floor at the fish market. And all my romantic notions of the drinking artistic life could not repair the wreckage that my behavior was creating.

Mondays were the day off at Cherokee, the "dark day," as they say in show biz. And occasionally on Mondays some of us from the cast would go over the mountains to a piano bar in Gatlinburg, Tennessee, and drink beer and caterwaul around the piano. After one such evening we stopped for coffee and eggs before the drive back over Mt. LeConte. When we went back out to our cars, our whole crowd was arrested and transported to Sevierville for the night. It seems the county made a little extra money in those days by picking up singing tourists. I was the only one in the bunch who had seen the inside of jailhouses. It was getting to be old hat for me. For some reason, I still remember the name of the Sheriff of Sevier County back then. It was Bat Gibson.

Back in Chapel Hill, my cousin Ty and I started a theater from the remnants of the defunct Triangle Theater. It was a traveling troupe called The Children's Theatre of North Carolina. In one production, he and I played Cinderella's ugly stepsisters, the only time I was ever a drag queen. I'm telling you, those stepsisters were some plug-ugly women.

We toured off and on for two years. When I didn't have shows lined up, I would take classes at the University. I think I took every writing class the University offered. The teachers whom I got the most from were Walter Spearman in the Journalism Department and Ralph Dennis, a drinking buddy of mine who taught film writing. Ralph and I hit it off. He had been a poor redneck kid from a mill town and during the hard times of the Depression he had been raised in an orphanage. He was a brilliant scholar who taught me more while we were shooting the bull in beer joints than I learned in all of those classrooms. But then, I spent a whole lot more time in beer joints than I did in the classrooms.

After patiently putting up with three years of my insanity, Vicki said she had to have a separation. Then I completely lost control. I went on a two-week bender that ended with me kicking down a motel door, trashing the room, and slapping her around. I was hauled down to the jail and awoke the next day with no idea of why I was there or what I had done.

Vicki left for Texas. She was one of the kindest people I have ever known, and I had hurt her deeply. I knew only one way to deal with the guilt and remorse that I felt so deeply. I drank to make it go away. I sold our books and bought an old car. The car was my home for awhile.

That was the situation when Mary Alice Beall came back from Europe. She was a young writer from Briarpatch, Georgia, and she had graduated from Carolina a year before and then took off hitchhiking through Europe. She had been a high-school beauty queen, and I thought she was quite a looker. Given the shape I was in, I have no idea what she saw in me, but within a few days of meeting her we were a couple. After the years of big cars and oil wells with Vicki, I was back to waiting tables at Harry's, which kept me in food and beer money.

The year to come brought a deepening of the Vietnam War, the assassinations of Robert Kennedy and Dr. King, and civil disorder on a scale not seen in America since the War Between the States. In Chapel Hill it was all played out in a sultry climate of sex, drugs, and rock and roll.

Please Don't Throw Me in Dat Briarpatch

Putnam County, Georgia, is as green as the deep South gets, covered with kudzu in summer and evergreen pines all year round. It is dairy country now, but until the late 1930s it was in the heart of cottonland. Briarpatch is so named because that is where an old black man, a former slave, told a young Joel Chandler Harris the African folktales of the trickster Brer Rabbit, including the tale of Brer Rabbit, the Tar Baby, and the Briarpatch, where Brer Rabbit was, of course, "born and bred."

Mary Alice was born and bred there, too. She must have been looking for a man like her daddy when she hooked up with me. Her father, "Honey" Beall, was an outrageous hell-raiser who rambled through Putnam County leaving a legend of laughter and a trail of empty likker bottles. "Honey" was a dairy farmer, but in truth it was Mary Alice's mother who seemed to do all the work. Landyce Beall was long-suffering, tough, and taciturn. She was an expert deer hunter and a Southern country cook of great reputation. I had the "Honey" shtick down solid, but Mary Alice was not nearly as long-suffering as her mother. We fought like North and South for two years before we called a truce and got hitched. That was when the real fireworks began.

My last year in Chapel Hill became even more hectic. A typical example was the night my buddy Stan and I were leaving a rowdy tavern called The Tempo Room. He offered me a ride on the back of his motorcycle and as soon as I hopped on, a squad car pulled up. Two cops we knew, one called "Jonesey" and the other called "Smitty," decided that Stan should go to jail for not wearing a helmet. He had left his helmet in the back of my car and was going to pick it up when he dropped me off. But we hadn't pulled out yet; the motorcycle was stationary. So I went off on Smitty while Jonesey was putting Stan in the police cruiser. Smitty pushed me and I pushed him back, hard, up against the trunk of the cruiser. He hollered and Jonesey came to his aid, but Stan grabbed Jonesey's mace and used it on both of them. This happened at closing time, just as the Tempo Room was emptying out, and it gathered a large and appreciative audience. Smitty ran to the radio and actually said, "Calling all cars!" The entire force showed up and hauled us down to the slammer.

Still feisty, Stan and I cussed Smitty and Jonesey even as the cell door was being locked tight. We hollered after them as they went back up the stairs. Before long, the whole place was dead quiet. We were left totally to ourselves. Except for us, the jailhouse was empty as a pocket. Finally we calmed down. We still had cigarettes. And matches.

Then Stan remembered something. "Oh, shit," he said, "I forgot." He pulled off his right boot and dumped out an aluminum foil square the size of a big toe. "I gotta stash of hash," he said. "We better smoke this stuff to get rid of it!" And so we did, emptying the tobacco out of our cigarettes to make room for the crumbly tar of the hashish. We smoked seriously for nearly an hour to get rid of the evidence.

When Smitty and Jonesey checked on us later that night, they couldn't believe what a change had come over us. We told them we loved them like brothers, that they were great human beings doing their duty, and that we forgave them and blessed them and wished them well forever. They left, shaking their heads and wondering what that odd smell was.

One night in those years I stopped by a party back out on Justice Street. I was standing in the backyard by a fence, taking a leak, when a guy staggered up next to me to do the same. He offered me a slug of his wine and we shot the bull for a little. The next day somebody asked me what me and Kerouac had been talking about. Well, I not only didn't remember what we had talked about, I didn't even know I was talking to Jack Kerouac.

It was clearly getting to be time for me to leave Chapel Hill.

Mary Alice and I headed out to Tahlequah, Oklahoma, in the summer of 1969. I had been cast in a summer show called *The Trail of Tears,* the story of what happened to the Cherokee after their heartless removal from the Smoky Mountains. That was a good summer. We rented a cabin on the wild Illinois River for thirty-five dollars a month. One Sunday we attended a "homecoming" Sunday at an Indian church in Vian, Oklahoma. After a splendid picnic under a grove of trees, the minister preached to his congregation in four languages: Cherokee, Creek, Seminole, and English. We were so transported by the beauty of the occasion and the warm humility of the service that on the way home we realized that we had forgotten what else was going on that day. High above us, it was the day of "one small step for a man, one giant step for mankind." Humans had made it to the moon.

I seemed to have had my drinking under control that summer. It was the first time in years that I managed to go for three months without getting totally smashed and losing control. But the fuse was still burning; it was just burning a little more slowly for some reason. The old drunks say that "alcohol is cunning, baffling, and powerful." It sure had me baffled.

That fall Mary Alice and I ended up in Atlanta. A friend of mine had told me that the movie business was going gangbusters there, there was plenty of work to be had, and that he was in the middle of it. It turned out my friend was creating small newspaper ads for a porno house, but the move was a good one for me.

I had been to Atlanta back in my railroading days and was impressed by the positive vibes of the city. It had vitality and a freshness that I had not seen in many other places. It had also been Dr. King's town, and the white business establishment had been slightly more forward-looking than other Southern cities like Birmingham, Charlotte, and Jacksonville. Atlanta liked to call itself the City Too Busy to Hate.

When I arrived at the Greyhound Station, Mary Alice picked me up and we drove directly to a bar on Peachtree Street called The Stein Club. It seemed like half of the customers there were old Chapel Hill people. The ongoing party had just moved a few hundred miles south. And Atlanta was a much bigger playground to get lost in.

That first night I heard about an audition for the part of the Giant in a production of *Jack and the Beanstalk.* The next day, my first in Atlanta, I got the gig, a union job at the Alliance Theatre. The producer/director of the Atlanta Children's Theatre at the Alliance was a man named Chuck Doughty, a chain-smoking, hard-drinking, hard-fighting workaholic. Naturally, we hit it off great. It was the first of about twenty shows I was to do with Chuck, some of which toured nationally and all of which were critically praised. Besides being a ten-foot-tall giant, among many other roles I played pirates, dragons, lions, outlaws, mountaineers, one of Robin's merry men, a James Thurber creature called the Todal, and Mark Twain. The kids' shows played during the day, and often at night I worked at the

Alliance Repertory Theatre. In the years I worked as an actor around Atlanta I did about fifty plays, over thirty television and film productions, and a gazillion radio and television commercials. I worked constantly, and I loved the idea of making a living as a performing artist in the South.

During my theater years in Atlanta I also wrote, directed, built sets and props, painted drops, stage-managed, was a company manager, served as Equity Deputy, wrote publicity, was a stagehand, and drove the tour truck. Like a borderline Big League baseball player, I discovered it was a good thing to be versatile. "Jack of all trades, master of none" seems to have been my calling card.

In October 1969 Mary Alice and I got hitched in an arbor down at the dairy farm in Briarpatch. On August 8, 1970, our daughter Rachel was born. She was extraordinarily beautiful, a bright-eyed blonde who turned out to be as pretty as her mom. Mary Alice and I rented a nice house in an old neighborhood, bought a new Plymouth Duster, and both had good jobs. Everything seemed to be going well, and *seemed* is the important word.

The relative moderation of my drinking during that Oklahoma summer was the calm before the storm. Although I never drank before a performance, as soon as the show was over I made up for lost time, drinking deep into the night. I spent more time in The Stein Club than anywhere else, and the same patterns that had driven Vicki away began to repeat themselves. This went on day after day, week after week, and month after month. Everybody but me could see the insanity I was living. By the end of 1972, Mary Alice had had enough of the turmoil and heartache. She left, and I reacted in the same way I had when Vicki left. I drank more and more, harassed her, and drove her further away. One night I crashed a party she was at and went after her date. The cops came and hauled me off. When I made bail I headed back to the party to continue the fight. So I went to jail twice in one night. Every decision I seemed to make was driven by alcoholic self-destruction. Booze was slowly building a prison around my soul.

There is an old saying that "Whenever one door closes, another one opens." I guess the only question is, "How long do I have to stand out here in this hallway?" Sometimes it seems to take forever, sometimes the new door opens right away. On the day that Mary Alice finally said good-bye, I went to an audition. There had been an ice storm in Atlanta and the whole town was like a skating rink. As I gingerly approached the hotel where the audition was being held, I saw a middle-aged couple in front of me, holding hands like teenagers. It was clear to me that they knew something I didn't. They seemed to know how to be in love, how to be married.

They were going to the same audition. The man was the director, Jeffrey Hayden. The woman was his wife, the wonderful actress Eva Marie Saint. I auditioned for and got a small part in a production, Tennessee Williams's *Summer and Smoke.* It was one of the best things that ever happened for me. The show played Atlanta, and then we toured for the rest of the year. We played Palm Beach and Fort Lauderdale, Coconut Grove in Miami, then the Kennedy Center, the Poconos, the Cape Cod summer theaters, Detroit's Music Hall, and the Huntington Hartford in Hollywood. Often I would just sit offstage and watch "Miss Saint" weave her magic. I would study her choices, trying to figure out the craft that went into her mesmerizing submergence into the part. She and Jeffrey were relentlessly positive and encouraging to me.

The next summer I rejoined them in a tour of Eugene O'Neill's *Desire Under the Elms.* Besides Eva Marie, the cast featured James Broderick and a young actor named John Ritter. John and I got to be good friends that summer. As everyone now knows, he was smart, funny, very talented, and very good-hearted. We got a kick out of Jimmy Broderick's little boy, Matthew, who hung around backstage a lot. Matthew later did alright for himself, too.

We were playing the Kennedy Center in Washington, D.C., when the Watergate Scandal finally came to its inexorable conclusion. On August 6, Secretary of State Henry Kissinger and Nixon's Chief of Staff, Al Haig, came to the show and were in great spirits. Something was clearly up. The next night we held the second act curtain and piped in Richard Nixon's resignation speech. The audience cheered wildly. It got the best hand of the night, by far.

Those travels with Jeff and Eva showed me a different side of life, one that seemed more glamorous than the circuit I had been on. In Philadelphia, Princess Grace of Monaco came backstage to say hello. At the Westport Playhouse, it was Paul Newman and Joanne Woodward who did the same. At the dinner after the Hollywood opening, I sat across from Tennessee Williams and his "date," Faye Dunaway. Tennessee was very cordial and was the only person there who got as loaded as I did. Miss Dunaway hardly spoke. She was wearing a surplus Army jacket. I thought it was all very cool.

In Detroit, we were given a lunch by a big muckety-muck from General Motors. We went out to Grosse Point and had lunch next to the nine-hole golf course that was the front yard of his mansion. I felt like I had come a million miles from Sugar Hill. The folks were very nice, but they should have known better than to feed a bunch of actors. Everybody left with their pockets full of finger sandwiches and beer.

Those tours were a lot like my railroad ramblings. In every town I found the bar and in every bar I found a lady friend. Being an entertainer, I came to know a lot about "one-night stands." There is no business like show business.

Somebody Stole My Moral Compass

I had a friend named Oswaldo Calvo, a comic Cuban actor who had fled Castro after Che Guevara had given him a long, cold stare one night in a Havana nightclub. Ozzie taught me a lot of Spanish profanities and showed me where to get the best black beans and rice in Miami.

There was a pop instrumental by Stan Getz called "*Desafinado,*" which the record company publicity said meant "slightly out of tune."

"No, no," said Oswaldo. "Is not mean 'slightly out of tune.' *Desafinado* means 'without brakes.' Just like you, Benito." I don't know if that was the right translation or not. But he sure had me pegged. I had no brakes at all. When I got to going, my brakes went right to the floorboard. And I was heading for the cliff.

I had a lot of girlfriends in those years after Mary Alice and I divorced. Sometimes I'd have two or three girlfriends going at the same time. I ended up getting married to one of them, a girl I had known back in Chapel Hill in 1962. Nancy Sasser was a nurse, and Lord knows at that point in my life I sure needed a nurse. She was also a talented artist. But by the time we hooked up, neither of us was in good shape, spiritually or mentally. Miss Nancy was as hard a drinker as I was, and the marriage was destined to be short-lived. In that case, getting hitched ruined a really good friendship.

In 1976 I worked on a magic show that Chuck Doughty put together. The magician was a fellow named Abb Dickson and he specialized in large illusions and we toured the United States and Canada. I learned how to disappear a lady into thin air, how to saw a lady in half, and how to turn a lady into two ladies. But I had not yet learned the magic of just living with a lady.

During that gig Orson Welles showed up with a camera crew, and for several days we filmed what Welles said was "a pilot for Japanese television." He was a wonderful fraud, so obvious in his shabby grandiosity that I wondered if he understood that we were in on the act. He was already so morbidly obese that when he put down his cigar he could not see past his girth to find it again. So he simply shouted for his assistant to bring him another. By the end of the day there were twenty barely smoked cigars lying all around him. He was also an infamous deadbeat when it came to money, but he met his match in Chuck Doughty. When Welles didn't drop off a large check for our services, Chuck beat him to the airport and was waiting at the gate before Orson could fly away. We got our pay, in the form of a money order from a local convenience store, the Magik Market.

I did a lot of odd jobs to get by "between engagements." I drove a delivery van for a photo service, worked as a billboard painter, ran a "follow spot" for concerts, worked as a carpenter, a roofer, and for awhile I loaded furniture into a bunch of new motels. I worked Christmases as a singing Santa Claus, and I worked up a character called "The Storyteller" to entertain children at schools and birthday parties. I also did a few illegal things, like selling lids of grass. Those profits immediately went up in smoke.

I had a small part in a film called *The Bingo Long Traveling All-Stars,* which featured James Earl Jones and Richard Pryor. I had an even smaller part in *Smokey and the Bandit,* with Burt Reynolds. I had only one line: "Ain't seen him." Three words. But the picture has been such a success that I still get an occasional residual check for something like $7.19. Over the years it has added up to maybe $2,000 a word.

Once I was in a low-budget sex comedy called *The Bagel Report,* a spoof on *The Kinsey Report.* I played a character whose fetish was wearing women's panties over his head. He was also a chain-smoker, and as he talked the panties caught on fire. For some reason, *The Bagel Report* was not nearly as big a hit as *Smokey and the Bandit.* It was directed by Hugh Wilson, who went on to produce *WKRP in Cincinnati,* among other successes. I think that by now he has probably destroyed all copies of *The Bagel Report.*

I was also in a strange Western starring Troy Donahue and Hervé Villechaize, the dwarf actor who played Tattoo on *Fantasy Island.* One night Hervé got drunk and went to Troy's apartment and attacked him. So Troy picked Hervé up and threw him out the window. The next day a new dwarf was flown in from New York.

One time I was in Augusta, Georgia, on tour and a bartender wouldn't serve me because I wasn't wearing a tie. I told him my money was as good as anybody who had the poor judgment to wear ties and that I wasn't leaving. He called the cops, and after a big hassle, they busted me and hauled me in. I was charged with "failure to move on." "Failure to move on" was sort of the story of my life in those days.

There were other films, and other plays, and I think I always did a good job. But I hated myself. Twenty years of hard living and harder drinking had brought me to the edge of that cliff. I was now filled with the self-loathing that comes from years of hurting the people whom I loved. Whenever I considered for even a moment the wreckage I had left in my drunken wake, the urge to drown those feelings in even more booze became overwhelming. As the old drunks say, "One drink is too many. A thousand isn't enough."

The Death of a Rebel Soldier

In the summer of 1977 I was playing a Confederate cavalry sergeant in a Walt Disney film titled *The Million-Dollar Dixie Deliverance.* It was a hard physical shoot, riding horses all day long in wool uniforms in the Georgia heat. It was unusual in that most of the leading parts were cast in Atlanta, and we more than held our own with the Hollywood actors. It was a rowdy bunch and we bonded like the best casts do. The director, an old pro by the name of Russ Mayberry, decided to compliment me by giving me a death scene on the next to last day of shooting. I was blown up by a Yankee cannon explosion and died bravely. So since I was dead, I decided to get dead drunk.

I went off that night with a couple of mountain boys and got into some Georgia mountain moonshine, the Dixie Express of alcoholic beverages. It hits you like a train, explodes your brain, and turns you into a werewolf. The binge continued through the night and into the morning light. I slept in the back of a car for an hour or two, then went back to the white shine. And since it was the last day of filming I went by to say good-bye to my old comrades in arms.

A busload of Union reenactors had been brought down from "up

North" for the day's filming. And, as scripted, they routed my cavalry company in a large battle scene. That was bad enough, but as the re-enactors headed back to their bus in formation, they had the bad manners to sing "Marching Through Georgia." That was the song of General Sherman's marauding army that devastated the Peach State back in 1864. These guys thought it was funny, but something in me snapped. A primeval rage boiled up from my Dixie DNA. I attacked the Yankee army. Insanely drunk, I stood in front of them and spit on their Captain. Two of his men turned and pointed bayonets at me, and I kicked them both as hard as I could right in their asses. The Union line collapsed as the Captain gave the order to run for the bus. And there I was, a large man with bright red werewolf eyes, standing outside their locked bus, screaming that I was going to kill every goddam one of them if they ever showed up in Georgia again.

That was the beginning of a five-week drunk, as I spent every dime I had made on the film. I have only vague memories of those days. It isn't a total blackout, but what I used to call "brownouts," when I had flashes of recall of what I had done and how I got to where I ended up. Nancy bailed out at some point during that binge. There were other women around, a couple of bar fights, a few cuts and bruises, and a screen door I fell through at some point. But what was different was that the brakes were completely gone. I could not stop drinking even for a few hours. I would sleep wherever I passed out, and then start drinking as soon as I got up. I felt like I could not get drunk enough, no matter how much I consumed.

I had fallen through the net, through any ability to stop. Now I was desperately free-falling toward the bottom of oblivion. I wanted out of life. I did not want to be me anymore. I wanted to erase all reality with the next drink. I was trying to escape the horror of drinking by drinking every drop of it.

On September 26, 1977, I came to on the living-room floor of my Atlanta house. I was lying up under a wicker couch, staring up at years of cobwebs and spiderwebs and dust and dirt. The electricity had been cut off for nonpayment at some point. I had thrown up during the night and was lying in the puke.

Something was different on this morning. My body was shaking and trembling, but that was nothing new. What was new was the sense that I was dying, dying finally and certainly, physically dying from what is called acute alcohol poisoning. I felt like I was falling away from the light, I could hardly breathe, and I knew only the terror of death. That was thirty years ago, and I still feel the shadow of the incomprehensible terror of that morning. I pulled myself up onto the couch, then fell forward, clinging to consciousness. On the floor again with the world fading away, I did something I had not done since I was a child. I prayed. With what I thought was my last breath, I pleaded, "Please, God, help me!"

Day Is a' Breakin' in My Soul

At some point during that binge, I had gone by to see an old drinking buddy. Bobby was a stage manager who was always ready to join me on a bender. I had a case of Pabst Blue Ribbon on my shoulder when I knocked on his door. But Bobby was different when he opened the door.

"Hey, man, let's go," I said.

"Can't make it today," he answered. "I'm building my little girl a playhouse."

"That's cool," I said. "I'll catch you later."

That was about all that was said. But there was a look in Bobby's eyes, a bright clarity I had never seen in him in all the years I had known him. He was a different man and even though I didn't mentally verbalize it to myself, I knew exactly what had happened, and it registered with me. And on the morning I didn't die, just after my prayer for help, I remembered the look in his eyes and called him. Bobby had gotten sober.

He came and got me and took me to a clubhouse for people like me who don't want to die from drinking. It was a fellowship of old drunks who helped one another. They had a drying-out room with a couple of cots, and I flopped around in there with the delirium tremens for a couple of days. Cold turkey.

There was a fellow in there with me, a great jazz trumpet player I knew named Sam. He told me that he had been sober for a couple of years, but had "gotten away from the program and slipped." He had gotten drunk again and it was worse than ever.

"Everything had been going great for me, and I got the big head again. You gotta be the most careful when all the lights are green." I saw him a few sober years later and asked him if he remembered our time together going cold turkey with the DT's.

"Sure do," said Sam. "The DT's was about the only exercise I got in those days."

That withdrawal was unvarnished hell. But I got through it. Even when I thought I was dying, I felt like I would rather die trying to get sober than die wanting another drink. I had come to the crucible of my life. And it was a miracle I was still alive.

When I took stock and added it up, it seemed even more miraculous. Over twenty years of boozing I figured I had knocked back at least a six-pack of beer every night and a couple of bottles of harder stuff every week. Truthfully, I always sloshed down a lot more than six beers, but just six beers a day is 42 a week, which is 2,184 a year, which comes to over 43,000 over twenty years. Plus over 2,000 jugs of whiskey, wine, gin, and vodka. There had been dozens of fights and there had been times that I faced guns and knives in the alleys. And there were all those times when I wasn't sure what had happened the night before. It all added up to an enormous amount of physical abuse, total spiritual demoralization, and an astonishing financial waste. That was a lot of dough that didn't go to pay the bills or to the simple responsibilities of home and family.

I had just turned thirty-six years old. There had been three disastrous marriages, and countless fractured relationships. I had been jailed for drinking in public, drunk and disorderly, public drunkenness, disorderly conduct, assaulting an officer, criminal trespass, battery, resisting arrest, and "failure to move on."

I owed two months' rent, the power had been turned off, and I was without a car. I had exhausted the patience of my friends. There was no employment in sight. I was broke, a financial zero minus a lot. Physically, I was on the verge of death. And I had long been spiritually bankrupt.

You might say I had nowhere to go but up.

Part Three

OUT

of the

HORRIBLE PIT,

OUT

of the

MIRY CLAY

I Meet a Man Named Howard

He brought me up out of the horrible pit
Out of the miry clay
And set my feet upon a rock
And established my goings . . .

PSALM 40

After three days of alcoholic withdrawal I was able to begin to listen to the people who met there at the clubhouse. They were all like me, lifelong alcoholic drinkers who had hit rock bottom and had become willing to do anything to stop drinking. I found out that a big part of alcoholism is the denial of the disease. So it is hard to acknowledge that there is a problem if the problem itself insists that you don't have it. That's weird, but it explains why somebody would continue to put something into their body which clearly creates an addiction which causes a schizophrenic reaction. Alcohol, these sober drunks told me, "has a contract out on your life."

One guy said to me, "Hey, if you ate asparagus and it made you act crazy and spend all your money and treat your family badly and wreck your car and lose your job, would you keep on eating asparagus?" I got his point.

What I couldn't figure out was how these folks had overcome alcohol and not only stayed sober but had reclaimed life and were living it happily and positively.

"It's real simple," a lady said to me. "You gotta get out of yourself and believe in something bigger than you."

Alcohol had inexorably narrowed my life until I was totally into myself, my pride, my fears, my insecurities, my resentments, my guilt, and my failures. I had painted myself into a very tight corner, from which I could see no escape. Although I had a great zest for life, I had finally come to a point where life did not seem to be worth living. And the slow suicide of alcoholism had led me right to the door of death.

My new friends spoke of a "higher power." At first I was confused. I thought they were talking about somebody named "Howard Powell." Finally I figured out what they were saying. And I had to agree. I sure as hell didn't have any power, and my way of thinking had led me to a terrifying destruction. It had been a long time since I had put much stock in spiritual things, other than a bit of lip service. I had searched for spiritual answers through drugs and alcohol, altering my consciousness with "spirits" but never getting as high as I wanted to get. Booze had been my "higher power," and it had laid me low. It was a false God.

I had to find something bigger than me. Outside the meeting room, next to a small stream, stood a large oak tree. The tree, I thought, was older than I was, and it was here in this place and on this planet before me. It would outlast me, too, I thought. It would be around for a long, long time. And something put the tree there long ago, and something put me here, and all I knew was that it wasn't me who put the tree there. So to whatever power had put the tree there I said, "You are a higher power than I am. You are the Creator. I cannot create trees. Or people. And if you can do that, you are probably powerful enough to help me. I know that's possible because others have been helped."

So it was as simple as that. It was simple, but not easy. There was a process to be learned, twelve steps to spiritual progress to be understood and practiced. But I was now among friends, fellow survivors who understood me better than I understood myself, because they had shared in the collective wisdom of this group. These people spoke straight from the heart with an honesty I had forgotten existed, and they spoke of hope and faith and redemption.

I stayed at the clubhouse until I was over the withdrawal and the shakes. I went back out to a new life, determined to stay sober by not drinking, a day at a time. The deal was to live completely in the present, and to use whatever means necessary to not take that first drink. I hadn't been back at my house more than an hour when I got a call from an agent. Even though I had absolutely nothing left after the five-week bender, the phone was still working. (Without a phone, an actor is really "s.o.l.") I was to guest-star in an episode of a television series being shot in the Tennessee hills outside of Knoxville.

The job was a Godsend. The show was called *Young Dan'l Boone,* and it was canceled while we were in the middle of a scene. An assistant director came climbing up the mountain on which we were shooting to tell us that the network had pulled the plug on the series. And then the crew literally pulled the plug. But they paid us, and paid us well. When I got home I paid the back rent, got the electricity turned back on, and bought a 1960 Chevrolet for $135. I had been sober now for almost two weeks, and I was clinging to my new sober life like a man clings to a life preserver at sea.

Then I almost immediately got a job at a dinner theater playing opposite Sandra Dee in a bedroom comedy called *Love in E-Flat.* It ran for about two months. During the day, I spent my time writing a screenplay called *Charlie Bing the Kudzu King.*

Rather than waking up in a haze of confusion and pain, I started waking up with enormous energy. That wasn't the only difference. I learned from the meetings with the sober drunks that alcoholism puts a clamp on the normal psychological changes that people experience. When we were kids we were warned that smoking cigarettes would "stunt your growth." Well, while smoking did nothing good for me, it was liquor that "stunted *my* growth." My spiritual and emotional growth was not only squelched by booze, it was put in reverse. I was a man approaching middle age who behaved like a twelve-year-old. To tell the truth, I behaved a lot better when I was twelve.

I had lived in the house in Atlanta for eight years and it was filled with memories, some good rowdy times, but mostly things I would just as soon forget. So one of the first things I did when I sobered up was to move out of the city, way out. I rented a farmhouse about fifty miles east of Atlanta, near a little town called Rutledge, not far from Hard Labor Creek. And it was there that I began to restore my physical health and reclaim a bit of self-esteem.

After only a few months sober, I saw Mary Alice. She had come down with Rachel from up north to her folks place at Briarpatch. She had remarried and long since moved up to Delaware. With a small smile she complimented me. "Looks like you have found God," she said.

"God wasn't lost," I said. "He found me. Cause I sure as hell *was* lost!"

I just blurted that out without thinking. Driving back through the green gentle hills of Piedmont, Georgia, I thought myself foolish and pretentious for having said such a thing. God the Creator of every speck of the endless timeless universe had nothing better to do than to seek out a poor old agnostic drunk in the gutters of Atlanta?

"Well, you must be a helluva alcoholic, Jonesey," I thought, "to have none other than God Almighty looking around for you."

Then came into my thoughts another voice, one different from my own stream of consciousness. "You have it right," the voice said. "I have been looking for you for a long time. Take my hand."

I've been hearing that voice every so often ever since. That is the way it was and the way it is, y'all. I reckon it is the voice of "Howard Powell."

It had been long years since I had done any exercise other than repetitions of bending my elbow and lifting countless bottles down at the taverns. But with my renewed energy, I started bounding around the farm like a dynamo, cutting the fields on the tractor and shooting hoops on a basketball goal I rigged up on an oak tree. I had always loved basketball, and was amazed that before long I was in good enough shape to touch the ten-foot rim with ease. But to get into really good health, I knew I would have to give up smoking. Again I did the math. I had been a two-pack-a-day guy for many years. But even if I figured only thirty smokes a day, that added up to almost 220,000 cigarettes since I took up the habit at fifteen. Add to that the regular marijuana habit I had and it was a wonder that either of my lungs still functioned.

Quitting smokes was a two-stage process. There was good news and bad news in the way I quit. Every time I wanted a cigarette I rolled a joint. This went on for two weeks, until I no longer wanted a cigarette. That was the good news. The bad news was that I was smoking more wackyweed than Bob Marley and his band. And I was reluctant to let it go. Finally I knew that if I really wanted sobriety, and if I really wanted a clear channel to my "higher power," I had to discard this last crutch. I realized that the only reason to indulge in dope was that I was afraid of reality, afraid of my potential, and afraid of life. And I came to understand also that until every crutch and every shield was thrown away, I would not know myself and I would not come to know God. And I prayed again for help from the Creator, and I got that help.

It wasn't long until I was playing full-court basketball every day, running 10K road races, and holding down left field for two softball teams. My body reshaped itself and I lost weight and added muscle. My buddy Ernie said that I looked as if I "had lost five pounds from under each eye."

That spring I was cast in a film, a prison comedy starring Tim Conway. I played a tough inmate named Lugs. My partners in crime were Richard Kiel, who played "Jaws" in the James Bond films, and Lenny Montana, best known for his role as Luca Brasi, the Mafia enforcer in *The Godfather*, the one who "sleeps with the fishes." It was a good shoot and I was literally having a second childhood. I felt free from the demons that had controlled my thinking for all of my adult life. Finally, I was healthy and happy and I felt like I was starting all over again. I felt that way because I *was* starting all over again. Not many people get that chance.

Over those months of personal restoration I dated a lot, playing the field almost like a new man around town. There were a lot of near misses, literally and figuratively. One of those girlfriends was a pal of mine named Louise, but I called her "Weezy." In February of 1979 she gave birth to a most beautiful daughter named Jeanne. And she is my beautiful daughter, too.

Then one day I walked into an audition for a commercial and struck up a conversation with the cute receptionist, putting on all the charm that Buster could muster. I waited with the other actors for my turn to read and when I went into the conference room, it turned out that the attractive lady I thought was the receptionist was actually the producer of the spot. I didn't get the part, but it wasn't long before I got the producer.

Her name was Vivian Walker. She was twenty-six and she was the daughter of "Rosey" Walker, a well-known Atlanta police detective. Two weeks after we met she was producing a series of TV commercials for a big chain of convenience stores in the Midwest. I got the ongoing part of a cowboy whose dog, Lamar, was smarter than he was. So Vivian and I started seeing a lot of each other, during and after work. Pretty soon she was the only girl I was interested in.

Ticket to Hazzard County

In late September of 1978, exactly a year since I had nearly died from drinking on that dirty floor, I went to an audition for a new television series called *The Dukes of Hazzard.* The show had been created by an Atlantan named Gy Waldron. I had met Gy back in 1969 when he was directing *The Tubby and Lester Show* on WSB-TV and I was playing the Giant in *Jack and the Beanstalk.* In 1975 he had written and directed a low-budget feature film, *The Moonrunners,* based on the tales of moonshiner Jerry Rushing. In that one, I played a Yankee revenuer who arrested a mule. The film was rough, but it had a great spirit and terrific music by Waylon Jennings. A friend of mine, Chuck Monroe, played a character in it named "Crazy Cooter."

Gy had headed west, worked for Norman Lear for awhile, and had then created a series idea out of *The Moonrunners.* The timing was perfect. Jimmy Carter of Georgia was the President. Burt Reynolds of Georgia was the number-one box office star, and it seemed like Waylon and Willie records were going platinum every other week.

Gy shopped it to Warner Bros. Television, who liked it and sold it to the CBS network. The plan was to make five episodes at first, to come on as a midseason replacement in January 1979. I was told that the show was to be made entirely in Georgia. That was the most exciting part for me.

I had spent all of my life in the South, and I was deeply proud of the region and the way Dixie had come through the Civil Rights Movement to a new beginning. And I firmly believed that the South, with Atlanta leading the way, could become a major international player in industry, communications, entertainment, and the arts. The old South had been unshackled and the Sun Belt was becoming a magnet for investment. And the new attitude was that nothing was impossible for us. Having lived in Hollywood and New York, and having traveled the country up one side and down the other, I was in love with the idea of the South's limitless potential.

Atlanta was filled with the talent necessary to film any production, and an ongoing television series could help lay the groundwork for a more permanent production community. Like Dr. King of Atlanta, I believed in dreams.

I went to the audition dressed as I usually dressed, in jeans and a work shirt, an old pair of boots, and a feed store ball cap. I was reading for Cooter, the good ol' boy mechanic with a wild and crazy streak. The producers didn't know the half of it. I not only understood this character, I had spent my whole life being this character. I was immediately cast in the role. My feet didn't touch the ground for a month.

"Hang On to Your Hats, Y'all"

The Dukes of Hazzard was to be a one-hour action comedy, following the adventures of Bo and Luke Duke and their fetching cousin Daisy as they battle the wily Boss Hogg in Hazzard County, a fictional place somewhere in the hills of Georgia. It was Robin Hood with cars. The outlaw Dukes were the good guys, because the law was corrupt.

The cast and crew gathered for the filming at the Holiday Inn in Conyers, Georgia. Conyers was then a small town just past the Atlanta suburbs, an old railroad town that was beginning to grow quickly as the city started bulging outwards. It was around the Holiday Inn swimming pool where the cast got together for the read-through of the first episode. There is almost always an upbeat glow at the start of a new film project. But this one had a special feel to it.

Denver Pyle was playing Uncle Jesse Duke, the patriarch of the Duke family. Denver was as solid as any character actor in the business. I remembered him as the Texas Ranger who was tracking Clyde Barrow and Bonnie Parker in *Bonnie and Clyde* and as Briscoe Darling in *The Andy Griffith Show.* Denver was one of those actors like Walter Brennan, who "had always played old." When we met in

Conyers that day, Denver was not yet sixty years old, but it seemed like he had always been older than that.

James Best was cast as Hazzard's sheriff, Rosco P. Coltrane. Like Denver, Jimmy had gone from World War II to an acting career and was a familiar face to a generation of moviegoers. Among hundreds of roles, I knew him as Paul Newman's sidekick in *The Left Handed Gun.* In fact, he was killed in that one by Denver Pyle. Jimmy was also known as one of the best acting teachers in Hollywood, in addition to being a world-class fisherman.

Sorrell Booke was to play Boss Hogg, the crooked, corpulent politician who runs Hazzard County. Sorrell was an actor's actor. A graduate of the Yale School of Drama, he had made a career on Broadway and in the great early television dramas. Sorrell was a consummate character actor. With Sorrell, Jimmy, and Denver in the show we had as solid a foundation as a show could hope for. Between them, they had appeared in more films than I had ever seen.

The role of innocent Deputy Enos Strate went to another Georgia actor, Sonny Shroyer. Sonny and I had worked together in a half-dozen film and television projects over the years, often competing for parts. I knew him to be a wonderfully subtle comic actor and also one of America's greatest souls. Perfect casting there, I thought.

As Daisy Duke, the tomboy cousin, the producers could not have possibly done better. Catherine Bach was a wonder of nature, the sexiest country girl anyone could have imagined. She had the best legs in the history of legs. And the rest of the package was all there, too.

Tom Wopat was to be Luke Duke, the cooler of the Duke cousins. Tom was a good-looking fellow, a Broadway singing veteran and a muscular athlete with a natural acting style. He had grown up on a dairy farm in Wisconsin, so the role of a reckless country boy came easily to him.

Rounding out the cast as Bo Duke was a kid I had seen around Atlanta auditions for a couple of years. John Schneider was making a name for himself as a young man with great looks, a lot of talent, and even more confidence. John was only eighteen years old but had told the producers he was twenty-four, afraid that they wouldn't hire him if they knew how young he actually was.

So there we all were, sitting around the pool at a Holiday Inn next to Interstate 20. And my feeling was that we were beginning an adventure that could not fail. The chemistry was magical, the feeling was electric.

After the read-through I blurted out, "Hang on to your hats, y'all, I gotta feelin' this one is gonna take off like a rocket!"

I felt like success was inevitable, but none of us could have had any idea of the ride we were about to take.

The show first aired as a midseason replacement at nine P.M. on Friday night, January 26, 1979. The reviews beforehand were decidedly mixed. Howard Rosenberg of the *Los Angeles Times* said, "This show will not last past the first commercial break."

Never has a critic been more wrong. From the first notes of the theme song during the opening titles, America was hooked. Waylon Jennings had been hired to reprise his role from *The Moonrunners* as the balladeer. Not only did he bring his mellow country voice and Texas humor to the narration, but he wrote the theme song "Good Ol' Boys" and along with his band set the musical tone for the show during the first season. It was a perfect match.

Within weeks, *The Dukes of Hazzard* was consistently in the top five shows on television, and it began hitting number one during its first season. In those years there were only three major networks: CBS, NBC, and ABC. In 1979 over 90 percent of the sets in the United States were tuned to those three networks, and on Friday nights most of those were tuned to CBS.

The way we receive information and entertainment has changed enormously since then. Cable television was in its infancy. Ted Turner down in Atlanta had begun the cable revolution by hitting a satellite with his signal at WTBS, a small UHF station on West Peachtree Street. Suddenly everybody in the country could watch the Atlanta Braves every night. In 1979, Turner's brainchild CNN was still a couple of years away from becoming the first cable all-news network. When *Dukes* hit the airwaves there was very little cable, no home satellite dishes, no Internet, no DVDs, no TiVo, and no iPods.

So every Friday night, tens of millions of viewers watched *The Dukes of Hazzard,* and they liked what they saw. During our first season, the network discovered that a large portion of our viewership was under twelve years of age, so they moved the show to the eight P.M. "family hour." We softened the rough edges of Hazzard County a bit to become more "family friendly." And all over the country, America's families started piling up on the couch on Friday nights with popcorn and pizza to watch the exploits of a bunch of rambunctious country folks as we tore around Hazzard County with as much horsepower as "Cooter" could get out of Bo and Luke's 1969 Dodge Charger.

The Charger was their dirt track race car, The General Lee. Painted reddish orange with a rebel battle flag on top and the number "01" on its doors, the "General" had the ability to jump obstacles with extraordinary ease, suffering nary a scratch on landing. It was a magic car, and became as big a star as any of us on the show.

The show's success perplexed the critics, annoyed the snobs, and infuriated the manners police. The national PTA condemned the show's recklessness. Prudes decried the shortness of Daisy Duke's shorts. But the show kept soaring in the ratings.

A former president of CBS told me years later that William Paley, the CBS founder and chairman who despised "cornpone" humor and wanted his network to have a more "sophisticated image," was on an extended European vacation when the *Dukes* came on the air in January of 1979. When he returned to the States, he was aghast at our show being on his network. But it was already too successful to kill off. No matter how embarrassed he was by it, he would have to wait years before he could cancel the thing.

Over its first three seasons, the show went from just being very popular to being an American phenomenon. Suddenly there were *Dukes of Hazzard* lunchboxes, *Dukes* Underoos, *Dukes* jigsaw puzzles, *Dukes* posters, *Dukes* T-shirts, *Dukes* bicycles, *Dukes* action figures, *Dukes* knapsacks, *Dukes* bedsheets, *Dukes* window curtains, *Dukes* bubblegum cards, and more *Dukes* toys and games than any other TV show ever. Not bad for a show that wasn't supposed to "last past the first commercial break."

To me, the show's connection with the public was simple. It had a lot to do with those Saturday morning B Westerns that my brothers and I went to see down at the Virginia Theatre in Portsmouth back in the 1940s. Like Gene Autry and Roy Rogers, we had great action, good-lookin' gals, slapstick comedy, and country music. And Bo and Luke Duke were like Autry and Rogers in other ways. They were not fancy superheroes, or urban sophisticates, or hard-boiled cynical detectives. They were blue jeans–wearing country boys, as down to earth and sincere as the folks who might live down the road. They did not have much in the way of material goods, but they had a proud sense of family and of life's possibilities. And above all, they had a very rooted sense of right and wrong. Like my childhood cowboy heroes, the "good guys" in Hazzard County always did the right thing. They always made the right moral choice under any circumstances, no matter what the consequences. And like the medieval "morality plays," that sense of morals and values might just rub off on the audience.

And of course, in our show the good guys always won, and nobody really ever got hurt. There was comic action and mock violence, but in the end nobody bled and nobody suffered real pain. Crime and greed never paid off, and virtue was its own reward. There was a dearth of that kind of programming by 1979. Now there is a total absence of it.

So the popularity of the *Dukes* is, I think, simply the heartland of America sending a message about the kind of programming they would like for their family to be watching. Well, at least for an hour a week at eight o'clock on Friday night.

Trouble in Hazzard

For a guy whose life was seemingly over a year before, it seemed as if I had gone from the bottom to the top in record time. Suddenly, after fifteen years of paying dues, I had hit the big time. I was where I had always dreamed of being. And in fact it seemed like a dream. But the deal did have its problems, like everything in life. And since I still had a little piece of that chip on my shoulder, I suppose I had a way of finding problems that were of my own making. For starters, the show that I had been assured would be made in Georgia was moved to Hollywood, actually to the backlot of the Warner Bros. Studio in Burbank.

This was a big disappointment to me. For as long as Hollywood had been making films, they had been making films that distorted the South in sometimes grotesque and demeaning ways. I had hoped that somehow the *Dukes* could be our own Southern version of our myths and foibles, but that changed overnight. The producers said it would be too costly to film on location. That was baloney. It would actually have been cheaper to film in Georgia, but I guess the producers thought it would be easier to move the whole thing to California than to spend a few months a year away from their swimming pools in Hollywood. So suddenly the Appalachian South of Hazzard County was filled with palm trees, cactuses, and burnt-out sandy hills. Except for Gy Waldron, whose role seemed to be diminished, there were no other writers, producers, or directors on the show who understood anything at all about the South or its people. And it seemed that one of the criteria for casting the Hollywood actors was that they had to have the worst Southern accents imaginable. So I was a bit frustrated.

"Cooter" had started as a minor character and through my improvisations it had grown more substantial. His clothes were my clothes and his behavior had to be true to what I believed he would do. Taking the character that personally was bound to lead to disagreements with the "suits," and soon enough it did.

It got worse when one of the producers decided he could jack me around. His name was Rod and he was a veteran Hollywood TV producer and director. He was a talented guy who had made a difference in shaping the show back in Georgia. But once we got to Hollywood he tried to bully me. One day he told me he had been Bugsy Siegel's right-hand man, and that if I knew what was good for me, I'd do what I was told. I told him that I didn't give a damn who he used to be, that Bugsy got what was coming to him, and that he could kiss my redneck ass. You might say the relationship deteriorated from there. Suddenly I was told that the character I had created was all wrong, that I should be playing a Stepin Fetchit sort, and that the beard I had been wearing had to go. They insisted that I be just unshaven and scruffy looking. I told them that maybe Stepin Fetchit was still around and they could hire him. And the next day I was back in Georgia.

After a few phone calls and a story in the *National Enquirer,* I was back on the set, the chip on my shoulder firmly in place. Then the same thing happened again. Rod said, "Cut your beard or you are off the show." I told him to fold it four ways, tie a ribbon around it, and put it where the moon don't shine.

And so I was out of the show for five episodes. And "Cooter" was badly missed for five weeks. We worked out a compromise. If I could be clean shaven, rather than scruffy looking, I would play the character as I wished, rather than the stereotype they wanted me to portray. I agreed, came back, and nobody ever tried to push me around again. Rod was fired the next season.

By standing up for my dignity, my craft, and my character, I gained a measure of respect from some quarters. And over time I developed a character that changed into a more dimensional person, wiser and more mature. It wasn't easy, though. I butted heads with everybody who wore a suit around there.

It wasn't just me. Even though we were the highest-rated show and the biggest moneymaking television project ever, we all felt that we were being treated like redheaded stepchildren by the studio. Other shows that came and went in weeks had bigger payrolls, nicer dressing rooms, and more publicity. Jimmy Best was replaced when he demanded the same quality dressing rooms as were used on other shows. John Schneider and Tom Wopat left the show for most of a season in a dispute over merchandising payments. All those *Dukes* posters, lunchboxes, and action figures were bringing in tens of millions of dollars and we weren't seeing our contracted share. In fact, we still haven't. In Hollywood it's called "creative accounting." We were supposed to receive 3 percent of the net profits when our likeness was used on a product. Unfortunately, in all these years there has never been a "net profit." Hmmmmm . . .

So much for the bad news. The good news was that even when the show was canceled after seven seasons, we were still getting a bigger audience than hit shows do now. And the show has had a very successful syndication run, a very successful cable run, and a very popular international showing. John Schneider and Tom Wopat became cover boys for every teen magazine around, and Catherine Bach and her "Daisy Dukes" became a permanent and iconic sex symbol. Sorrel Booke, Denver Pyle, and James Best capped off long careers with their contributions to a beloved hit show, and Sonny Shroyer starred in a spinoff series, *Enos.*

Filming for the *Dukes* ended in 1985. But Hazzard County was not going to become a thing of the past. In some ways, the best was yet to come.

The Cabin in the Pines

In the fall of 1979 Vivian and I were married in Atlanta. I was thirty-eight years old. She was twenty-seven. I had been sober for two years and a part of *The Dukes of Hazzard* for a year. I had made more money in that year than I had made in my whole life. We bought a home near Covington, Georgia, the town where the *Dukes* had first filmed. It was a beautiful log cabin set back on a pine-covered hill. It was surrounded by azaleas and dogwoods. I had never lived in a house that didn't belong to someone else. To own a home this special was a thrilling event for me. For months afterward I would go out at night and just look at the place, feeling a gratitude that perhaps only a boy who grew up without electricity and plumbing could feel. Vivian and her family gave me rock-solid support, and as the months of my newfound way of life went by, I discovered new depths of energy and creativity within me that had been stifled for decades. I wrote screenplays and songs and created a children's radio show. None of this stuff ever saw the light of day, but it is still in the trunk as a reminder that I had to go through there to get to here. And in every little ol' scrap there may be something that sparks something better down the road. I've got a barn full of old notions.

On most weekends we were making personal appearances at car shows, racetracks, and charity events. And I was still doing those commercials with Lamar the Dog. I did some singing with a country rock band and made a five-song cassette that we sold at the weekend events. I figured I wasn't a singer, but I could carry a tune, and I was a good enough actor to act like a singer.

In 1980 I became active in Jimmy Carter's reelection campaign. I had never really done any public speaking, but I wrote up a stump speech and gave it throughout West Virginia in the days before the election. President Carter lost that election, of course, but I have reminded him that wherever I spoke on his behalf, he won overwhelmingly. I could tell by his smile that he knew I was just kidding.

The political bone that had been fired up in the 1960s now came back around. I worked for several candidates and discovered that I could help draw a crowd and that I could be an effective speaker when I was advocating for something I believed in. I was elected President of the Georgia Branch of the Screen Actors Guild and was asked to serve on several boards, including the Chairmanship of the State of Georgia's Film Commission.

And I knew as sure as I knew anything that all of this was happening as a result of those four words I had spoken as I lay dying on that floor in 1977. "Please, God, help me!" I was finding out that as long as I asked for the help, I would continue to get it. My reading led me to the philosopher William James, brother of the novelist Henry James. I came across this line: "We and God have business with each other; and in opening ourselves to His influence our deepest destiny is fulfilled." I felt the truth of that as I fumbled along, trying to alter the ingrained grooves of twenty years of heavy addiction.

James said something else that astounded me in its simplicity: "The greatest discovery of my generation is that a human being can alter his life by altering his attitudes of mind." So what I had to do was to admit and accept the fact that if I wanted things to change, I had to change. I had to get rid of all of my stubborn self-assurance and become open to the fact that I was seeing things through eyeglasses that were thirty years old. I had long believed that drugs and alcohol were my friends and that they would make me happy. Well, I had been dead wrong about that. So I had to understand that I might be full of crap about everything else, too.

Over the seven seasons of *The Dukes of Hazzard* I flew roundtrip from Atlanta to Los Angeles at least a hundred times. That's a lot of jet lag and a lot of frequent flyer miles. Sometimes I would leave the cabin in Georgia at 5 A.M., drive to the Atlanta airport, catch a flight west at 6:30 A.M. EST and arrive at LAX around 7:30 A.M. PST. I kept a car at the airport there and would drive out to the set in time for my first scene. When I left home back in Georgia, I would pass the original "Boar's Nest," the roadhouse from which Boss Hogg ran his operation. And when I arrived at the location, there would be the exact same building. Only now it was not only a replica painted exactly like the original, but simply a façade, behind which was nothing but scrub oak, sandy dirt, and a little cactus. There is the saying that "Hollywood is all front and no back."

Integrating Hazzard County

Whenever I would drive onto the Warner Bros. lot, I would remember that time back in 1966 when I was demoralized just by walking past the imposing wall around the studio. I dreamed of the day that I would be working on the other side of that wall. And now my picture was on a billboard on that wall, forty feet high. It was for me a marker of how far I had come since I had hit bottom. The first time I saw it, I went and bought a Polaroid camera and took a few pictures of it. In show business, you never know when it might come down.

For several years I stayed at the Tolucan Motel on Riverside Drive in Burbank, just a long block from the Warner Bros. Studio. It was a simple, blue-collar place run by a retired couple named Fred and Doll. They were salt of the earth people and treated me like a son. I had no interest in becoming a Californian. By flying back and forth, I avoided California licenses, leases, utilities, and any absorption of the vapid lifestyle that was so pervasive. I was a proud Southerner and I felt deeply that I should be a part of the rapidly changing South that had been liberated by the Civil Rights Movement.

A lot of people thought I was crazy for resisting the life of a

Hollywood celebrity. When they asked me why in God's name would I want to live somewhere like Georgia when the glitz and balmy glamour of La La Land was beckoning, I had a ready answer.

"I live in Georgia because my house is there. My wife is there. My friends are there. My doctor, my dentist, and my lawyer are there. My books are there. My heart is there. And dammit, my dogs are there." That sort of shut them up.

In those years we had an office apartment in Atlanta in the King District, just around the corner from where Dr. King is buried. And the black folks in the neighborhood got a kick out of "Cooter" being around there. It turned out that everybody I met there loved the *Dukes*. They could sure tell that there was no racism in Hazzard County. I had a theory that black folks related to the show because they had spent generations dealing with characters like Boss Hogg. They had to always "fight the system," too.

On a trip out for filming I dropped by Paul Picard's office. He was the show's executive producer. I told him that everywhere I went in the South, folks loved the show. It transcended class or color. And since black folks were such a big part of our audience, and since black folks were such a big part of the South the show was supposed to be representing, then shouldn't we see a lot more African Americans on the show?

Within a few days, Paul sent a memo out to the assistant directors, who did the extras casting, that the percentage of blacks on the show should reflect reality, and suddenly Hazzard was integrated. We often had fine black actors on the show, including the great Woody Strode. And the running character of Sheriff Little of Chickasaw County was played with gusto by Don Pedro Colley, a very large gentleman of color. Hazzard County was probably the most color-blind place in television history.

But a really good example of how Hollywood misconstrues Southern culture happened a bit later. I had gotten to know the great soul singer James Brown from events we attended together in

Georgia. He had invited me onstage with him at a show, and I danced up a storm. I once shared a flight with James to L.A. and he told me that he was a big fan of the *Dukes* and would love to appear on the show.

We had an occasional piece at the end of some episodes called "Boss Hogg's Speed Trap," a musical ending that featured Nashville stars who had been stopped in Hazzard's speed trap and had to perform at the Boar's Nest in lieu of a huge fine. Boss, who owned the joint, would make a killing when Tammy Wynette or Roy Orbison did a show at his honky-tonk.

So I mentioned the idea of having James Brown in the speed trap to the cast and they thought it was more than cool. Catherine Bach said we should have James play for the Boar's Nest dance contest. James Brown was an icon of American music and everyone was excited that he might join us. I took the idea to Paul Picard. He said he would get back with me on it. I didn't hear anything for a couple of weeks, so I went by and asked Paul what was going on.

"The network nixed it," he told me. "They said James Brown is not right for the show."

Not right for the show? A guy from Georgia who is a world-famous artist and who loves the show? Think about it. Why wouldn't James Brown and the Famous Flames get caught in a speed trap in Hazzard? It not only wouldn't have bothered us, we would have loved it. And so would our audience. Was the network implying that the people who watched our show wouldn't like it, that they were bigots? Why would some nameless, faceless corporate executive in a Los Angeles high-rise office building owned by Northeastern urbanites be making decisions about the nature of Southern culture? Why would our fans be deprived of that kind of fun? Not right for the show? It wasn't like we were doing *The Importance of Being Earnest* on *Masterpiece Theatre.*

So the South and its people were once again reflected and defined by some nerd in Hollywood as a place where the people have narrow tastes and narrow minds. And diversity was "not right for the show." James Brown!!? Mr. Dynamite!? The Hardest-Working Man in Show Business!!?? Soul Brother Number One!?? Those number-crunching MBAs didn't understand that my friend James was right for any show, any time. Rest in Peace.

One spring evening I was on the Tolucan Motel balcony watching a classic California sunset over the palm-covered Hollywood Hills. A late-model Lincoln pulled into the parking lot beneath me and a couple in their seventies got out. She was stout, with gray hair tinted blue and a pretty face that wore a worried responsibility. The man was small and slight, dressed in a brown western suit, and he walked like a bantam rooster. As they crossed the lot, coming toward me, I recognized Roy Rogers and Dale Evans. They went into the room directly below mine.

Now, I was used to meeting movie stars and even U.S. presidents. I had met Grace Kelly and Paul Newman and Elizabeth Taylor. But the sight of Roy and Dale walking across the parking lot was a close-up view of American royalty. My first thought was something like, "I oughta call all those guys who picked on me in the second grade and tell 'em, 'Hey man, I'm out here in Hollywood living upstairs from Roy and Dale.' "

But I didn't. It was quite enough just to know it. Doll, who ran the motel, told me that whenever Roy had appearances in the city they would drive down from their ranch at Apple Valley and stay in the same room. "They've done that for years," she said. The next morning Roy was getting coffee in the tiny motel office. We spoke hello and talked about the weather. He struck me as the real deal, just an old cowboy who did not have a phony bone in his body. He was down to earth, unpretentious, and a straight shooter. What I had seen as a little boy at the Virginia Theatre was what I got as a grown man.

I flew Mama out to see "beautiful downtown Burbank." She had gotten to Hollywood long before me, back in 1950 when she won that trip to be on *Double or Nothing*. Besides taking her to the set and introducing her to "The Dukes," I gave her a tour of the old Hollywood she remembered. Grauman's Chinese. The Brown Derby. Mulholland Drive. Musso and Frank's. The Farmers Market. The Hollywood Bowl. And I took her to the theater on Hollywood Boulevard to see Rex Harrison play Henry Higgins in *My Fair Lady*. Mama's favorite part of her trip happened just before the opening curtain. Eva Gabor, looking splendid and classy and dressed to the nines, took her seat right in front of Mama's and gave her a sweet and sincere smile and "hello." I had never paid much attention to Eva Gabor, but after that I was a big fan.

The travel wasn't so tough. Sometimes I'd fly in, do my scenes in a day or two, and not be needed again until toward the end of the next episode. So I'd check out of the hotel and head home for a week or so. But if my role was heavy in an episode, I'd spend the week out there. If I found myself in L.A. for a weekend, I'd go exploring around California. I kept a 1968 Mercury Cougar at the motel and I'd point it toward Big Sur or Yosemite or Death Valley or up the east side of the Sierras to a place called Lone Pine. California is another country altogether.

Another thing I did in those years was to get in shape. Full-court basketball became a daily ritual. I got up a team in the Covington Industrial League back in Georgia and that is how I learned the game, by playing with really good players who were all in their twenties. I had played a little as a kid, but I was short and fat and uncoordinated back then. Now sober and full of energy, I discovered that underneath all of that chronic insanity was a pretty fair natural athlete.

I was the only "white" guy on our team. At first I named the team "Cooter's Garage," but the guys voted me down. They thought "Slammer-Jammers" was a much cooler name. They were right.

Being an owner of a city league team had its responsibilities. One time I had to bail our six-foot, nine-inch center out of the slammer for having pilfered two pork chops from a local supermarket. But we won the game that night. All of these guys had played serious high school ball and some of them had played college hoops. And all of them played over the rim. I was forty-one years old and had never played organized ball, but I loved the game with a passion. After two years with those guys, mostly sitting on the bench, I joined an over-forty league at the YMCA and was unstoppable. I was the Magic Johnson of the over-forty bunch. Just as I was beginning to get pretty good, age and gravity began to catch up with me. I went from playing like Magic Johnson to playing like Lyndon Johnson. But for a few months there I was in a league of my own.

My knees began to ache when I hit forty-five. It could have been the hoops, but it was more likely the compulsive jogging I started doing at age forty-two. One spring I decided to run the 10K Peachtree Road Race in Atlanta on July 4. It was symbolically important to me. I remembered one Fourth of July when I was sitting in The Stein Club on Peachtree Street, already drunk and swilling pitchers of Pabst Blue Ribbon as if they were going to quit making the stuff, and chain-smoking Pall Malls until the smoke was coming out of my ears. That was when I saw them coming, hundreds of runners chugging merrily along, all thin and smiling and positive looking. Although I scoffed at them, a deep part of me envied whatever it was that enabled them to do that. As I watched them I felt very old and very wasted away. I was about thirty-two years old then.

Now, ten years later, I determined to make the race. After all that damage to my body and my soul, I figured that running "the Peachtree" would be a good testament to my recovery. I trained hard and ran a couple of 10K races to prepare for the distance. July 4, 1983, was a scorcher as it always is in "Hotlanta," and I ran the race along with twenty-five thousand other folks. I managed the distance in about forty-nine minutes. Slow, but everything being relative, it was miraculous. During the race, every time I passed a bar I said a prayer for the ones I saw with that bloated, sad alcoholic look around the eyes. I have rarely felt the euphoria that I experienced when I crossed the finish line that day.

So I started jogging a lot and running a lot of 10Ks, just to get the T-shirts and keep my weight off. For five years, I ran every day, averaging about fifty miles a week. That's over ten thousand miles, and along with the basketball, my knees were really starting to protest. I played a lot of softball, too. That was something I could do well. I had a lot of power and a Big League arm. I was on two teams. On one of them, in the Atlanta Music League, I played left field. Isaac Hayes was the catcher. Yep, how could we lose with "Cooter" and Black Moses?

One part of filming that I have always enjoyed is "all that waiting around." I have heard actors complain for years about the downtime on the set while scenes are being lit and prepared. On Johnny Carson's show even big stars would gripe about "all that waiting around." So I decided to get very good at waiting around. I figured that I might never be the actor that Paul Newman or Marlon Brando was, but I could "wait around" with the best of them.

Sitting around and shooting the bull with veterans like Sorrell Booke, Denver Pyle, and Jimmy Best was easy, much like sitting around the taverns in the old days. The difference was that I was sober, and getting paid to sit around. But the stories and jokes were endless. Sorrell Booke was not nearly as outgoing as the others, but he became my best friend on the show. He was a polymath, the kind of learned man who could do the Sunday *New York Times* crossword puzzle with a fountain pen in less than five minutes. He had not only played most of Shakespeare, I do believe he had memorized all of it. He spoke at least seven languages fluently and could communicate in many more. During the Korean War he had worked in Army Intelligence and I was told on good authority that the CIA had used Sorrell as a code breaker.

Jimmy Best and Denver Pyle had the kind of careers most actors would give an arm for, working with the best in the business and working constantly. But I believe that they had more fun and were prouder of their work on the *Dukes* than anything else on their long résumés. We spent many an hour sitting in our canvas-backed director's chairs with our names on the back, telling tales and solving the world's problems. Just talking and laughing. That's the part of filmmaking I miss the most. Just waitin' around.

Besides being a teenybopper idol, John Schneider started making hit records in Nashville and making feature films in Hollywood. It seemed like to me that every week he would show up with a new automobile, a Ferrari or maybe a Lamborghini. I couldn't relate to that. For awhile he was married to a Miss America, Tawny Little. And then he wasn't anymore. That I could relate to.

Tom Wopat spent a lot of his set time working on his music, mostly picking his guitar. He traveled by motorcycle and was more of a loner than Schneider. But they bonded through their work and always seemed as close as the Duke cousins.

The other Duke cousin, Catherine Bach, was every adolescent boy's first love. The boys liked Bo and Luke until they were eleven or twelve and those hormones started kicking in. Then they turned their attention to Daisy Duke. Catherine was so magnetic that she could just walk onto a busy set and all work would seem to stop for a few seconds. Studio security had a problem with wannabe stalkers. Several men were arrested scaling the studio walls in an attempt to propose to Daisy Duke. Cathy had a big old German shepherd to protect her and a bodyguard named Billy Blanks. Yeh, the Tai-Bo guy on the infomercials.

I mellowed out over the years of the *Dukes.* Occasionally I would butt heads with a director, but mostly they just let me do my own thing. I got pretty pissed off one time when I arrived at "Cooter's Garage" to find that it had been completely done over by a new art director. I had decorated the old set over the years as authentically as I could, trying to replicate the country garages back home, and "Stump" Rountree's place, where I had been the worst mechanic he ever had. Every little thing had its place. So when the character "Cooter" walked into his garage, he was absolutely at home. But not on this day. "Cooter's Garage" had been gussied up to look like something out of a Judy Garland musical. The supervising producer, who was also new, thought it was none of my business. It took me a day or two to straighten it back out. That producer avoided me for the next two years. If he saw me coming down the street he would scoot off in his little golf cart.

At the end of each shooting season I would drive home to Georgia, taking my time and meandering along any road that looked interesting. And out there in the vastness of America, I have never found a road that wasn't interesting. So I cruised the country twice a year in an old Mercury and that was one of the best parts of the *Dukes* years for me.

The very best part was in November of 1983. I was finishing an episode and ready to fly home for something special. But Walker Jones wouldn't wait. I got the news at "Cooter's Garage" on the backlot of Warner's studio. I was a father again. Vivian had given birth to a big blue-eyed boy, close to nine pounds, healthy and hungry and with a big round face like his daddy. I got there the next morning and he was already walking and talking. Well, that's a bit of an exaggeration, but he was and is exceptional.

The last episode of *The Dukes of Hazzard* was filmed in January of 1985. We had finally started losing in the ratings war for eight P.M. on Friday nights, beaten out by a cute little kid named "Webster." Nobody around the production office ever asked for my opinion, but being very opinionated, I gave it to them anyway. And it was my belief that if the *Dukes* had been just a little less of a cartoon, and had developed the characters just a little bit more, and had just a bit more red meat on the stories, then it could have lasted for fifteen or twenty seasons, like *Gunsmoke.*

The writers were good fellows, but they knew about as much about Southern culture as I knew about shopping on Rodeo Drive. Rather than recruiting some really sharp Southern writers, our writers were all old Hollywood guys who had done *McHale's Navy.* They did find a little formula that worked for awhile, but if you look at a *Dukes* script and then compare it to what we did onscreen, you'll see that most of the regulars on the show improvised practically every line. And it worked. We called it "making chicken salad out of chicken guano." No telling what the writers were saying about the actors. Anyway, by the time it was over it seemed like we were doing the same show over and over every week. And as Hemingway once said, "It's alright to borrow from each other, as long as you don't borrow from yourself."

Now What?? Again

In 1985, when it was over, I hopped in the Cougar and roared east across the Mojave, heading for the hills of Dixie. I was forty-three years old and I had a lot I wanted to do. I still had income from *The Dukes* coming in and I still had those commercials going.

Then, along with my old writer pal from Chapel Hill, Ralph Dennis, I developed a detective series to be shot in Atlanta called *Gunnarson.* Ralph had written a series of paperback hardboiled detective novels about an ex-cop named Hardman, but he thought we should tailor something more specifically to me. It was really good stuff. But I couldn't get through any doors to shop it. A few years later I managed a meeting at Paramount, but all I got was, "Nobody does detective shows anymore." This from a twenty-six-year-old whiz kid who wasn't familiar with Raymond Chandler.

I did some demo tunes with a band and took them up to a big shot in Nashville. "You ain't got the pipes," he said. "Clint Eastwood thinks he can sing, too. Did you see *Paint Your Wagon*? Jeeezz. He ain't got no pipes, either!" Me and Clint. SOL.

There was a good-sized hill near us called Cornish Mountain. I'd always end my daily jog by taking the trail up to the top, where there was a rock outcropping that had a view of Atlanta, thirty miles to the west "as the crow flies." And I'd sit and rest and meditate on the rocks. And I would pray. I would pray that God put me to the use that He intended for me, and that He instill in me a desire to do His Will. And then I would listen for the voice of "Howard Powell." Because as I jogged along, thinking about the future, I really didn't have a clue as to what to do next.

Part Four

The MOST UNLIKELY CANDIDATE

An Old Alky Versus Ken and Barbie

In the spring of 1986, I was at the Georgia State Capitol to be sworn in as Chairman of the State Film Commission. After the ceremony, a fellow named Doug Henson approached me and asked if I had ever considered running for Congress. "No," I said. "I could never run for office. I've got more bones in my closet than the Smithsonian Institute."

But Doug was serious. "Think it over," he said. "We really need somebody to take on Pat Swindall." The "we" he was talking about was the Democratic Party. And the reason they really needed somebody to make the race was that none of the ambitious local politicians thought anyone had a chance against Congressman Swindall. But I did tell Doug Henson I would "think it over."

Pat Swindall was a young lawyer and businessman who had beaten a five-term Democratic incumbent in the Reagan landslide of 1984. A lot of people thought that Swindall, a right-wing evangelical, had used anti-Semitic tactics in upsetting Elliott Levitas, who was Jewish. One of those people was Levitas himself.

There was some evidence for that. Swindall's wife, Kim, had sent out a letter proclaiming Pat's Christian righteousness, and ended by saying, "Best of all, Pat is one of us!" Although Levitas' ethnicity had never been an issue at all, suddenly it was being talked about. But Swindall had a lot more working for him than that.

After the 1982 redistricting, a large portion of the African American population in Georgia's Fourth District was put into the neighboring Fifth District. Those neighborhoods had traditionally voted overwhelmingly Democratic. Now the Fourth was comprised almost entirely of Atlanta's suburbs, mostly white and generally upscale, and tilting Republican.

Before the 1970s, the joke was that Georgia had an active two-party system, "The Democrats who were in, and the Democrats who were out." But that was changing rapidly. As Atlanta boomed, many of the newcomers were white-collar "Yankees" who had no allegiance to or tradition with the Democratic Party. And Southern whites were defecting to the Republican Party in droves. Much of this was due to Richard Nixon's "Southern Strategy" of appealing to the disaffection of Southern whites with Democratic leadership on the civil rights issue. And there was no doubt that the National Democratic Party was out of sync with the more traditional South on hot-button social issues.

Historically, those Southern blacks who could vote tended to vote Republican, the party of Lincoln. Franklin Roosevelt's New Deal changed that. And now, with the leadership of the Kennedys and Lyndon Johnson on civil rights, blacks formed a crucial and important bloc in the Democratic Party down South. That, and the fact that the national Democratic Party had veered to the left on issues like gun rights and school prayer created wholesale defections from traditionally conservative white Democrats in Dixie. So race was being played in a more subtle way than in the past, but played nevertheless. Suddenly the word *liberal* became a pejorative, a code word for everything that was anathema to this new right-wing coalition.

Pat Swindall wore his evangelicalism on both his sleeves, and preached the gospel of supply-side economics along with it. Pat had been student body president at the University of Georgia and his wife, Kim, was a former Duke University cheerleader. He was a nice-looking fellow, articulate, and driven. The conventional wisdom was that this guy was a genuine rising star in Republican politics, perhaps a Senator, perhaps then a potential Vice Presidential nominee. He had raised more money than Levitas and had beaten him easily. His wife, Kim, had been very pregnant during that campaign, and darned if she wasn't expecting again.

Vivian and I considered the proposition. At first glance, we both thought my past made any candidacy not only unlikely, but almost laughable. I was the guy who had been drunk for twenty years, married four times, and seen the inside of a whole lot of jails. I had never run for office, had no organization, had no war chest, had only a newspaper reader's knowledge of policy and issues, and I didn't really know what was involved in a Congressional race.

But there were also reasons to run. I really didn't like Swindall's politics. It seemed to me that he represented a viewpoint that was based upon sanctimony and insensitivity. The sanctimony was evident; whoever didn't agree with the so-called "religious right" was morally inferior and lacked the values necessary to governing. The insensitivity was reflected in his votes against the school lunch program, the Head Start Program, Ethiopian famine relief, and the Clean Air Act. For a man who claimed to have Christian compassion, it seemed like Swindall had somehow skipped the part where Jesus talked about feeding the hungry, clothing the naked, and housing the homeless.

Now, I wasn't a bleeding-heart liberal myself. I didn't subscribe to the notion that every social problem demanded a federal program in which the bureaucracy would throw a lot of taxpayer money back and forth around the bureaucracy. But I believed that many social problems were the result of past mistakes, such as the legacy of slavery, and that government should take the lead in attempting to solve them. If our national leaders didn't care about creating opportunity, fairness, and equality, then what good were they? If they didn't care about those who were hungry and sick and had no help, then what good were they? If in the most prosperous nation in the world these conditions exist and are not being reached by religious organizations, or charities, or corporations, then surely government should try to help. But the evangelical Swindall did not think that this was the role of government. And a lot of voters in the Fourth District agreed with him.

And no one was going to challenge him. If there was one thing that I was sure of, it was that in a democracy there had to be choices. If there was only one name on the ballot, there may as well not be an election. Hell, there may as well not be a democracy. The way I figured it, our political system was like our economic system. It works a lot better with competition. And the founders really wanted it that way. They wanted that fiery competition of solutions, of ideas, of visions.

The attitude of a lot of the career politicians was that beating an incumbent is next to impossible. "Unless," they said, "he gets caught with a dead woman or a live boy." But Swindall himself had beaten an incumbent only two years earlier.

There was no doubt that I was a Democrat. I liked Harry Truman. I liked Jack Kennedy. And I liked Jimmy Carter. I did not like Richard Nixon. I liked Ronald Reagan but I didn't like his politics. My gut instincts had always been sort of blue-collar egalitarian. And I had seen in the Civil Rights Movement how a small group of dedicated people could make a big difference in moral persuasion and ultimately in shaping the conscience and the actions of a nation.

Unfortunately I was, as Mark Twain described himself, "educated beyond my intelligence." I really wasn't very sophisticated when it came to policy and politics, so if I were actually to become a candidate, I would have to learn a whole lot in a very short time.

The first thing I learned was that the Fourth District was a lot more diverse than I had thought. It contained urban areas of the City of Atlanta, many of the suburban areas surrounding it, and ended in rural areas which were just beginning to be touched by Atlanta's booming growth. The District contained great ethnic diversity. It was 17 percent black, and had fast-growing Latino and Asian populations. There were substantial ethnic communities of Jewish, Greek, Lebanese, and Italian populations. And the District contained Emory University, Agnes Scott College, Oxford College, Oglethorpe University, and the DeKalb Community College system. It was home to the Centers for Disease Control, and home to a number of first-class medical facilities. In short, it was a microcosm of the best in the South and the nation.

I got a lot of encouragement to run from Manuel Maloof, a tough, wily old "yellow dog" Democrat who ran a popular tavern in Atlanta. Manuel was the Chief Executive Officer of DeKalb County, which held 70 percent of the Fourth District vote. Manuel was not a man who minced words.

"Why in the hell wouldn't you run? Gawdam, you're still young, you've got good sense, and it's the right thing to do. Hell, if I was as good-lookin' as you, I could be the damn President. So you ought to get off your ass and run. There are a lot of people ready and willing to help a guy like you. So do it."

So I did it. And Manuel was right. There was an immediate outpouring of support from all over the district. All the doubts that I had were washed over by the positive reinforcement I was suddenly getting from hundreds of Democratic activists. Vivian and her parents, "Rosey" and Roberta, had been involved in many Atlanta campaigns, and they went to work relentlessly.

The *Atlanta Constitution* ran a story announcing my candidacy and asked the Republican chairman what he thought of my entering the race. "We think it's hilarious," he said. "A two-bit actor from a stupid television show running against Pat Swindall!"

The paper asked me to respond. "I work in a very tough profession," I said. "And I have been blessed to have worked at a very high level of that profession. And it is a profession I share with the head of the Republican Party, Ronald Reagan!"

The GOP quickly dropped that line of attack against me. It also seemed that a lot more people had heard of *The Dukes of Hazzard* than had heard of Mr. Swindall. So what I had working for me was the curiosity factor. Folks just wanted to see if that grease-covered redneck mechanic "Cooter" could walk and chew gum at the same time when it came to politics.

On a radio interview I was asked to name some of my heroes. "Stonewall Jackson and Dr. Martin Luther King," I said immediately. "Well," said the host, "I guess that just about covers the field."

I tried to position myself as a thoughtful moderate and I tried to characterize Swindall as an extremist who was out of the mainstream of sentiment in the district. He, of course, tried to paint me as a "Hollywood liberal."

I had confidence about everything but fund-raising. Never in my life had I asked anyone for money. I went down to see former Senator Herman Talmadge to ask for some advice. Herman had grown up in politics. He had been a segregationist "back in the day," but had become as progressive a Senator as any from the South. He had done a lot of good things along the way. Herman was also a recovering alcoholic. Booze had played a part in his political downfall.

"Senator," I asked, "do you have any advice on the art of raising campaign funds?"

"Well," he drawled, "I just call 'em up on the telephone and I say, 'This is Herman Talmadge. Send me some money.' "

"Ol' Hummun" was right. The direct approach is best. But I could never pull it off without stammering. I reminded myself of the kid who appeared in an ad in the back of the comic books I read when I was a kid. The company hired kids to sell mail-order Salve. In comic book panels, they showed the right way for a kid to sell salve at someone's door: "Good day to you, sir, you look like the kind of person who would really enjoy this wonderful salve I am offering to you today!" Then they showed the wrong way: The kid at the door says, "You don't wanna buy this salve, do you?"

I always related very strongly to the second kid.

I went up to Washington to talk to the Democratic Congressional Campaign Committee. Basically they just blew me off as not having a chance. "We don't think this is a competitive race," they told me. I figured that with that sort of help, their opinion could easily become a self-fulfilling prophecy.

So I wasn't very good at shaking the tin cup. But I got pretty good with my stump speech, outlining my positions and stating the case to replace Swindall. Basically, I was "pro-education, pro-environment, pro-choice, and pro–health care." That might seem simplistic, but it rallied a lot of folks to our campaign. The Congressman was none of those things, and he had the voting record to prove it.

I went on the attack and stayed on the attack. The Georgia delegation was mostly a conservative group, but Swindall had been a little to the right of Generalissimo Franco. In a delegation that included Newt Gingrich, he had been the only Georgian to oppose Head Start, the only Georgian to oppose the School Lunch Program, the only Georgian to oppose African famine relief, and the only Georgian to oppose the Clean Water Act. Although he himself had borrowed five hundred thousand dollars from the Small Business Administration, he voted to reduce the very fund that had made his success possible. And he insisted that "there is no Separation of Church and State Doctrine in our Constitution."

I got some help from a couple of my *Dukes of Hazzard* pals. Jimmy Best and Sonny Shroyer came to a picnic out in Rockdale County. Jimmy is pretty much a conservative Republican and Sonny is an independent, but they were both ready to pitch in for "Cooter." Our *Dukes* cast had become like family over the years. A slightly dysfunctional family, perhaps, but the kind that sticks together out of a common bond. The only other help I got from Hollywood was a five-hundred-dollar check from Ed Asner. Ed had been the national President of the Screen Actors Guild when I had headed up the Georgia Branch. He and I never saw eye to eye on anything, so

I was especially pleased that he would remember me with a contribution. Swindall jumped on Ed's support as evidence of my being in cahoots with the "ultraliberal Hollywood counterculture." Well, I guess he was right in a way. I thought Ed was too much of a leftist myself, but I sure appreciated the five hundred bucks. Asner is a very decent fellow, and when Swindall made an issue out of the contribution, a lot of people just thought it was cool that "Cooter" knew "Lou Grant."

I got right out front about my drinking and hell-raising. "I'm a recovering alcoholic," I said. "I've seen a lot of jails and done a lot of things I am not proud of. But I've been sober now for almost nine years and my life has changed in ways I could not have imagined." The reaction didn't really surprise me. Most people have good hearts. And just about everybody has dealt with alcoholism in their own family. Rather than seeing it as a negative, my recovery was accepted as a positive thing. Only the hardcore right-wing political operatives tried to make hay out of it. "A drunk is a drunk," one said. Swindall said that "alcoholism is a disease, not an excuse." He was right on both counts. Although I had never used it as an "excuse," there was pretty clear evidence that my life had changed dramatically when I found a way to overcome the addiction on a daily basis.

I was actually surprised at how little of an issue it was. There were a lot of rumors and gossip going around about me, but in my case I figured most of it was true. "There was a time in my life when I spent 90 percent of my money on whiskey and women," I said. "The rest of it I just wasted!" That quote made the "wires" and went all over the country.

A reporter asked me if I had ever smoked marijuana. The standard political answer was, and still is, a bit too cute by half. "I experimented with it a couple of times in college," they would say. "But I didn't like it." Everybody remembers Bill Clinton's phony "I didn't inhale" line.

I did a variation on that theme. "I experimented with it twice," I said. "Once from 1957 until 1961 and once from 1963 until 1978." I could have said that I was the guy who never exhaled.

I didn't go into much detail about my past. A lot of it was genuinely hazy to me, and I didn't see any point in rehashing every awful incident. What I said was, "There isn't much that I haven't done, and I would have probably done that had I been given the chance. But I am not like that now." That seemed to satisfy the inquisitors.

The real reason my opponents weren't attacking me on my past was that they had a huge lead in the polls. Incumbents don't "go negative" until they have to. And so far, they weren't really taking me very seriously.

But the press was having fun with it and that attention helped me more than Swindall. They saw it as a good story in a dull campaign year. Former badass alcoholic actor challenges fair-haired evangelical Congressman. It helped too that Pat could seem arrogant and sanctimonious and I could easily crack jokes and be what the press called "colorful."

I had a steep learning curve, but I studied hard. I'm what actors call "a quick study." Memorizing is a big part of what actors do. There has been a lot more attention paid recently to the confluence of show business and politics, and I've been asked about that connection a lot. Show business celebrities are in the public spotlight a lot and many of them are politically involved. They have found as I did that just by showing up they can bring attention to a cause, a charity, or a political point of view. And often these showbiz folks have the kind of charisma and communication skills that lend themselves to advocacy. Actors like Rob Reiner, Paul Newman, and Robert Redford are smart and savvy spokespersons for their causes, and though none of them have run for public office, if they did, they would, like Arnold Schwarzenegger, immediately be formidable candidates. But there is another factor that I think has been helpful to actors in politics. If they have succeeded in show business, most likely they have developed a very tough hide. The entertainment industry is tough as tenpenny nails, and for every job a performer might get, he or she has probably been turned down ten times for other gigs. Rejection is an inherent part of the territory, and perseverance is the most important ingredient for success. There are a lot of folks with talent, but they can't hang on through the lean and hungry years. As my hero Gene Autry said, "If show business was easy, everybody would be doing it."

One of my favorite memories of that first race was going with Mayor Andrew Young to several black churches. I had always been a great admirer of Andy, since his days at the right hand of Dr. King. He had afterwards been elected to Congress, had then been our Ambassador to the United Nations, and after that was twice elected Mayor of Atlanta. He is one of the most respected and recognizable people on the planet, but as I got to know him I found him to be down to earth, humble, and very helpful to me. I asked him to visit some churches with me and he immediately said, "Sure!" The last church we visited was in what would now be called a "transitional neighborhood," one that had once been an all-white neighborhood, but was now a mixture of black and white working folks. Outside, after the service, while I was chatting with the congregation, I saw Andy talking animatedly with a couple of white guys, "good ol' boys" who were working under the engine of an old car. They were all laughing and joking together. Andy was pointing at me. Then I watched as Andy, in his Sunday suit, knelt down on the pavement and put my campaign bumper sticker on their car. He introduced me to them. They were "Cooter" fans. And two more votes, maybe. As we drove off, Andy gave me a political lesson. "Always make sure the bumper sticker gets stuck on the bumper," he said. I love Andy Young.

It turned out that there was a Democratic primary I had to win. An adherent of the crackpot conspiracy theorist Lyndon LaRouche entered the race. At one forum he remarked that the ultraconservative Swindall was a "communist dupe." I mentioned that comment to Senator Sam Nunn and he said that the fellow had gotten it "half right."

We built a strong campaign organization and won the primary overwhelmingly. It was my first electoral win. At that point I had a perfect batting average. That night I was asked by the press about the public's perception of the race. I said that it could be construed as "me being just an old alky running against Ken and Barbie. But it is my job to change that perception." The part about "an old alky running against Ken and Barbie" is the part they printed. And on New Year's Eve, they reprinted it as one of their quotes of the year.

As the race went into October, all the polls (mine included) had Swindall comfortably ahead. But I figured that when it came down to it, at least 40 percent of the voters weren't going to vote for him because of his rigid ideology. So I had to somehow get another 10 percent plus one voter to win. That would take some kind of miracle, but I really believed it could happen. After all, it was a miracle to me that I was alive, that I was sober, that I was healthy, and that I was even running for Congress.

Everybody who runs for "higher office" gets a pile of questionnaires from various special-interest groups attempting to define where that candidate stands on the issues of interest to that group, whether it is the National Rifle Association or the Brotherhood of Left-Handed Grommet Makers. Just after the primary I received a questionnaire from a group calling itself The Freedom Council. The questionnaire was labeled a "Biblical Scorecard." It had about ten yes-or-no questions asking if I was a born-again Christian, and how I felt about things like prayer in school and abortion, and whether or not I thought homosexuality was "constitutionally protected."

It said, "This questionnaire shall be published and mailed to all churches in your voting district. Should you decide not to participate, next to your name shall read: CANDIDATE DID NOT PARTICIPATE. We are committed to bringing back the Christian values which were so dearly held to by our Founding Fathers."

The thing was signed by a Mr. John Sauers, the regional director of The Freedom Council.

Something about it bothered me deeply. I consider myself a Christian. I believe that Christ is who He said He was, and I take my relationship with Him very personally. I was always taught not to wear my religion on my sleeve and that when folks started going on about how devout they were, then you'd better watch your wallet. The Reverend Jerry Falwell had created The Moral Majority a few years earlier, and his modus operandi was to create political power through his ministry. In fact, that was his stated purpose. He and his movement seemed to think the Democratic Party was a humanist tool of the devil, and The Moral Majority quickly became a major power broker in the GOP.

The Freedom Council was the creation of another Virginia evangelist, Pat Robertson, the same guy who had once preached at Pinners Point Church and had gone on to create a Christian-based media empire. Robertson's dad had been a U.S. Senator from Virginia when I was a kid there, so he had always understood political power.

Rather than answering "yes" or "no" to the complex and nuanced issues, or simply throwing the "Biblical Questionnaire" in the trash can, I sent a letter back to Mr. Sauers and a copy of the questionnaire and my response to the Atlanta media outlets.

Dear Mr. Sauers:

I have received and considered the "questionnaire" you sent to me on the stationery of an organization called "The Freedom Council, Fourth Congressional District."

When I called the number to inquire as to who you represented, I reached the Creative Realty Co. On further investigation, I discovered that The Freedom Council is a "front" organization for the Rev. Pat Robertson, Republican candidate for the Presidency.

Since you feel it is your business to publicly publish my personal views regarding my spiritual relationships and con-

victions as part of a political campaign, I'm sure you don't mind my making your request public, and also making my response to you public.

Sir, as an American and a Christian, I am offended by your letter and by the "Biblical Scorecard" you enclose. Contrary to what you say, the Founding Fathers of this great nation were men and women of varying religious beliefs and creeds. Many had come to these shores seeking refuge from religious intolerance and doctrinal bigotry in their native lands.

Freedom of religion, freedom of worship, and the separation of church and state are cherished tenets of their enduring legacy. Surely men like Jefferson, Adams, and Washington would condemn the narrowmindedness of a "Christian" litmus test designed for political purposes. As Christians they understood that, by definition, no Christian is better than any other Christian. As Americans, they risked their lives to create a nation where people of all faiths could live and work together in freedom.

We must beware, I think, of those who practice business and politics in the self-righteous guise of religion.

My positions on the political and social issues of the day are well known and will be more publicized during the coming weeks of our campaign.

My religious beliefs are best expressed in Matthew, Chapters 5, 6, and 7. I believe that I should try to live as Christ instructed in the Sermon on the Mount.

As for your questionnaire, I would like for you to mark mine "See Luke 20, Verse 25. 'Render therefore unto Caesar the things which be Caesar's and unto God the things which be God's.' "

Yours truly,
Ben Jones

A lot of people saw me differently after that. Several ministers came by, thanking me for my "courage." I really didn't understand what they meant by that. I had just said what I thought and laid it out there. Apparently a lot of people felt that way about the "religious right," but no politician had spoken up about it. It was considered a kind of political suicide to take on those organizations. One preacher, well into his eighties, told me that if anybody questioned my faith I should just continue to point to The Sermon on the Mount. That, he told me, is just about all the Christianity one would need, if one could live by it.

Swindall said he had absolutely nothing to do with the "Biblical Scorecard." When asked, he did say that he had scored "a 100" on it, though.

With about two weeks left in the race, two things happened almost simultaneously. Someone came by the campaign office with evidence that Swindall had been arrested for driving under the influence (DUI) and had somehow covered up the matter. I had to decide how to deal with that. I felt that it would be hypocritical of me to bring up somebody else's drinking problems, but then I wasn't really hiding anything. There were shameful incidents in my life that I didn't advertise, but my arrests were all a matter of public record. What this seemed like to me was a question of influence and of political favoritism. And it was coming from someone who had become a public scold and who presented himself as a model of moralism. So rightly or wrongly, I got the evidence and called a press conference.

What happened then was that Congressman Swindall completely blew his cool. He started attacking me for the dastardly act of pointing out the incident, and he attacked the media for bringing it to light. Of course his overreaction just created more press attention and he overreacted to that, too.

Then Doug Henson dropped by the campaign office with a document. "Take a look at this," he said. It was the building permit for Congressman Swindall's new house in Stone Mountain. It stated that he was building a 16,000 square-foot home and paying approximately $350,000 for it. Doug said his contractor friends had told him that a house that size in that location was at least a million-dollar house.

Then I noticed the kicker. The permit was signed by Swindall's contractor. John Sauers. The same guy who had sent me the Freedom Council letter.

At the Conyers Rotary Club the next day, someone asked me if I was a churchgoer. I explained that I was a person of faith, but did not belong to an organized denomination. I added that I didn't think it had a whole lot to do with my qualifications for office. I then said that the Freedom Council letter had concerned me. And I closed by saying, "And it turns out that the guy who sent me that letter is the same guy who is building Pat's million-dollar house over there in Stone Mountain and only charging him a third of what it should cost."

The reporters present seized on that remark. I showed them the copy of the building permit. When they called Swindall to comment, he went totally ballistic. "It is absolutely nobody's business," he said. "This is the worst kind of mudslinging imaginable!" He said he would not allow the press anywhere near his new mansion. That just increased the interest in the house and its price. And the Atlanta television stations had a field day with the story, flying news helicopters over the gigantic house. It was a pretty spectacular pad. It looked like the opening shot from *Falcon Crest.*

As far as I knew, Pat Swindall hadn't done anything illegal, and I had not accused him of doing anything illegal. But the impression of impropriety was there, and his blistering overreactions to the heat I was putting on him raised a lot of eyebrows.

In the weeks before the election, we had three major debates. I had a lot of trepidation about debating an incumbent Congressman who had been a trial lawyer. But I more than held my own in the first debate. I thought he won the second debate, but on the morning of the third debate, the *Atlanta Constitution* endorsed me and Pat was really rattled. He was angry and distracted and condescending. If that debate had been a prizefight, the referee would have stopped it. I really KO'd him. I thought he was just bugged by the *Constitution* endorsement, but he knew something that I didn't. The *Atlanta Journal,* the conservative afternoon newspaper that was reliably Republican in its views, had also endorsed me.

There were just a few days left and the momentum was all mine. But our campaign was broke, with absolutely zero resources left. Swindall dominated the airwaves with positive commercials on the last weekend. On election night, the Swindall/Jones race went late into the night, with live coverage from both "victory" parties. When the last returns from overwhelmingly Republican areas in Dunwoody and North Fulton came in, Swindall won, 52 percent to 48 percent. But in the public perception I had come off as a winner.

We had been outspent by six to one, but we had almost pulled it off. We had just run out of time and money. I felt that if the election were three days later or if I had been able to spend another few thousand dollars, I could have won. But then, if frogs had wings they wouldn't bump their asses.

They say that "close only counts in horseshoes and hand grenades." But sometimes it counts in politics, too. I had won respect and credibility. Our strong showing had helped Democrat Wyche Fowler to win a squeaker in the U.S. Senate race. And our race had also revealed Swindall's vulnerability, so I knew that a lot of other folks were going to be eyeing the next election. I got up the next morning to start running that next race. I felt that I had come too far and fought too hard and learned too much not to continue the fight.

Another little consequence of my race had been the demise of Pat Robertson's Freedom Council. The Federal Elections Commission saw through the gambit just like I had. Pat was using The Freedom Council as a national organizing tool for his planned

Presidential race in 1988. But the political money was coming from religious contributions to his *700 Club* television show. That's against the law. And so the FEC and the IRS put the ol' kibosh on The Freedom Council.

Several ambitious state legislators started talking of making the 1988 race against Swindall. But then a State Senator named Bud Stumbaugh called a group of Democratic leaders together and made it clear that he thought I deserved everyone's support. There was agreement in the room and pledges of endorsement. Bud Stumbaugh's being a stand-up guy made my life a whole lot easier. Those are the things we never forget.

I worked away through 1987, solidifying the support I had gotten, raising what money I could, and studying the Congressional process on a daily basis. Vivian continued to produce award-winning television commercials and was named Atlanta Business Woman of the Year. I knew it was going to be hard to sustain the wild momentum we had at the end of the '86 race, and sometimes it seemed like I was just out in the desert by myself, but that perseverance in 1987 paid off. I went into 1988 with a solid foundation.

Things got complicated when a couple of other guys announced their candidacies. Nick Moraitakis was a polished, thoughtful attorney who was popular in Atlanta's large Greek American community. As Michael Dukakis was firing up Greek Americans nationally in his presidential bid, so was Nick around the Fourth District. He was working hard and raising serious money. Another fellow, John Stembler, apparently already had money. Somebody told me that Stembler was a "wealthy redneck playboy." That sounded alright by me, but his campaign was bizarre. He hired some sleazy guy to follow me around with a telescopic lens to take pictures of me looking goofy. Hell, they didn't need a telescopic lens for that. And Stembler announced that he was going to walk the entire district. Taking a reporter from the *Atlanta Constitution* with him, he started way out in the northern extremes of the district, which was then a long way from any population. It was a scorcher of a day. He was quite a bit overweight and he walked for hours without seeing hardly anybody. Then he hopped in an air-conditioned car and the "Great Walk" was put on hold. Forever.

Once again I got help from Hazzard County. Sorrell Booke came to a big picnic fund-raiser. Well, actually "Boss Hogg" came to the picnic. Sorrell came rolling up in a Cadillac convertible, dressed in that white suit and totally in character. People just loved it. The highlight of the day was a mock debate between Boss Hogg and me. He was hilarious and I have to admit that Boss won that debate hands down.

Swindall, meanwhile, was doing all the things incumbents can do to raise his positive profile and mend his fences. And his wife, Kim, was preggers again, for the third election in a row.

At one scheduled debate with Swindall, Kim showed up instead, looking beautiful but looking also as if she might give birth right there on the speaker's platform. I spoke first. "Ladies and gentlemen, I am at a distinct disadvantage here today facing Mrs. Swindall rather than Mr. Swindall. Not only is she much better looking than him, but in my opinion, she is also somewhat smarter!" Everybody laughed but Kim.

The race kept a low profile throughout 1987. Then it heated up in a hurry.

One day in February of 1988 there was a small mention in the Atlanta papers that Swindall had been asked to testify before a grand jury. That was about it. The nature of the jury's investigation was not revealed, and Swindall's testimony was secret. He acted as if it were a trivial matter of which he had some slight knowledge. And that was all. To my disappointment, the matter disappeared into wherever news stories go when the editors decide it ain't news anymore.

But it bubbled up that the grand jury was investigating a money-laundering scheme involving a Swindall supporter, Charles LeChasney. And then it turned out that LeChasney had been caught in an

FBI sting operation. Swindall reported that he had been interested in securing a "mortgage" on his home from LeChasney because of cost overruns. He had been bamboozled by his contractor, he said, and the place was now at 1.2 million bucks.

Seems like that good deal on his mansion wasn't such a good deal after all.

Pat seemed to have finessed the whole grand jury business until June 16, 1988. That's when the story broke big-time in banner headlines on the front page of the Atlanta papers. Someone had leaked tapes to the newspapers of the secret meetings between Swindall, LeChasney, and an undercover FBI agent posing as a Florida Latino businessman.

Despite the best spin Swindall could put on it, it appeared from the tapes that he was willing to launder $850,000 in what he was told was possibly narcotics money. He had accepted a check for $150,000 and had continued to deal with the undercover agent for a month before getting cold feet and backing out of the deal. Swindall's defense was that he had ultimately done the right thing, and had done nothing illegal. "They tried to tempt me," he said, "but I was strong." So instead of willingly being a drug money launderer, he was presenting himself as Christ in the wilderness.

Pat Swindall's world changed that day, and so did mine. I went from dark-horse challenger to a candidate who was now favored to win. I declined to comment much on the revelations. "If a crime has been committed, the system will play out. But right now, Pat has not been charged with anything and he hasn't even been accused of anything. So he should be presumed innocent until he is found otherwise." That was me being sanctimonious and phony. Already I was sounding like a congressman. Of course, being human, down deep I was really hoping that he was guilty as hell of something.

I really didn't need to say much. Every time Swindall opened his mouth he ate more of his shoes. But he still had a very strong core of support, and perhaps not surprisingly it came from the "religious right." They trusted him and believed him. And that summer, the Georgia delegation to the National Republican Convention chose him as their Chairman. They were "standin' by their man."

I won the primary easily and that is when the ructions really began. As I was beginning to celebrate our victory that night, Swindall stood in front of the cameras and announced that this was going to be a campaign focused on Ben Jones's dishonesty about his life, and about Ben Jones's lack of candor regarding his criminal past. Pat said the issue was character. He said his had been impugned by the liberal media and that the voters didn't know Ben Jones's real character.

In the conventional political playbook, this was the equivalent of a "Hail Mary" pass. Pat's negatives were now so high, and his odds for election so tarnished, that his only chance to win was to raise my negatives to a higher level than his. And in my case, of course, he had a lot of material to work with. And he went to work with the determination of a cornered rat.

He sent a detective up to Chapel Hill and the detective found a police report from the night I had pursued Vicki to a motel back in 1967. The cops had thrown me in jail for my own good, and Vicki hadn't pressed charges. But I had hurt her, and the shame of that night was a terrible burden. She and I had communicated every so often since those days, and she had forgiven me and we both knew that we still cared deeply about each other. We were dear friends, plain and simple. When Swindall made an issue of that incident, I felt a lot of that old pain again. I said the facts spoke for themselves. I got in touch with Vicki and she said she was sorry that deal had come back around on me. That's the way she was. She was very proud of how I had turned my life around. She said that the Swindall campaign had pointed reporters to her, but that she had told them off.

In twelve-step recovery meetings, the fourth step is, "We made a searching and fearless moral inventory of ourselves." It is one thing to do that when you are among fellow recovering addicts in a private setting. But it is quite another to have your political opponent make "a searching and fearless moral inventory" of you on the national news and in thirty-second attack commercials. But my support not only held, it was strengthened by his attacks. And I was determined to stay on the high road. Or at least the highest road I could find under the circumstances.

"My life is not a story about falling down," I said. "It is a story about getting up."

We had an outdoor debate in Conyers, the town where the *Dukes* cast had first met ten years before. By now, the race was getting national attention. There were a lot of television cameras there that night. Dan Rather of CBS had called it "the dirtiest race in the country." The mud was flyin' for sure, but I was just duckin'. Swindall went on the attack. "Mr. Jones has been less than forthcoming about his past," he said. "We should expect more honesty from our candidates."

It was the perfect setup. "Pat," I said, "being called dishonest by you is like being called ugly by a possum!"

The audience roared with laughter. The press roared with laughter. And I swear to you that my timing was so good that Pat Swindall laughed too. And since that was the sound bite that everybody liked, that was the one they used on all the local channels on the eleven o'clock news that night. It was all making Pat more and more desperate.

On October 18, about two weeks before the election, Pat was indicted on ten counts of perjury to the grand jury. Desperation became something more like sociopathic schizophrenia, if there is such a condition. He was bonkers. At our last debate, held at the Jewish Synagogue auditorium, he came out with a gigantic poster which magnified a tiny notice in a local gay newspaper. The notice in the paper was about one inch by two inches. It encouraged gay folks to help out with our phone bank. The poster Pat brought out was about four feet by six feet. At the top it said, "Ben Jones says he's mainstream. But this ad shows he is NOT!" His face was contorted with anger, and it just got worse as the crowd starting hissing at him. He shoved the poster at me and I tossed it to the floor. The crowd cheered. "I happily accept the support of any eligible voter," I said. I had a lot of gay friends in showbusiness and I had learned to judge people by their actions and their hearts. What they did in private was none of my business.

Pat Swindall's desperate tactics backfired. He was a gone goose. The election itself was almost anticlimactic.

In a staunch Republican District, running against a well-funded incumbent who had been the rising star of the GOP, and running against the powerful "religious right," we won by a landslide. At our celebration a young gospel singer belted out "Amazing Grace." That was exactly the right song for that victory. "I once was lost, but now I'm found, I was blind but now I see . . ."

Pat Swindall phoned and I went into a private room to take his call. "I just want to congratulate you and wish you well," he said. And then, with the celebration outside almost drowning him out, I heard him say, "Hey, I've got some real nice office furniture up there I can make you a good deal on. It's really good stuff." And as always, he wasn't kidding.

The Honorable Cooter

Back in 1974, when I was working at the Kennedy Center in *Desire Under the Elms,* I had slept in the basement storage room for the Folger Shakespeare Theatre, just a few blocks east of the U.S. Capitol. A buddy of mine lived upstairs, and I got the storage room for free, thus saving a few bucks to spend on more beer. And every evening I walked the three miles or so down the National Mall to the Kennedy Center.

And so I passed the Capitol. This is a bit hard to explain, but I was afraid of the place. I was intimidated by its grandeur and by its authority. For some reason, I was reluctant to enter there. I thought maybe they wouldn't let me in. I don't know what I thought because I was thinking like the alcoholic I was, but I did not enter that great building the whole time I was there. I simply did not feel worthy.

Now I was being welcomed into "America's office" like a conquering hero. Well, certainly to the Democratic caucus, I was a conquering hero. And I was in a state of euphoria. The whole deal seemed like a dream. It seemed that everyone in Washington had kept up with the race, and there were a lot of eyes on me. Some folks expected to see the Wild Man of Borneo, or even a grease-covered mechanic named "Cooter." And though there was a fairly large freshman class with many more gifted public servants and learned legislators than me, the press made me the story. I took the train up from Atlanta and there was a TV camera waiting for me at the station. I was profiled in *People* magazine and the *New York Times* did a big piece on me. *Life* magazine had a great column about "Cooter" going to Congress. I did all the orientation things, made the rounds of parties and receptions, started trying to put a staff together, paid homage to the leadership, and explored every square inch of the Capitol Building like a kid at the beach.

Speaker of the House Jim Wright was an old Texan with a homespun, syrupy style that could be deceiving. I had a feeling that his raising had been similar to mine, kind of hardscrabble. He gave me some advice: "When you first get here, you'll wonder what in the world you are doing here. But after just a few months, you'll be wondering what in the world all the rest of these fools are doing here."

I heard there was an early-morning meeting of sober drunks somewhere in the Capitol Building. I wandered around until I heard the sound of deep, heartfelt laughter. Sure enough, that was where I found Howard Powell.

One night I met President George H.W. Bush at a White House reception. A couple of days later I was in the House Gym, exhausted from a hard hour of full-court basketball. I was sitting naked, soaked with sweat, at my locker when Congressman Sonny Montgomery, whose locker was across from mine, asked me, "Ben, do you know the President?"

I looked up and there was President Bush, as naked as I was. Being an old exhausted gym rat, I just nodded at him and said, "Yeh, I know him. Hey, howzit goin'?" Then I thought, "Holy shit, that's the President of the United States! The leader of the Free World! And you just brushed him off!" So I jumped up and said, "Oh, yes, Mr. President! Good to see you, sir! How are you, sir!?" It was as neat a piece of syncophancy as you'll ever see. And it reminded me of Bob

Dylan's old line: "Even the President of the United States sometimes must stand naked . . ."

When Bush chose Congressman Dick Cheney of Wyoming to be his Secretary of Defense, it set off a fuse in the Republican caucus that was to have consequences for all of us. Cheney had been the Republican whip, and when the GOP House Caucus voted to replace him, back-bench firebrand Newt Gingrich of Georgia took on the Republican Leader Bob Michel's candidate and won the whip's job.

I had known Newt slightly down in Georgia. After Pat Swindall was indicted, before the election, we crossed paths at an event. "Looks like we're going to be colleagues very soon," he said. "I don't think either one of us should be counting those chickens until they hatch," I said. Gingrich had a tougher race on his hands than he thought, but he won. And when he became whip, his strategy was to do anything and everything possible to destroy the Democratic majority. In that endeavor he was obnoxious, relentless, and ultimately successful. But that was still a ways off.

I was just trying to sharpen my spikes and learn my way around the bases. It was a heady time, and I had some really good help. Dotti Crews, Wendy Herzog, Jim Watkins, and Chester Benton stayed on after the campaign. They gave up their regular jobs to become a part of our Congressional staff. And we hired some terrific people who knew their way around the Hill and the bureaucracy. I realized that as a freshman legislator, I was not going to have much influence on major issues. I thought we should focus on learning the process and doing the best constituent services possible. So my speech to the staff went something like this: "We represent about six hundred thousand Americans in all of their dealings with the Federal Government. We work for the taxpayers. They are our employers, our bosses. So if anybody calls with a problem involving the Federal Government, it is our job to investigate it, to solve it, and if we need to, we will advocate on their behalf. Most of the time about half of those people are going to be upset about some position I've taken or some vote I've made. That is their right. Just remember that our door is their door. It belongs to them. So let's just do the best we can and let the chips fall where they may." And that's what we did. Our constituent services were as good or better than any office on Capitol Hill.

I asked for and was assigned to the Public Works and Transportation Committee and the Veterans' Committee. Atlanta is about transportation. It exists because it is at a natural geographic crossroads. The Chattahoochee River there was the border between the Creek and the Cherokee Nations, and the Native Americans had long since found the trails which were the paths of least resistance to the river. European settlers followed these trails and they became the first wagon roads. Then later the railroads came along the same way. Atlanta began as Terminus, the last station of the railroad line. Now it is an international crossroads, so the Transportation Committee was a good place for me. The Fourth District also had a Veterans Administration Hospital in Decatur, and a large population of veterans. So I was on committees that were practical and dealt with issues I cared about.

But there were a lot of issues I cared about. I gave my first lengthy floor speech during Special Orders. If you have watched C-SPAN you've seen those members pontificating in the late afternoon in front of an empty chamber after the regular business of the day is done. If nothing else, it is a good way to put in your two cents worth, and maybe somebody back in the district will see you on television and think you are a big shot. There were a couple of members who seemed to be there every day, having a great time extemporizing on whatever crossed their minds. There also seemed to be a bit too much praise going around than was warranted. You know what I mean: "I am honored to yield to my good friend, the distinguished gentleman from Winnemucca who has done so much for this nation in his tireless efforts in his important role as Chairman of the Subcommittee on Fan Belt Safety!"

But the remarks become a part of the Congressional Record, the daily printed record of all of Congress's proceedings. They become part of history.

I asked John Lewis to join me in a Special Order honoring the twenty-fifth anniversary of the murders of three civil rights workers in Mississippi in 1964. Michael Schwerner, James Chaney, and Andy Goodman had been registering voters when they were brutally beaten and shot. Congressman Lewis represented the Fifth District of Georgia, which bordered the Fourth and contained most of the City of Atlanta. John Lewis is a legendary leader of the Civil Rights Movement, a man rightly respected for his humility and courage. It was personally important for me to speak of those young men and their legacy. I spoke of the remarkable changes in the South since those days and of how blacks and whites had shared so much for so long. We had a culture in common and through that bond we were building a South that would honor those three kids and all the others who had sacrificed for the fulfillment of the American promise.

Having been witness to the great changes in the Southland, I now had an opportunity to see an extraordinary change in Eastern Europe. A lot of folks, myself included, had predicted the eventual fall of the Soviet Empire. But very few people were not astonished by the speed with which it disintegrated.

I had good timing about when to show up in Washington. Nineteen eighty-nine was in many ways the most important year of the twentieth century. The Communists had controlled Russia for over seventy years and had been engaged in a struggle with the Western democracies for world dominance since the end of World War II. Yet within a year, the Soviet Union would come apart, and Hungary, Poland, Czechoslovakia, Romania, Lithuania, Latvia, Estonia, and East Germany would begin making the transition from dictatorial state-controlled economies to democratic market economies. And the myriad Soviet "republics" from Georgia to Uzbekistan would break away from Moscow's grasp.

The Cold War had suddenly ended and the United States had emerged as the most powerful and influential nation on the planet. The Republicans immediately gave all credit to Ronald Reagan, who surely was a factor, but in truth the victory was one that was achieved through decades of bipartisan leadership in the United States and from our allies in NATO. It came too from the people who had stood tall in our military, and from all of us American taxpayers who had backed our commitment and resolve. Communism, which promised empowerment to all, had empowered no one except the Kremlin chiefs. It was a bane to the individual human spirit. And I got to see it fail and fall firsthand. In Hungary and Poland I was part of a delegation working with the new private sector to help them make the leap to an entirely new way of living. The excitement throughout the region was palpable in 1989. There is no more spirited feeling than the deliverance of newfound freedom.

In Czechoslovakia we witnessed the success of the "Velvet Revolution." On a snowy night in Prague, we celebrated with the new Czech leaders at our American ambassador's house. The ambassador had an Academy Award on her mantelpiece. That's because she was Shirley Temple Black, the former child star of the late 1930s. The original Little Miss Sunshine.

As we chatted with the ecstatic Czechs beneath Shirley Temple's Oscar, a slight fellow smoking a cigarette came over to me and introduced himself. This was the great playwright Václav Havel, soon to be the new President of his country. I mentioned the recent passing of Samuel Beckett. Havel, intrigued, asked me, "And what is your profession?"

"I am an actor by trade," I said.

"Ahhhh," he said with an approving grin. Then, referring to the recent uprising that brought down the dictatorship, he said, "The actors were the first ones out!"

In Berlin our delegation was given pickaxes and chisels, and we had the honor of whacking away at the Berlin Wall. A large cornerstone of the Wall is now a part of my walkway. I thought about jok-

In 1988, debating Boss Hogg (Sorrell Booke) was tougher than debating my real opponent.

At age 43, finally getting in shape.

My election got a lot of attention. People *magazine, 1989.*

My boy Walker was a great campaigner. Primary victory night, 1988.

Newt Gingrich chickened out of our televised debate in 1994.

Jimmy Carter may be the most respected American in the world.

The elder Bush's term as President coincided with my two terms in Congress.

Andy Young is one of the finest people ever to come out of the Southland.

Me and Alma in New York. The background says it all.

LEFT TO RIGHT: *Walker, Rachel, Michael, me, Alma, Michelle, and Wes—a happy family.*

Alma and I were married in 1992 in the Chapel of the United States Capitol by the House Chaplain, Jim Ford.

Dynamite and a match.

In La La Land, Catalina Island, 1997.

Freelancing as a body guard for Sarah, the Duchess of York, 1995, in New York City.

At our Blue Ridge Mountain home, which has been there since the 1700s.

June 2006, on stage at the Grand Ole Opry. I'm always amazed at the affection the American heartland holds for our crazy ol' show.

Happiest day of my life! August 30, 2006. Three of the smartest, best lookin' kids ever show up to wish me a Happy 65th Birthday. LEFT TO RIGHT: *Jeanne, me, Walker, and Rachel.*

My pride. Miss Alma and the five grandbabies, summer 2007.

ing to my constituents that none of this had happened before I got to Congress, that I was clearly the tipping point that brought down the Soviets. But then I was afraid they might think I was serious and that the job had already driven me into delusions of grandeur.

Back in the House of Representatives, Newt Gingrich claimed his first victim when Jim Wright resigned as Speaker. Jim had written a book and gotten some special interests to buy a bunch of copies. That was clearly unethical, but the GOP was acting as if he was a serial killer. Finally, Wright had had enough and graciously bowed out, still syrupy, but graciously syrupy. Tom Foley of Washington became the new Speaker. He was not nearly as tough as his predecessors, Wright and the avuncular Tip O'Neill. Even with a forty-seat majority, Tom was always playing defense against the tirelessly attacking Gingrich. Maybe he was just too nice.

During 1989 two of my colleagues, Larkin Smith of Mississippi and Mickey Leland of Texas, were killed in plane crashes. Larkin had come in the same time I had, and he was a younger guy. His office was right next door to mine, on the fifth floor of the Cannon Building. He was a Republican and we joked that Richard Nixon and Jack Kennedy had both started out up on the fifth floor of Cannon back in 1946. After his passing, Larkin's office was taken over by Dennis Hastert of Ohio.

I had played basketball with Mickey Leland a few days before he headed off to Ethiopia to help in famine relief. He was one of the good guys.

In early 1989, after the Battleship *Iowa* suffered a fatal explosion in the Mediterranean, I went down to those "war games" at the request of the Navy. A lot of the sailors wanted to get their picture taken with "Cooter." Before the weekend was over I was a member of the Tailhook Society because I had landed and taken off from the carrier U.S.S. *Coral Sea.* I guarantee you that there isn't any ride at Six Flags quite as thrilling. As Rosco P. Coltrane used to say, "It'll put a quiver in your liver!"

It never failed that every time I dealt with the military I was always impressed with the quality of our young servicemen and women. I can't necessarily say the same for the brass.

Back home in Georgia the Republicans were gearing up to win back the Fourth District. They felt that my victory was clearly a fluke and that I would surely be a one-term Congressman. A well-known State Representative named John Linder was the candidate of choice to take me out. Linder was from "up north," had been a dentist, and now called himself a "venture capitalist." He loaned money to entrepreneurs at high interest, and if they defaulted he took their assets. "Rosey" Walker said, "Venture capitalist. That's what they used to call a 'loan shark.' "

Meanwhile, Pat Swindall was convicted on nine counts of perjury. The prosecutor was another Republican named Bob Barr. If you keep up with politics, you've probably heard that name, too. Pat ended up pulling a year in a federal slammer.

Then there was the trip to Alaska in 1989. One of the subcommittees I served on was tasked with going up to deal with the mess created by the *Exxon Valdez* oil spill. However awful you might think that disaster was, it was worse. It doesn't take much for mankind to desecrate Mother Earth in horrific ways. And this one was just a case of drunk boating.

There were things about being a Congressman that I really loved. I felt like I was in the best graduate school in the world, with the best library, and some great teachers. As often as not I would go to sleep at my desk well past midnight, trying to catch up with the enormous pile of paper that seemed to grow on my desk like kudzu. Then I would wake up in my chair, go over to the couch, and sack out for a few hours before the next twenty-hour day started. I loved the competitive nature of debate, I loved the opportunity to move people with words, I loved the camaraderie, and I loved being surrounded by the history of the place.

There were also some things I didn't like about it. And the things I didn't like about it then are much worse now. Through partisan redistricting, a majority of the 435 seats in the House are not competitive. They are "safe" seats. They change hands when a Congressman retires or dies. Or is indicted. As we know, that happens too.

And, of course, incumbent Congressmen almost inevitably have bigger campaign war chests. That's because well-heeled individuals and special-interest PACs make it their business to curry favor with the powerful. Now, everybody knows this. That is how the system works. And it is unfortunately how it is probably going to continue to work. The process has evolved into this racket over many decades, as everyone naturally learned to "game the system." But the system sucks. It really does screw the individual. "Damn the public interest," the thinking goes, "what really matters is what our special interests want." Sure, sometimes the public interest and the special interest may coincide, but that is just a happy coincidence. I'm afraid, friends and neighbors, that most of your fine elected representatives are bought and paid for, no matter how they like to phrase it. And as the costs of campaigns go up, the special interests accrue more power. And whenever someone points out this unfortunate truth, the entrenched power structure in Washington scoffs at their "naïveté."

And that is the part I didn't like. Every relationship becomes a quid pro quo. And the sycophancy in D.C. is as thick in the air as the humidity in August. I had spent years in Hollywood being a "celebrity." "Celebrity" is, of course, a total illusion. The so-called celebrity is the same old doofus that used to fart in eighth-grade Geography class. He just got lucky and has a cool job now. But when you are sitting in a chair with your name on it, and people are powdering your face and bringing you coffee and your messages, and folks want your autograph and want their picture taken with you and have a business proposition they would like to pitch you, and now it's time for your close-up . . . well, it is both unnatural and seductive. And the person involved gets to thinking that somehow they are perhaps more deserving of this attention and luxury than your average

Joe Schmoe. And they tend to get their head wedged up into the lower end of their alimentary canal.

Well, in Washington the ones who cast the votes are the "celebrities," and they are subjected to ten times the sycophancy that a Hollywood star deals with. Everybody is forever kissing everybody else's ass. And everybody wants something from the member of Congress. As a rule, they are usually so sweet about it that sugar won't melt in their mouth. They want that vote. And if they get that vote, the Congressman will get their support and money. You scratch my back and I'll scratch yours. And the Congressman, like the "celebrity," starts thinking that somehow he is more deserving of this attention and luxury than your average Joe Schmoe. Well, that ol' hubris will get you every time.

The Monkey Wrapped His Tail Around the Flagpole

It seemed to me that there was a constant tension between idealism and practicality. And I had never been a very practical person.

There is a great maxim that has been attributed to several statesmen which goes, "You must never be afraid to take the vote that will get you defeated." For me, that says it all about political principle and courage. I was enjoying the experience I had worked so hard to get, and I planned to run for reelection. But I never intended to be a career politician. I figured that six or eight years of this would be plenty of public service. I felt like I was getting better at the job week by week and that in a few years I could be a very effective spokesperson for the issues I felt needed addressing. That was my only vague ambition. And I really didn't understand being afraid to do what I thought was right. I have been afraid in my life, but never over something as insignificant as losing an election. Losing might make you feel bad, but it ain't gonna kill you.

And then suddenly, right in front of me, was the vote that would probably get me defeated. Every few years the "Flag Amendment" comes up for a vote. It is a proposition to amend the U. S. Constitution to prohibit the desecration of the American flag. It is obviously a visceral issue. Every once in a blue moon, some clown will burn a flag and there will be ten TV cameras there to cover it. And it makes a lot of people upset, which is probably what the perpetrator was hoping for. But to make this action illegal, the Flag Amendment would change the Constitution's Bill of Rights, our basic freedoms. It would put an asterisk on the First Amendment's guaranteed right to dissent. It is easy to understand why The American Legion and other veterans' groups support the Flag Amendment. "Protecting the flag" is seen as a way of honoring our nation and honoring the memory of those who fell under that flag. So there it was. And I hated that amendment. I hated it because I love America and I think the Bill of Rights is the greatest public document in history, and I don't think you strengthen our nation by screwing around with The Bill of Rights. There was no way I was going to vote for that amendment. There were two bodies of opinion from my friends and supporters. The first was that I was foolish and the vote would lead to my defeat. The second was that I was right and the vote would lead to my defeat.

My thinking was that the flag is a symbol and what it symbolizes is our great freedoms. And one of those freedoms is the freedom of political expression. And if burning a flag isn't political expression, then what the hell is it? It is that and only that.

Senator Bob Kerrey of Nebraska, who left a leg in Vietnam and brought home a Congressional Medal of Honor, agreed with me. So did a lot of other veterans. But I got scads of very angry letters and calls from people who were stirred up about it. At a parade in Alpharetta, Georgia, a couple of hecklers went over the line. I hopped out of the car and went after them. If someone is going to question my patriotism, they had better be prepared to duck.

In the end I not only voted against it, I helped to lead the fight against it in the House. And when it came up short, the Republicans back in the district started writing their TV attack spots. They thought I had cast the vote that would beat me, too.

Up in the office in D.C. I asked our scheduler what was on my "to-do list" for the weekend back in the District.

"On Saturday morning you have to go to Savannah to speak to the state American Legion Convention," she said. Y'all, God has a great sense of humor.

I got up very early Saturday morning in Atlanta and drove the four hours down to Savannah. I prayed all the way. I hadn't gotten ten steps into the Convention Hall before a man was in my face. He was literally gasping for air he was so mad. Most of the folks there were polite, if not particularly friendly. When it was time for me to speak I could sense the tension in the hall. I told them of my work on the Veterans' Committee, how we were trying to improve the health care system, and how we were upgrading the care of our Veterans' cemeteries. I told them how I supported compensation for Agent Orange sufferers and how my vote had made the difference in its passage. And then I said, "I know that a lot of you disagree with my position on this flag business. And I respect that. For me, though, it seems like a choice between our flag and our Constitution, and that shouldn't be. I think we respect our flag by the kind of citizens we try to be. As for these people who burn American flags, well, it seems like to me that the best thing to do with them is to drop them off at an American Legion Hall around ten-thirty on a Saturday night!"

The building erupted in cheers and I left to a standing ovation. Like I said, God has a great sense of humor.

Something else was going on in those years. Vivian and I were drifting apart. Both of us had become workaholics, she at her production company and me at my new career. And she hated the country life as much as I loved it. We bought a townhouse close by her parents' place and I found myself alone in the country. This slowly created more and more real distance between us. But we had a lot to hold us together. We were both committed to progressive causes and we had a son whom we both adored beyond anything. But the cracks in the foundation were starting to form. Looking back with the clarity of hindsight, I'd say we were both in a lot of denial about our basic stubbornness. A lot of marriages come apart from "irreconcilable differences." But the trouble with our relationship was that we had "irreconcilable similarities."

A longtime Republican activist and legislator, John Linder had much more political experience than I had. But the Fourth District was clearly trending to the right, and though I had a centrist voting record, that didn't matter. Every vote I cast was fodder for their attacks. Linder was a savvy campaigner, a good debater, and a relentless fund-raiser. At one point, Vice President Dan Quayle came down on his behalf and badmouthed me a bit. Quayle, who is now largely forgotten, was considered to be a mediocre Senator and a worthless Vice President. But he and I got along just fine.

I had a nice comeback for Quayle's remarks on Linder's behalf. Everybody remembered Lloyd Bentsen saying to Quayle in the 1988 debate, "Senator, I knew Jack Kennedy. Jack Kennedy was a friend of mine. And believe me, you are no Jack Kennedy." So I said, "I know Dan Quayle. Dan Quayle is a friend of mine. And believe me, John Linder is no Dan Quayle."

I also pointed out that the taxpayers had paid for the Veep's trip down from D.C. for the political rally. For some reason that didn't bother all those "conservatives" who were always yapping about how our tax dollars are spent on "welfare queens."

On August 2, 1990, over 140,000 Iraqi troops with 1,800 tanks poured across the border with Kuwait, overwhelming that defenseless nation and proclaiming it part of Greater Iraq. Saddam Hussein acted as if there would and should be no consequences. But the United States, working with a coalition of United Nations allies, put Operation Desert Shield in place. It was a massive buildup of troops in Saudi Arabia to put pressure on Saddam to withdraw his forces from Kuwait or face enormous reprisal. He refused to budge, and tensions increased throughout the rest of the year.

Linder made the "flag vote" the centerpiece of his campaign. But he had plenty of other red meat to throw to the hounds on my heels. The National Endowment for the Arts had become a particularly easy target for demagogic attacks. Although the Endowment had at that time given over seventy-five thousand grants, a handful of them had been extremely controversial. A movement led by Senator Jesse Helms and strongly supported by Jerry Falwell, Pat Robertson, and others had vociferously targeted the Endowment for elimination. Although he had not received direct grants, exhibits of male nudity and homosexual themes by photographer Robert Mapplethorpe had been sponsored by galleries which received Endowment money. But perhaps the most egregious work was a thing called *Piss Christ* by Andrés Serrano, which consisted of a crucifix in a container of urine. It wasn't hard to figure out why taxpayers were upset about their dough being used for this sort of stuff. By its nature, art is sometimes going to offend, but I was one among many who thought *Piss Christ* was indefensible. To me, it didn't rise to the level of deserving to be called "art," nor did it rise to the level of deserving a defense.

But as an artist myself, and a strong supporter of the Endowment, it seemed to me that the religious right wanted to "throw out the baby with the bath water." Almost by definition, *art* is going to mean different things to different people. Everybody has dissimilar tastes. But most Americans understand the value of the arts to our civilization, its inherent place in our culture, and the need to encourage our children's creativity. Despite the occasional controversy, the

National Endowment has done a terrific job of supporting and enhancing the arts in America.

Again I was told that supporting the Endowment would cripple my reelection chances, and again my position was that if I had to pander to foolishness to hold the job, then the job wasn't worth it. I would say what I believed and let the chips fall where they may. We worked to change and tighten the grant process, creating a thorough review of works in progress. And I made it clear that an Endowment grant should come with a responsibility to excellence and was certainly not some sort of entitlement.

My best argument came right out of Atlanta. A young composer of musicals received an eighteen-thousand-dollar Endowment grant to spend a year writing his first nonmusical play. It was set in his hometown of Atlanta, and when it was ready, it had its successful premiere at Atlanta's Alliance Theatre. It went to Broadway from there and won the coveted Tony Award as the Best Play of the Year. It also won the Pulitzer Prize for drama. It was made into an Oscar-winning film which was shot in Atlanta. The play and film have generated hundreds of millions of dollars over the years and continues to be produced around the world. *Driving Miss Daisy* by Alfred Uhry is an example of how the Endowment quietly succeeds 99 percent of the time. That's surely a higher percentage than any other federal program. And oh yeah, every "taxpayer dollar" had to be matched with privately raised funds. In 1989, the entire annual cost of the National Endowment for the Arts was less than the cost of one wing of one B-2 bomber.

That wasn't a bad argument, but it was overwhelmed by the thirty-second attack ads that Linder's crowd was running. One day I was driving my boy, Walker, to school. He was about six years old at the time. A commercial came on the car radio that went something like this:

> ANNOUNCER: (In a serious, astonished tone) "If you live in the Fourth District, there's something you need to know. Your

> Congressman, Ben Jones, says that he stands for family values. But did you know that Ben Jones took your hard-earned taxpayer money, went to Washington, D.C., and spent it on pornography!!?

Walker looked up at me with a confused look of sadness and fear. "Dad? Did you do that?" "No, buddy," I told him. "And people who tell lies like that are bad people." It was paid for by some "Christian" organization. But it is like my mama always said: "A person isn't a Christian because of what they say, but because of how they behave."

And then there was the Brady Bill. It would have mandated a "five-day waiting period" for the purchase of a handgun, to give law enforcement the opportunity to do a background check on the buyer's criminal record. The National Rifle Association opposed it vehemently, supporting instead an "instant check" system that was some years away from practicality. My position was that Brady should be in place until the new technology became available. That sounds reasonable enough, but the NRA is no longer the kind of *Field and Stream* outfit of the old days, back when they were mostly hunters who were interested in gun safety and training. Back when they were reasonable. Now they seem mostly interested in protecting gun manufacturers rather than gun owners. My support of the "five-day waiting period" brought down the wrath of the NRA and their shock troops. They supported Pat Swindall, who looked as if he wouldn't know which end of a rifle to point. But if you get a 100 percent on their questionnaire, and suck up to them for the PAC money, they'll put up big signs saying, "SPORTSMEN FOR JONES." But, since I wouldn't be their boy, they supported John Linder. SPORTSMEN FOR LINDER. Make that "POWERFUL LOBBY OF GUN NUTS FOR LINDER."

I am an armed man. And I'm not one of those guys who thinks the Second Amendment is only about state militias. I think I've got a right to buy guns, fire guns, and have them around for hunting and self-defense. But we have long had gun control laws. You can't own an automatic weapon legally. Or a 50mm Howitzer. Or a bazooka. Or a heat-seeking missile. Our culture, working through democratic government, has had to decide what is in the public interest when it comes to serious hardware. And the fight is over where to draw the line.

There are roughly 52 million gunowners in the United States, and I'm one of them. And 50 million of us don't belong to the NRA because we don't respect the way that outfit does business. They are bullies.

Once, at a parade in Tucker, Georgia, I was riding in a carload of kids on a beautiful afternoon, with happy people everywhere, smiles, balloons, flags, fun. And there was one angry NRA weirdo screaming at me, "Ben Jones wants your guns. Ben Jones wants your guns!" I hopped out of the convertible and walked over to him and smiled. "I don't want your gun, pal," I told him. "I've got one." I looked him square in the eye and added, "And it's loaded, you sumbitch . . ." I guess you could say it disarmed him.

By now I had managed to piss off a lot of folks.

One of Linder's supporters said on a radio talk show that "Ben Jones is just a tax-and-spending, baby-killing, porno-supporting, flag-burning Hollywood liberal leftist!"

It looked like I was headed into another real high-toned campaign.

One Republican businessman snapped to me that Linder had some surprises for me. "I understand that we have got a lot of stuff on you," he smirked. "You don't have nearly as much stuff on me as I've got on myself," I replied. He just stood there, slack-jawed and dumbfounded. Nobody had ever said anything like that to him before. For all I know he is still standing there.

I had a slight lead in the polls, but there were a lot of "undecideds," and the conventional political wisdom is that the "undecideds" tend to break for the challenger. So as we entered the stretch, it was neck and neck. And I could feel the stress as if it were a head cold. I was angry and exhausted, and it took every bit of my actor's skills to keep smiling and forging ahead with something approaching genuine confidence. My tough hide was beginning to look like a worn-out alligator suitcase.

In my opinion, John Linder won our last televised debate on substance. His answers were more succinct, he attacked better, and he was more relaxed. But I had a hole card. In his many years in the State Legislature, Linder had missed a lot of votes. Many of them were procedural votes, but nevertheless, he was being paid to be there. We did a little research, made an accurate tabulation, and printed them out on a long scroll. There were well over a thousand. When I brought the subject up, I pulled the scroll out and unrolled it across the studio floor. It went out past the podium, past the cameras, and it kept on rolling until it hit the back wall. It was about twenty-five feet long. Suddenly Linder was tongue-tied. He sputtered like Porky Pig. Now that is what I call an "effective visual."

I hadn't snatched victory from the jaws of defeat, but at least I had managed a tie.

Two days before the election, Linder ran a blistering negative TV ad that contained all the usual distortions. Political advertising uses all the techniques of show business. I'm sure that they thought it was too late for me to respond. But I had done a little showbiz myself. I saw the ad in the afternoon, immediately wrote a thirty-second response attack ad, got a buddy of mine to do the "voiceover," threw some still pictures together, went to a studio, put it together in about an hour, and had it delivered to the TV stations that night. It was on the air the next morning. If I say so myself, and I'm about to, it was a dynamite spot. It "worked," and now it was John Linder who didn't have time to respond. Gotcha.

And we won the election. It was close, 52 percent to 48 percent. That night, for the first time in my life, I felt as if I had really earned something. I felt a sense of validation. Getting elected by beating Pat

Swindall may have been a "fluke," but now the voters of this wonderfully American district were giving me a "thumbs-up" for the job I had done. It was the greatest honor of my life.

Some months later I shared a flight with Ed Rollins, who had been running the Republican Congressional Campaign Committee. "I gotta hand it to you," he said. "We really thought we had you down there. We threw everything we had at you." Well, gee, Ed, thanks for the compliment. And good luck to you in the hottest recesses of hell. . . .

Things Come Undone

Some months after that election, Vivian and I parted ways. We had lived in separate homes for several years and though we shared a deep love of our family, and a continuing affection for each other, I told her that I had to end it. The relationship had long since deteriorated into a daily ritual of shouting matches and recriminations. It was hard. Vivian and I had met when I was still "drying out," and with the support of her and her folks, I had found success in television and in politics. But once I was elected to Congress, our personal relationship really went to hell. It was not her "fault." It was not my "fault." It was not our "fault." It was hard for both of us. We had changed away from each other and it had created an impossible situation. In the end, I guess it was those "irreconcilable similarities."

And yes, I had met somebody else. At a small dinner party for several of us Congressional members who were all in recovery from alcoholism, I was seated next to a little blond-haired gal in a red dress. I knew she wouldn't have been there if she wasn't in recovery, so we had that in common. And she was a theater executive, so we shared a background in show business. I asked her where she was from. "I was born in Washington, North Carolina," she replied. "I know that town," I said. "Been there many times. I was born just up the road in Tarboro." That started a conversation that has been going on for almost twenty years now. Alma Viator was, and is, cosmic electricity in the form of a woman. And it was like meeting the other half of me, a mystical thing, a genuine soul mate whom I felt like I had known for a million years. And it scared me. Because I felt the magnetic energy and I had to pull away. I was a Congressman and I was married and suddenly I was confused in a way that I had never expected to be again.

That was in late 1989. We both felt what was going on, and we both resisted it for over a year. But somehow we kept showing up at the same Capitol Hill functions. I had loved before in my life. I had loved deeply and sincerely and, I had thought, forever. And I had been hurt by love and I had hurt others. I had felt great affection and empathy and occasional joy. But this was new. Yes, I had loved. But I did not know until I met the girl in the red dress what it was like to be "in love." Not like this. And neither had she.

Good Guys Gone

I'm not sure I could handle two years like 1991. Just after Christmas I went with a Congressional delegation to see our military buildup in Saudi Arabia firsthand. I could only think that if Saddam Hussein was to see what I was seeing, he would immediately withdraw from Kuwait and hightail it back to Baghdad. Our troops were filled with steely resolve and were fully prepared. The tension on the bow was full. The arrow was pulled back tight, ready to fire. In Egypt, President Mubarak told us that Hussein was "a crazy person, like the men who sell cars on your television." He could not be reasoned with, he said. In Jerusalem, the city was preparing for Iraqi missiles should war begin. As we were heading home, Secretary of State Baker came out of a meeting with Iraqi Defense Minister Tariq Aziz with the news that their discussions had been fruitless. Now we were going home to vote Yea or Nay on a major war.

On the flight back to Washington I thought about the troop trains that rolled in and out of the Pinners Point freight yard back in World War II. And I thought of the sound of "Taps" being played across Scott's Creek at the Naval Hospital. The vote took place on

January 12, 1991, and I voted an unequivocal "Aye" against the preference of the Democratic leadership and most of our caucus.

On January 17 the world watched via CNN from a Baghdad hotel room as that city was lit up by a massive bombing attack. Operation Desert Storm had begun. I was in Atlanta. As I headed to the airport to get back to Washington, I saw an ambulance at "Rosey" Walker's house. He was suffering serious chest pains and was taken to the hospital. By the time I got to my office at the Cannon Building, he had passed away. My relationship with my own dad had never been an easy one. We had little comfort with each other and the only thing we could talk about was our common interest in sports. My father and I were not close. But "Rosey" was like a father to me, and I think he felt like I was the son he didn't have. We had a ball together over the years and I still think of him a lot. When he hit the beach at Salerno he was just a kid. When he retired from the Atlanta police department forty years later, he was a man's man. My son, Vivian's son, is named after him. Robert Walker Jones.

The war ended but Saddam Hussein was still around. Since he didn't seem to care about anyone but himself, I think he felt he had won a victory. And while thousands of rebellious Shiites and Kurds were murdered by Saddam's remaining forces immediately after the "cease-fire," our troops were not allowed to do a thing.

In 1990 my father became ill with throat cancer. Over the years, I had made hundreds of trips to see the folks in Wilmington. And the trips became more and more depressing. After my kid brother left home around 1968, there was no one left in the house with him but Mama. And he turned all of his drunken, carping criticism on her. That had always been there when he drank, but it got worse. And after he was forced to retire in 1975, he became a daily drinker, not just a weekend drunk. The situation grew progressively worse.

The old man would be in a stupor and Mama would be a nervous wreck. I'd take her out for long rides and she would spend a lot of the time worrying about how mad he would be when we got back. One time he staggered about, waving a loaded pistol at me. Around 1985 it had finally reached the point when Mama had to get out of the house. This was after forty years of marriage and forty years of enabling codependence. I drove up to Wilmington and moved her into a high-rise for seniors. My father reacted like an alcoholic would. He drank more. And naturally Mama got depressed and worried about him. One winter day she drove by the house and something didn't seem right. She looked in and saw him unconscious on the floor and called Emergency Services. Daddy had been real drunk and the heat had gone off. He had passed out on the floor and was in a coma from low body temperature. I headed up there as quickly as I could. The doctor told me that it didn't look good and that I should be prepared to tell my brothers of his passing. But he rallied. Then he slipped back again and the doctor told me it was a matter of an hour or two at most.

Well, let me tell you how tough my old man was. He survived, and he gradually recovered. He was seventy-five years old and he lived for six more years and he never touched another drop of alcohol. He had been drinking bad whiskey for sixty-two years and he stopped cold turkey. He was a sick man for awhile, but he lived to be eighty-one years old. In those last six years he was as solicitous of my mama as she had been of him. Her health was beginning to slide and he waited on her hand and foot. And in the end it wasn't the whiskey that got him. It was the cigars, the pipe, and the chewing tobacco. He always told me that he "never inhaled." But that cancer didn't care about that. His throat was like the cinders from the steam engines. When he finally kicked the old water bucket, my brother Bryan and Mama put a railroad spike in his coffin. A retired railroad man who had been his District Superintendent took me aside after the funeral and told me, "Son, your daddy was the last of the John Henrys. He was an old-time steel drivin' man. Yessir, the last of the John Henrys." He didn't know the half of it, and I'm sure I didn't, either.

So my father was gone, "Rosey" was gone, and my marriage was over. And I began to feel like I was fifty years old. Because I was. My knees began to ache incessantly, throbbing and waking me up during the night. The doctor told me to knock off the athletics. I quit the compulsive jogging and gave up softball, but I continued to play hoops every day. Now that was a crazy thing. I was a mediocre player to begin with, and getting slower by the day, but basketball was my high, my meditation, and my time "with the boys." So I kept on and the pain just got worse.

The Little Man in the Tan Cap

During the Congressional recess in August of 1991 I was asked to join a human rights delegation sponsored by a nonprofit group. We were to go to China to express concerns about the situation there. I was joined by Nancy Pelosi of California and John Miller of the state of Washington. We all had sizable Chinese American populations in our districts. Surprisingly, the Chinese community in Atlanta was large and very active. They had appreciated the strong position I had taken against the Beijing government before and after Tiananmen. One of the student leaders who had escaped China had visited me in Washington and shown me pictures of the Tiananmen Massacre that had been smuggled out of there. From what I saw, the event was even more brutal and grisly than we had seen and heard.

August 30, 1991, was my fiftieth birthday. I spent it en route to Hong Kong. Hong Kong was still British then, and filled with democratic resistance to becoming part of China. To me, Hong Kong was like Manhattan in fast-forward mode. It made Times Square look like Mayberry. The ferry ride over to Kowloon was like a demolition derby on water. I really loved Hong Kong.

We met there with the leaders of the Chinese Democratic Resistance, including the courageous Martin Lee, who asked us to be certain to check on the hundreds of political prisoners in China. They gave us lists of who they were and where they were. They also asked us to address some very real concerns regarding political dissent. And before we left, Martin Lee asked us to do one more thing, if it was possible and we were willing.

"It would mean a lot to the free Chinese in the world if there could be some gesture at Tiananmen Square as a reminder and a memorial to those who died there."

I looked at Nancy and John. We were all nodding in agreement at the same time. And that is why I smuggled a banner into China in my drawers.

The Chinese officials and "handlers" who met us at the airport immediately tried to disabuse us of the notion of visiting any prisons. And for several days, in all our meetings with high-ranking officials, we got the same repetitive line. "There are no political prisoners in China. We have political freedom here. Freedom of speech. Freedom of assembly. The only people arrested at Tiananmen Square were criminals and thugs. There were no students killed there. The entire business was a fiction created by The Voice of America and CNN."

We also knew right away that our hotel rooms were bugged and that our every move was being monitored by "the handlers" and by undercover security. Beijing is a city of 20 million people, and on the first day I saw the same Chinaman three times. He was a slumping middle-aged man in a tan cap. It was the tan cap that was the giveaway. The third time, he saw me looking straight at him and he knew that I had "made" him.

Our diplomats at the American Embassy told us that all of this was, of course, business as usual. "These walls are most likely bugged, too."

Late on the first night I slipped out of the hotel and was taken to meet the wife of a dissident. There was great risk involved, especially for the lady. Her husband was critically ill, she told us. He was dying. Could we try to find out his condition?

We tried and it was reported to us that the man was in wonderful health. Besides, he was a criminal who had knowingly violated regulations and was being rehabilitated. "You see, in China, everyone is perfectly free to protest, free to speak, free . . ."

On our last day in Beijing, we were scheduled to visit the Great Wall, but we begged off, claiming jet lag and exhaustion and the need to rest before our journey home. As soon as the "handlers" were out of sight, I called Mike Chinoy of the CNN China Bureau. We talked in the code of those whose phones are bugged. "Eleven A.M. at the Square will work for me," I said. He knew we were planning something.

John, Nancy, and I went out the back of the hotel, walked a block, and hopped into a cab. We had three small white flowers to place at Tiananmen, and the banner was in my inside coat pocket. In the cab on the way there, I wrote a brief statement of tribute.

When we arrived at the vast square, we were spotted by an international reporter who showed us to a spot where tanks had crushed the life out of hundreds of students two years earlier. Suddenly there were television cameras and print reporters converging on the same place. Apparently Chinoy had put our intentions on the underground grapevine.

Then I pulled the banner out and the three of us unfurled it. It was beautifully sewn by the Hong Kong democracy movement. In Chinese and English lettering it said: "TO THOSE WHO DIED FOR DEMOCRACY IN CHINA."

From the corner of my eye I saw that we were drawing a crowd. Our whole tribute couldn't have taken more than two minutes, but our little gaggle of Americans had drawn the attention of a lot of men in uniforms. The proverbial shit hit the fan.

We were swarmed over by "police," actually soldiers whose job was to keep a very tight rein on anything that went down on Tiananmen

Square. John Miller got shoved around, but the press got the worst of it. I watched as several cameramen got whacked on the head with batons. They took it like it was routine, wincing as if they were being buffeted by high winds. One officer came bounding at me yelling, "NO!" which was probably the only English word he knew, or needed to know. He came up to about my navel. I leaned over to him and shouted back, "NO!" That confused the hell out of him. He backed off and went after somebody else.

In one of the photographs of that chaos I am standing there smiling. The reason is that just after I ran the little soldier off, I looked up and there not fifteen feet away, sitting at the base of a statue, was the little man with the tan cap. And I smiled at him. And I'll be damned if he didn't smile back at me.

It was right about then that I started thinking that these soldiers were under some strict orders. And these were the same guys who had no compunction at all about killing their own young students at this same spot. Then the words of an old Waylon Jennings song came to my mind. "If You See Me Getting' Smaller, It's Cause I'm Leavin'," he sang. I took ol' Waylon's advice and got the hell out of there.

Bill Whitaker of CBS, whom I had known in Atlanta, was nearby on the Square. He shouted a question as I was motivatin' for a cab. "Congressman, what made you think you could demonstrate in China?" he asked in astonishment.

"Well, hell, Bill," I replied, "they said they had absolute freedom of speech and assembly here. I was just testin' 'em out!"

That night, at a formal dinner with the Chinese Foreign Minister, the air was as chilly as the iced lobster. But our American ambassador had a very, very slight grin that he couldn't disguise.

The next morning we headed out to the airport with twice as many "handlers" as before. Everybody but me flew back to the States, for I was heading the other way, and my plane was delayed for hours. So I spent the day debating with four Chinese officials about the concept of "freedom." I doubt if my own little "cultural revolution" made any impression on them. They lived in regimented fear and the only time they smiled was when I got on the plane and headed for Tokyo.

I had been invited to join a bipartisan group sponsored by the Helsinki Commission. I flew from Tokyo to Moscow on Japan Air Lines and transferred to Aeroflot in Moscow for a flight to Vilnius, Lithuania. Aeroflot lived up to its reputation as the worst airline in the world. It was truly an adventure in travel. There must have been a dozen employees behind the Aeroflot desk in Moscow. But none of them paid any attention to their only customer, ol' *moi.* The joke among the Russians was, "We pretend to work and they pretend to pay us."

But it wasn't a joke. They were all smoking profusely, eating candy bars, and doing a lot of grab-assing. For hours I tried to pin down what flight was taking me to Vilnius. Finally a supervisor put me on a crate that looked as if the Germans had shot it up in World War II. The interior hadn't been cleaned in months and the seats were covered with a film of greaselike grime. The pilots, in mismatched ill-fitting uniforms, climbed aboard in the dim, smoky light. They did not smell like vodka because vodka doesn't smell. I looked down and could see the runway through the cracks beneath my feet. Atheism had been the official policy of the Soviet Union, but I assure you there were no atheists on that plane. We were all praying up a storm just to get off the ground.

When I finally hooked up with my colleagues in the Baltics, they all knew what had happened in China. The Chinese had detained the press at Tiananmen Square and had confiscated their videotape. But after a few hours, they let them go and gave them back their tape. So for three days, CNN had been running the story. And CNN goes into every government office in the world, just as it goes into every motel in North Dakota.

One colleague gave me a Chinese-sounding name: "Wun Dum Fuk."

From Vilnius, we flew to Tbilisi, Georgia. Things there were unstable, to say the least. There were a large group of rebels in the north of the country, pointed toward the Capitol. The President, Zviad Gamsakhurdia, was also under siege from his own Defense Commander, who had taken over the barracks above the city. When we went up to meet with those troops, they were all drunk. I was sitting by one of the commander's bodyguards, who dropped his matches as he was trying to light a cigarette. When he bent over to fetch them, a grenade rolled off of his belt and through my legs. It reminded me of some beer joints I had been in down South.

That night, back at President Gamsakhurdia's house, there was great tension as reports were coming in that the rebels were approaching the city from the north. Gamsakhurdia responded to this crisis as I would have back in my drinking days. He got loaded on vodka. The evening dinner turned into a marathon affair. Some of us speculated he wanted us around as witnesses, or perhaps felt we might give him cover. Soon it was impossible to tell what was going on because the English interpreter got as drunk as the President and they were both incoherent.

We left the next day. Tbilisi was still intact. The whole rebel attack had been a rumor. Gamsakhurdia was still in charge of something, and I assumed he was ready for a little hair of the dog.

After a short trip to Armenia, we flew back to Moscow. This was just after the attempted coup on the Russian government, when Gorbachev had been briefly held prisoner. Boris Yeltsin had climbed onto a tank at the barricades and had catapulted himself to a position of leadership. The city itself was burdened as usual with shortages of basic needs. There were long lines for available bread. Only the black market was thriving. The contrast with Beijing was striking. The Chinese capital was busy and bustling. There had been no shortage of anything there, except the joy of freedom. The Chinese populace was walking a tightrope at every moment. They had everything they needed, except the thing they wanted. In Moscow, the citizens had nothing they needed, but they had what they wanted. They had thrown off the yoke. There was in that city a palpable spirit of freedom. The excitement of animated argument and conversation was everywhere. And the air was filled with the spirit of potential, of what could be. That was then.

When I got home I realized that I had flown around the world. There was a lot of mail waiting for me. I had hundreds of letters, mostly from Chinese expatriates, thanking Nancy, John, and me for standing up in Tiananmen Square. That token of remembrance meant a lot to a lot of people. But I also got a letter from an American businessman in China who said that he was embarrassed and appalled by our action. He told me that China's affairs were nobody's business but China's. He had found very cheap labor in China and very big profits. By his reasoning, I guess Germany's business in 1938 was nobody's business but Germany's, as long as there was a buck to be made.

Nowadays the Chinese government is a giant corporation, and all of its people "work for the man." And they've got the Olympics. I'll be watching, to see if I can spot the man in the tan cap.

Laws and Sausage

Every ten years, after the census, the seats of Congress are reapportioned among the states. States which have proportionately added population add Congressional seats and those who have lost population lose seats. So the growth states like Texas, Florida, and California have seen big increases in their Congressional delegations in recent decades. And after the 1990 census, Georgia was poised to add a district.

I figured that I would come out of redistricting in good shape. The process is controlled by the State Legislatures, and Georgia's Legislature was completely controlled by Democrats. In 1992, both the state's House and Senate had overwhelming Democratic majorities, with a powerful Democratic Speaker of the House and a Democratic Lieutenant Governor in control of the State Senate. And Democrat Zell Miller was the state's Governor. At that point, Georgia had two Democratic Senators, and nine Democratic Congressmen. There was one Republican Congressman, the redoubtable Newt Gingrich.

Everybody and his brother-in-law started bringing in redistricting maps which would protect themselves. I presented a map which I thought was fair to both parties, and which would create Districts which were competitive. And since the Voting Rights Act required that the map be approved by the courts, I made certain it would pass that muster by assuring that no minority would be adversely affected by the redrawing.

But the State Legislature could have cared less about my map or my feelings. I had never served in that body, and although I had a few friends there, I wasn't "one of the boys." It seemed that the Lieutenant Governor's priority was to create a district for an old fraternity brother, and I sensed that Governor Miller hadn't forgotten that I once campaigned against him when I went with Herman Talmadge to Miller's home county. He had always looked at me sort of slaunch-eyed. (But then, he kinda looks at everybody that way.) So things didn't turn out so well in that redistricting for me, or for the Democratic Party.

One person who was accommodated by the Legislature was Newt Gingrich. Newt had come within an eyelash of losing his seat in the previous election, but he was rewarded with his own district in a completely different part of Georgia, drawn by himself, one which guaranteed him a seat for a long, long time. I got the short straw. I had nowhere to run. Newt got the goldmine and I got the shaft.

Because George Bush's Republican Justice Department had to approve the maps, a kind of apartheid situation was created. The Justice Department insisted that districts be created which would guarantee the election of African Americans. By putting blacks into new districts, the Democratic strength in the old districts was greatly weakened.

I was not on anybody's "radar screen." Every suggestion I had made was snorted at. And that's when I made my first big political mistake. My home county was put into the district which was created for the Lieutenant Governor's pal. And since I had no chance in what was left of the Fourth District, I decided to run from where I lived. But it was dumb of me. I ran into the "Courthouse Crowd" in counties where the Governor and Lieutenant Governor had a lot of pull and I had zero. In the primary I just missed a runoff and that was that. I was whupped.

A very troubling thing happened during that primary. My Democratic opponent's allies got very busy spreading the rumor that I had started drinking. They carried it to the Atlanta papers, where apparently it got some credibility. They spread it around pretty good, from and to some serious offices. At that point I had been sober for fifteen years and was a well-known speaker at recovery meetings and a high-profile advocate for issues like warning labels on alcoholic beverages. What hurt was that it was coming from my party, from people I knew, and who I thought were my friends. One of them, a State Public Service Commissioner, was spouting off about it in an Atlanta dentist's office to a dental tech who was one of my supporters. She let me know about it and I called the guy on it. He stuttered and stammered and he lied that the incident had not happened. The kind of guy who will do that sort of thing is the kind of guy who will lie about it. The only consolation I had was that I knew that he knew that I knew he was lying.

There is an old saying: "The two things you don't want to see being made are laws and sausage."

If you know someone out there who is looking for a thesis subject in political science, tell them to check out the Georgia Redistricting of 1992. It will show them how "the best-laid plans of mice and men sometime go awry." In 1992, Georgia had nine Democratic Congressmen and one Republican, and the state was adding a seat. There were two Democratic Senators. Within four years there were eight white Republicans, and three black Democrats and one Republican Senator. One of those Republican House members was Newt

Gingrich. He had almost lost his seat in 1990. Thanks to the legislature he was now planning the "Gingrich Revolution."

And thanks to the Democratic legislature and my own stubbornness, I was now former Congressman Jones.

Alma and I got married in the Capitol on October 10, 1992. It was a very happy ending to a gnarly year or two.

Cooter Tries to Neuter the Newtster

On November 6, 1992, we were in Little Rock as Bill Clinton became the forty-second President of the United States. I had known Clinton for a few years and I was impressed with his "smarts" and his extraordinary focus. When George H.W. Bush had a 90 percent approval rating at the end of Operation Desert Storm, I was one of the few folks who thought he could be beaten. And I felt that Clinton was the best chance the Democrats had of getting the job done. I had been a national surrogate speaker for him very early on, and I started working the Democratic caucus in the House on his behalf. In July, I had left my campaign in Georgia to attend the nominating convention in New York City as a Clinton delegate.

In the heady excitement of that victory, I felt that I could find a place in the new Clinton Administration. There were possibilities. I had a lot of support from the recovery community for the so-called "drug czar's" job, overseeing the country's efforts to combat addiction. But I had no support outside of recovering people. I had been outspoken about the scourge of alcoholism, the worst addictive drug problem we have in America. But because it is a popular and a legal drug, it is hard to bring it into the national agenda. The liquor lobby spends hundreds of millions of dollars making sure that the problem is always swept under the rug. Anyway, the drug czar thing didn't happen. Nor did my interest in the National Endowment for the Arts get any traction. When a new administration comes in, there is some vicious elbowing going on for access, influence, and jobs. And though I had been totally supportive, I wasn't a part of the "in crowd" with the Clinton bunch, either. I had to face the fact that maybe some people around the President found me to be a bit gauche. Must've been that "Cooter" thing they couldn't relate to. I also let it be known that I would be more than happy to be the Ambassador to Barbados. That job went to a friend of mine who was adamantly opposed to Clinton back when I was the only House member outside of Arkansas to be for him. In the scrum for appointments, I had gone from fair-haired boy to persona non grata. Yeah, I know life isn't fair, but I needed a job, y'all.

Nineteen ninety-three was a year in the desert for me. Alma was a vice president of the National Theatre overseeing the interests of the powerful Schubert Organization there. So at least one of us had a job. But I couldn't seem to hit the ground with my hat. I started a little nonprofit advocacy organization for recovering people, but couldn't seem to get it off the ground. Suddenly I couldn't pay my bills and the creditors were getting less forgiving by the week. On top of that, my knees were constantly throbbing. I went to a "jock doc" in Atlanta, the orthopedist for the Atlanta Falcons and Hawks. His taciturn manner reminded me of Jack Webb on *Dragnet.* He brought in my X-rays. "No wonder your knee hurts," he said. "You don't have one."

There was a hole where there used to be a knee joint. The condition is called "Avascular Necrosis." Bo Jackson lost his hip that way. A bone takes a whack somewhere along the way and it doesn't get blood properly. So it decays. It dies. Apparently my knee had been falling apart for years. "You are a little young for it," he said. "But I recommend a total knee replacement."

So I got my right knee replaced. And sure enough, a few months later it didn't hurt. I was able to get around well enough to hike hills and even to limp about shooting hoops every once in awhile. But I still didn't have a regular job. I gave a few speeches for which I was paid, and that helped. But mostly I just worked on a novel about Stonewall Jackson's amputated arm, the one he lost at Chancellorsville before he died. I know, I know, it doesn't sound like a marketable idea, and it wasn't. I think I got the inspiration while under the influence of the industrial strength morphine they used after the knee operation. Hmmm, maybe that is where I got the inspiration to run against Newt Gingrich, too.

In 1994 the Democratic Party was in trouble. Clinton's first two years had been a bust, and it seemed that the Democrats controlling the House had been on the job too long—for forty years, to be exact. And Gingrich, the GOP whip, was seemingly everywhere. It was said that the most dangerous place to be standing in Washington was between Gingrich and a television camera. Through his GOPAC network, he had recruited a large number of like-minded, well-funded candidates to run in 1994, and he provided them with the rhetoric to go for the jugular. And it looked like it was working. The GOP was predicted to pick up a number of seats in 1994. When, how, and why I got the idea to take him on, I really can't say. But I convinced myself that *(a)* somebody had to take him on, and *(b)* that I probably had the best chance of anybody of making a race out of it.

Like I said before, most of us can convince ourselves of just about anything. I had represented part of Newt's district before the redistricting, and after two terms I was pretty well known around that neck of the woods. I figured I'd just get in there and start slugging away, and maybe I could land a lucky punch. And since I really thought the overwhelming influence of special interests was not in the public interest, I announced that I would forgo PAC money and limit donations to $250. That was wonderfully idealistic, and people from all over America sent in small donations, but there was a built-in problem with that. Running without PAC money is a great idea if you're Ross Perot and have a few million lying about that you can throw into a campaign, but if you're running on a shoestring, it is very difficult to bring attention to what a fine thing you are doing. I was just smart enough to be that dumb.

I had figured on "free media" to get the word out. That is, the race itself would have a high enough profile that the press would be all over it. There was a lot of that, but it was not a good idea to get into a publicity contest with Newt Gingrich. He always had more cameras following him around than Madonna.

But of all the things I have done in my life, I don't think I've ever enjoyed anything more than that race in 1994 against the Newtster. When I first announced one reporter asked me, "Aren't you just tilting against windmills, Mr. Jones?"

"Nope," I replied. "I'm tilting against windbags."

Not at all concerned about my candidacy, Gingrich refused to engage in any give-and-take. Although he had always wanted to debate before, now he was silent, leaving it to his subordinates to fling the occasional insult my way. But I was rallying a lot of volunteers for whom the mere mention of the word *Gingrich* brought out a determination to rid our government of his pompous gasbaggery. He seemed to be a symbol of the low road in politics. Though he presented himself as a visionary man of ideas, the part of his political technique that dominated was a constant stream of invective, hyperbole, and personal attacks. He was quick to judge the character of his opponents with a stream of negative adjectives. Anybody can do that with a little practice, if that is really what you want to do.

I did a bit of that myself. "Newt Gingrich is the man Will Rogers never met." "Gingrich talks so much he must think he's getting paid by the word." I pointed out that Newt, who fancied himself to be an entrepreneurial business genius, had been supported by the government all his life. As an Army brat he benefited from subsidized housing, subsidized schooling, even subsidized toothpaste. He had attended public schools and public universities and had worked for a public college. And then he had gone on the taxpayer's dime as a Congressman. Far as I could tell, he had never hit a lick at a snake as far as manual labor was concerned.

And so on. It didn't matter. He was traveling the country promoting his "revolution," and his strategy was to act like I wasn't there.

All that changed one Saturday in May when Steve and Cathy Bruning met me at a McDonald's for a late breakfast of coffee and supersized fries. Steve and Cathy were Democratic activists from Cobb County. They had brought me several hundred pages of photocopied documents they had procured under the Georgia Open Records Act.

Gingrich had arranged with Kennesaw State College to teach a televised course titled "Renewing American Civilization." Since Kennesaw was a public, state-supported school, that enabled the Brunings to obtain copies of the paper trail regarding the class. It was a shifty business that was intended to further Newt's political agenda and included a scheme to use political money raised by GOPAC from Newt's wealthier supporters. That money could then be used in a tax-exempt way by contributing it to the College. And the clear and convincing evidence was right in front of me. What they had done was obviously unethical and possibly illegal. They had commingled political and charitable funds and purposes. GOPAC, under Gingrich's direction, had become a secret operating fund with various tentacles to serve his goal of taking over Congress. One infamous GOPAC memo instructed candidates to refer to their Democratic opponents as "bizarre," "antifamily," "traitors," "corrupt," and "evil." For years GOPAC, which took in millions of dollars annually, had not disclosed the source or the amount of the contributions it received.

When Gingrich had first proposed his "course" there had been a bit of a flap in the Atlanta press because many faculty members objected to the idea of a serving politician in the classroom. Of course, Newt denied any political connection whatsoever.

On September 7, 1994, I challenged that contention by filing a formal complaint with the House Ethics Committee. Though few in the national media took notice, my presentation was serious and substantive.

Up until then, Gingrich had acted as if my candidacy was at best an amusing annoyance. But now he went ballistic. In the press he started calling me "pathetic," dishonorable," and "dishonest," among other things. I figured then that he knew I had him dead to rights. At that point, he had an enormous spending advantage and a comfortable lead in the polls. Why would he be overreacting like that if he had done nothing wrong?

I had always had a grudging respect for his tenacious style of attack politics. But I'd also come to believe that he was a pontificating poltroon, a bully and a blowhard who could dish it out but couldn't take it.

And he wouldn't debate me. So to have some fun, and to get some badly needed attention to the race, I took to trailing him around the country. In Alabama, where he was speaking, I tracked him with two gigantic bloodhounds. There was a great AP picture of me and those hounds that ran in a lot of papers around the country. We were a handsome threesome. Then in Wisconsin, I waited for him on the sidewalk outside of a restaurant. But he got the word and snuck in through the back. I followed him up to Connecticut and that time I caught him. With cameras flashing I yelled to him as his limo went by, "Hey, Newt, when you gonna debate?" He looked at me like I was rotten fish. So, I figured if nothing else I was "messin' with his head." They don't teach that in Government 101.

Georgia Public Television had set up a debate that it looked like he couldn't wiggle out of. But then, as I was walking to my car one day, an *Atlanta Constitution* reporter told me that Newt had said I was "scurrilous." Jokingly I said, "Oh, f**k him and the horse he rode in on." I knew the reporter wouldn't print it, and he knew I sure wouldn't want it printed. But it was overheard by a writer for Atlanta's alternative paper, *Creative Loafing*. He printed it verbatim.

Gingrich withdrew from our only debate, saying that he would not dignify someone who could use such language as worthy of sharing a podium with him. He demanded an apology. On television I told him that I was immediately apologizing to his horse and that I would apologize to him at the debate. But he bailed out anyway. He had more important things to do, like raising money out of state.

I have never enjoyed anything more than that Quixotic campaign against Gingrich. We had two chances to win: slim and none. But if I had not run, I wouldn't have had any chance to win. And I wouldn't have slept well.

In the end, Gingrich beat me like a rented mule. He spent more money in the last two days than I spent during the entire campaign, but I'm not sure he needed to. Nineteen ninety-four was simply Newt's year, the year all of his hard work and conniving paid off. The Republicans swept to victory nationwide, and he realized his boyhood dream of becoming Speaker of the House.

Soon the "Gingrich Revolution" was the talk of the town. "Newtie," as his mother called him, was the media's darling, *Time* magazine's "Man of the Year," and the undisputed king of Capitol Hill. His newfound admirers in the mainstream press called him a "brilliant visionary" and predicted with confidence the impending demise of Bill Clinton and the defunct Democratic Party.

Meanwhile, I was trying to keep the ethics story alive, banging on the side of my old fax machine just to get it to halfway work. I was being ridiculed by Newt as a classic example of a disgruntled "countercultural defender of the liberalsocialwelfarestate." I was among those whom he regarded as an "enemy of normal Americans." Gingrich and his shadow Tony Blankley would waddle out to the waiting cameras to denounce any attack on the Speaker's ethics as an "unconscionable" and unsupportable partisan character assassination. The

Ethics Committee, with all the deliberate speed of molasses flowing uphill, was sporadically dealing with my complaint.

When Gingrich's ascension to the speakership brought him into the spotlight, the glare revealed some warts the size of a Rupert Murdoch book deal. The press was starting to ask questions, and House Democrats, led by David Bonior of Michigan, were beginning to raise ethical hell. When I amended my complaint on January 26, 1995, some members of the Washington press corps actually read the thing. Editorials started to appear here and there calling for the appointment of a special investigative counsel and for Gingrich to disclose his secretive GOPAC operations.

The real change in public and media attention in the ethics case came when the committee finally voted in December of 1995 to hire a special counsel, James Cole, to investigate the questions surrounding GOPAC and Kennesaw State College. Asked his reaction, Newt looked at the cameras and said the charges were "mindless, baseless, and frivolous." Then he said they were "phony." Then he said they were "phony" eight more times. Really. I saw it on the news. It's on videotape.

But he knew they were not phony. And the committee should have known because I had written to Chairperson Nancy Johnson (R., Conn.) long before, responding to Gingrich's attorney, Jan Baran. I pointed out the inconsistencies and inaccuracies of Gingrich's defense. Johnson never responded to my letter, nor did she respond to my request to testify before the committee. In December of 1996 Special Counsel Cole came to the same conclusions I had come to thirty months before over ketchup and French fries in that McDonald's down in Georgia. His conclusion was that Newt had done what I said he had done.

So now it was for the House to decide Gingrich's fate. But a new House had to be sworn in, and Gingrich demanded that no business could be decided until he was sworn in as Speaker. Republican whip

Tom DeLay was assigned to assure the Republican caucus that the Ethics Committee's decision was a "slap on the wrist" and there was nothing in it that would prevent them from reelecting Gingrich as Speaker. The caucus, believing DeLay, voted Gingrich in. Only then were the Ethics Committee's sanctions revealed.

Gingrich's punishment was the first reprimand of a Speaker of the House in more than two hundred years and a three-hundred-thousand-dollar fine, the highest ever assessed against a member of Congress.

The disingenuous shell game that reelected Newt as Speaker was not forgotten by his caucus. They had been knowingly bamboozled one time too many. Two years later they dumped Gingrich as Speaker, and he resigned from the body.

In the Presidential election of 1996, Bill Clinton won handily over Republican Senator Bob Dole. Gingrich's obstinate and arrogant behavior was generally thought to be a contributing factor. A few years later, in the green room of the show *Hardball,* I chatted with Senator Dole as we waited to go on. "You know, I believe if you had whipped Gingrich in 1994, I woulda been elected President," he joked. At least, I think he was joking.

Newt always fancied himself a "historian." Perhaps he should have learned this lesson from a wonderful old history book: "He that troubleth his own house shall inherit the wind."

And in this case, the windbag.

Here Be Dragons

I'm now at the age where we talk about our operations. You tell me about your operations and I'll tell you about mine. We can sit around on benches and complain about our back problems and our neck problems and our knee problems. And maybe some kind soul will come along and wipe the drool off of our chins.

Shortly after Gingrich beat the tar out of me in that 1994 election, I started having troubles with my new prosthetic knee. One day after working out it started swelling up and hurting like hell. So I put some ice on it and took some Advil. The next day the swelling had increased, it hurt worse, and I had a little fever. So I put some ice on it and took some Advil. The third day my knee was the size of a volleyball, the pain was excruciating, and I had a serious fever. After more ice and Advil, my stepson Wesley pleaded with me to go to the Emergency Room at Georgetown Hospital. So I went grudgingly, remembering that 50 percent of doctors graduated at the bottom of their class.

My body temperature was 104 degrees. The doctor stuck a big needle into the swollen knee. "I really don't care what else you do to me, ever," I told him. "As long as you never do that again." He gave me some serious painkiller as they ran tests.

"The knee has to come out immediately," he told me a few hours later. "You have a virulent and potentially fatal staph infection." The staph had been hiding in my body since the knee replacement a year and a half before and had gotten loose with a vengeance. The knee came out the next day, and I spent the next few kneeless months taking copious amounts of antibiotics to kill off the staph before another total knee replacement was performed. And then the long, tedious rehabilitation process began again.

Three months later, I knew that something was wrong. The second knee replacement just wasn't responding well and there was still a lot of pain. The orthopedist decided to go in and take a look, to "clean it up," he said. But when I came around in the recovery room, Alma told me that the doctor had not only found that there was still staph in there, but that I had developed a very weird fungal disease as a result of all the antibiotics I had been taking. They had killed off the good stuff, too. So now I was back without a knee, having gone through two total replacements that didn't work. And I now had two potentially deadly infections. At one point after that operation, I had to be packed in ice because of a temperature of 106 degrees.

I had just gotten back to the apartment from the hospital when the phone rang very early one morning. Alma was in New York on business and I was afraid something might be wrong. It was a tow truck driver telling me that he was repossessing my Explorer and that I had better get everything out of it. This was the first I had heard about a repo, and since I could hardly move an inch, there wasn't anything I could do but watch him through my sickroom window as he hauled all my stuff off in the first light of morning. Three weeks later I got a letter from the creditor, which had been sent to an address I hadn't used in years. I prayed that morning that all this would even out someday.

Many more months went by as we dealt with the infections. But the fungal infection was resistant to the conventional treatments. Heavy doses of amphotericin completely debilitated me, and I developed anemia to the point of going back into the hospital for a couple of days of blood transfusions. A doctor at Johns Hopkins contacted Dr. Anthony Fauci at the National Institutes of Health. Fauci identified my fungal infection as extremely rare, but he knew how to treat it. He had heard only of two other cases in the world, he said. So finally we got the infections under control, but the consensus was that my leg would have to be amputated at the knee. Fortunately, Dr. Mark Connell, who had taken out the first knee and who had put in and taken out the second knee, insisted that he could jerryrig a third knee that would hold up. And he did it. It took two more operations, but he did it. That was in 1996, and it's still holding up. The only problem is that all that whittling on my right leg left it about two inches shorter than the left leg. And all of these surgeries have left me with absolutely no chance of making the U.S. Olympic Basketball Team. But hope springs eternal.

Now tell me about your operations.

Going Back to Hazzard County

I was still doing rehab after my last knee replacement when I got a call from Warner Bros. TV that a *Dukes of Hazzard* reunion movie was scheduled to be shot in September of 1996. It had been eleven and half years since we had said good-bye to Hazzard in primetime. But it was still a beloved show, and we couldn't wait to get back together. A lot had gone down over the years.

In February of 1994 my buddy Sorrell Booke had died of cancer. After the cast gathered in Los Angeles for his funeral, we went to dinner and talked about getting together for a reunion film. Finally it was happening.

Cathy Bach had done a series in Africa with Robert Mitchum, and then had started a family with a baby girl. Tom Wopat was constantly in demand for Broadway musicals, but also had a singing career in Nashville, and had done extensive television work. John Schneider had scored a number of hit country songs, had done television and film roles, started a production company, had remarried, and lived and worked out of San Antonio for a few years. Once when I was in Congress, I went up to New York City for some meetings.

Tom and John were both there singing leads in Broadway musicals. Not bad for "Luke" and "Bo" and "Cooter."

Jimmy Best had continued to write, paint, act, and fish. He and Dorothy were living in Florida and staying very busy with various projects. Sonny Shroyer had done a lot of film roles, including the role of Bear Bryant in *Forrest Gump.*

The joy of our reunion was dampened by the illness of Denver Pyle. He was suffering from lung cancer and was taking radiation treatments during the filming. It was to be his last film of the many hundreds that he worked on.

There really wasn't much to the reunion movie. It wasn't bad, but it wasn't particularly good, either. It tried too hard to be cute, and it lost the innocent spirit of the original. It managed to be silly without being endearing. It also lacked the authenticity of Waylon Jennings, who didn't go for their offer. But the show did well enough in the ratings that another one was put on the drawing board.

One nice touch for me was that "Cooter" returned to Hazzard County as the Congressman for that district. In that case, it was art imitating life. They even did a "flashback" to when "Cooter" had gotten elected. So I finally did win another election.

I stayed with a buddy of mine named Bill Dial who had a large bungalow in Studio City. Bill had been one of a group of Atlantans who had come out to work with Hugh Wilson, the Atlanta advertising guy who created *WKRP in Cincinnati.* Now a veteran writer and producer, Bill was busy as the Executive Producer of *Sliders* on the Sci-Fi Channel. So, after ten years of politickin' and knee surgeries, I figured it was time for me to go back to doing what I loved to do. I got an agent and went back to being an unemployed actor.

It was just like the old days. I was immediately "between engagements." Alma had opened a Manhattan office in the Sardi's Building and was handling press and public relations for several Schubert shows, including *Cats* and Steve Martin's *Picasso at the*

Lapin Agile. At one point I went to New York for the opening night of the award-winning Broadway production of *An Inspector Calls.* Alma needed someone to escort Sarah Ferguson, the Duchess of York. So there I was, all tuxedoed up, bringing "Fergie" through the paparazzi. And I was thinking to myself, "Buster Jones, this is a long way from Sugar Hill."

Alma and I hated being apart from each other for even an hour, but I figured that if I got reestablished as a character actor, things would somehow work out.

It started off that way. The first audition I went to was for the brilliant Mike Nichols, one of the geniuses of American stage and film. The project was the movie version of *Primary Colors,* a novel which was an only slightly fictionalized version of Bill Clinton and the events of the 1992 Democratic primary. The book had been written "By Anonymous," but because it was a huge bestseller, it wasn't long before "Anonymous" had been identified, by "scientific methods," as none other than Joe Klein, a well-known Washington journalist.

I knew Joe pretty well, and I liked him. He caught a lot of flak because he had originally denied being the author, and a lot of people sniffed about his credibility. But he is still as good as anybody writing about politics, and he probably did well enough on *Primary Colors* to start his own newspaper.

But there was a greater coincidence. I had been a part of the Clinton campaign in 1992 and was quite familiar with the people and the situations that *Primary Colors* was based on. In the film, Clinton was named Jack Stanton and was played by John Travolta. The Hillary Clinton character was played by the marvelous English actress Emma Thompson. Billy Bob Thornton played the campaign manager based on James Carville. And I was cast as the media consultant, Arlen Sporkin. That character was based on Frank Greer, whom I also knew. So I knew all of the people these characters were based on, I knew the novelist, and I was in on the campaign when it happened. So art and life were getting a bit difficult to separate.

During the filming of *Primary Colors* I was asked to do a cameo part in *Meet Joe Black,* which was filming in New York City and was directed by Martin Brest. I had a wonderful scene opposite one of my heroes, Anthony Hopkins. Later I got a note from the director saying his "rough cut" was over three hours long, and though he hated to do it, my scene had to hit the cutting-room floor. But, oh yeah, I still get paid for it. So I was two for two, and it looked like my little plan was gonna work out just right.

And then the well went as dry as a bone. It is one thing to be hobnobbing on sets with great actors, with famous muckety-mucks all about. That is my idea of the ideal life, practicing my craft and getting well rewarded for it. But when the phone stops ringing for a week or so, I get a little crazy. And when nothing happens for a month, I get more than a little crazy. The same view from a window can take on different meanings. Rather than seeing the sun-washed, palmy paradise around me, I started seeing the Day of the Locusts, an entire city that was based upon greed and lust, and which had long since lost any claim of civility or culture. I was now living in a tiny studio apartment for which I was paying an outrageous rent. My agent wouldn't return my calls. My fierce ambition was to establish myself as a busy character actor, well known and respected "in the industry." But that sure wasn't happening on my schedule. Or my agent's.

And I hated every second that I wasn't near Miss Alma.

I guest-starred in an episode of a series called *Michael Hayes* with David Caruso, who is famous for being redheaded. It was not a good experience. Caruso, who has a reputation for being difficult, more than lived up to that reputation. He spent a lot of his time pouting and demanding this and that. Life is short, Caruso, and it is too short to be spent with screaming egomaniacs.

Then Bill Dial wrote a nice detective part for me in *Sliders.* That was a good group to work with. But that was it for many months. The phone just stopped ringing. And I was back to hating Hollywood.

It really became a crisis in my life. I wanted that success so badly that I had lost my way. I was past impatient. I was past frustrated. I was in a deep box of sun-soaked misery. And all I knew to do was what the sober old drunks had told me to do. "You win when you surrender," they said.

Now here is what I did and what happened. I got down on my knees and I asked my Higher Power to take complete charge of the situation. I surrended my pride, my ego, and my temporal ambition. I asked to be relieved of that ambition and to be given direction as to where I should go and how I could do the most good when I got there. And I swear I could almost immediately feel the weight of my own foolish expectations come off of me. And within a day a plan came clear. I decided to head back to D.C., rent an old farmhouse out in the Blue Ridge, get an agent in New York, and start all over again. I piled all my clothes and books in my ragtop Chevy and I headed east across the desert as I had so many times before. After spending the first night in Lordsburg, New Mexico, I didn't stop until I got to our apartment in D.C.

Part Five

PARADISE FOUND

South Toward Home

It was late May when I drove out Highway 211 from Warrenton, Virginia, toward the Blue Ridge. Those hills had been a part of my life since I was a kid back in Portsmouth, always beckoning to the romantic in me. And they called me now, a magnetic enchantment that pulled me into those green hollows. The nearer I got, the stronger the pull. I ended up in a village called Sperryville, where I saw a small house for rent on a shady street. I had a déjà vu of a moment in Petersburg, Virginia, when I was five. I felt like I had come home to a place I had never been before. I immediately rented the house.

Alma felt the same enchantment. The town was in Rappahannock County, an hour and a half from Washington, D.C., and less than an hour from Dulles Airport. Alma was now the International Director of Operation Sail, that wonderful gathering of "tall ships" which was created by John F. Kennedy as a way of fostering international friendships through sailing. She was in the process of planning the largest gathering of tall ships ever, to celebrate the millennium, on July 4, 2000, in New York City's great harbor.

I hadn't been in Sperryville for two weeks when I dropped into an antiques store out on the highway. Browsing about, I saw a *Dukes of Hazzard* lunchbox and asked the proprietor if she had any other *Dukes* memorabilia.

She said she had a *Dukes* TV tray somewhere about, and then she said, "You know, you look an awful lot like 'Cooter' on that show."

"Well, I am," I said.

"You are not."

"Am, too."

"Are not."

It took a lot of convincing, but I won out and we started chatting up a storm. "Are y'all planning to buy a place out here?" she asked.

"Maybe someday. That would be a dream come true for us. But right now I'm just renting a little house."

"The reason I asked," she said, "is that there's a real nice place that just came open yesterday back in our hollow. You really ought to take a look at it."

She gave me the directions and I drove by. Set back behind a plank bridge across a stream was the most beautiful log cabin I had ever seen. It had perfect feng shui. (I have never figured out how to pronounce *feng shui,* but I know exactly what it means.) Surrounded by oaks and apple trees and dogwoods, it called to me just as the Blue Ridge around me had. I had plans to go down to Atlanta the next day to get a truckload of "stuff" out of storage, but Alma could take a look while I was gone. This was on a Wednesday.

"I can't get out there until Saturday," she said. When I got back to Virginia on Sunday evening, she had a little bitty smile like the cat that ate the canary. "Did you take a look at that place?" I asked.

"Yep," she said. "And forty-five minutes later I was signing a contract on it over in Front Royal."

The cabin had not only taken her breath away, but had overpowered her with a feeling of destiny revealed. We weren't exactly sure if we could pull the deal off, but Alma sold the D.C. apartment in no time flat, and suddenly we owned a piece of paradise, Southern style. The oldest part of the cabin dated from 1741 and was attached to the "newer" section, built around 1770. The hand-hewn logs that surrounded us were hacked out in the colonial frontier, years before a fellow from down the road, Tom Jefferson, wrote America's Declaration of Independence.

So we now lived near the town of Washington, Virginia. The village of Washington is called that because it was laid out by a seventeen-year-old surveyor in 1749, a kid by the name of George Washington.

I finally found an acting agent in New York who would occasionally return my calls. I was cast in a wonderful Stanley Tucci film called *Joe Gould's Secret,* which also featured cameos by Susan Sarandon and Steve Martin. There are no whizbang effects or explosions in *Joe Gould's Secret.* Basically it is a film about writer's block. After thinking about that movie, it took me three days just to write that last sentence.

My buddy Al Franken was doing a sitcom called *Lateline* and asked me to play a part titled "Big Redneck." I don't know why he would have thought of me for a part like that. It was quite a stretch. One thing I found out while we were filming was that Al's real name is not Franken, but Frankenstein. He had shortened it to fit on marquees. Not only that, but one of his ancestors was a famous doctor in the old country. (Hopefully, he will sue me for that remark, and we'll both get some publicity.)

I also appeared on a couple of soap operas. Other than the fact that the studio was air-conditioned, it didn't seem a whole lot different from working back at Corbett's Basket Factory back in North Carolina. Actually, the people at Corbett's had a whole lot more fun, and did not take themselves so seriously.

I also revived my novel about the supernatural spirit in Stonewall Jackson's amputated arm. It is set in the present. An editor at a big publishing house who read it said that Civil Wars books "are a hard sell." My book owed a lot more to Kurt Vonnegut than to Shelby Foote. Besides, Civil War books aren't a hard sell at all if you're selling them to me. I've got an entire room of books about The Late Unpleasantness. And when friends come down from "up North" they have to sleep there. We call it "The Yankee Room." Only one person complained. He said, "It is hard to wake up during the night and have Nathan Bedford Forrest staring at you with those murderous eyes."

Hazzard Nation

At some point in the 1990s, a now-defunct cable outlet, The Nashville Network, starting showing reruns of *The Dukes of Hazzard.* Suddenly something happened that hadn't happened since the days when we ruled prime time on Friday nights. I started being recognized by little kids whenever I went to the supermarket. That was a good feeling for several reasons. First of all, I am one of those actors who really appreciates being recognized. It means that people enjoy what you have done. Secondly, the fact that young children were faithfully watching our show over ten years after we stopped filming meant that we had done something lasting, something timeless.

So I got to thinking that it would be fun to open a little roadside stand called "Cooter's Place" and sell apple butter and cider and pork barbecue. And we would have really good bluegrass music and fine country pickin'. I'd hang out and sell "Cooter's Place" T-shirts and be around to autograph stuff. And the more I fantasized about it, the more it appealed to me. And then I happened by the perfect location, an old fruit and souvenir stand surrounded by the Blue Ridge and only a half-mile from the Shenandoah National Park on the main highway. Plenty of parking, and the cool Thornton River running right off the mountain through the property. And on the door was a big sign that said "FOR RENT."

I had just enough dough set by to give it a shot. I needed something to sell, for sure. But good honey and apple butter aren't hard to come by in the Virginia mountains. For that matter, neither are T-shirts and ball caps. I found the wholesalers who still stocked General Lee models and *Dukes of Hazzard* posters and licensed merchandise. I poked around in the barn for two days and came up with enough memorabilia to start a *Dukes* museum. My brother Bryan came up from Kitty Hawk and built some sturdy showcases for my odd collection of costumes, props, scripts, cast photos, and old collectible merchandise.

Then Wayne Wooten, founder of the Dodge Charger Registry, pointed me to an affordable General Lee replica down in South Carolina. I figured that putting the "General" out in front of the place would create a large orange magnet for anybody who was cruising along Highway 211.

When I first told Alma of my idea she said, "That's the craziest thing I ever heard. But you go right ahead!" She was a bit bemused at what had "come over me," but she was totally supportive, as always.

Within a few short weeks, "Cooter's Place" was ready to open. We needed a "cold opening," sort of a shakedown cruise to get the hang of it. A lot of folks dropped by and got a kick out of the store. Then Alma got to work publicizing a "Grand Opening Weekend" over July the Fourth. All of the local papers in the nearby towns talked it up.

Rappahannock County has a population of six thousand, and according to our county newspaper, about two thousand people descended on "Cooter's Place" that weekend. We ran out of T-shirts and apple butter, and we even ran out of our Blue Plate Special, a MoonPie and a Royal Crown Cola for only a dollar.

It wasn't long before I had hooked up with Robby Meadows, a bass player who ran a recording studio over the mountains in the

Shenandoah Valley. Robby and his wife, Lisa, whose singing is reminiscent of Patsy Cline and Tammy Wynette, formed the backbone of our house band. Since "Cooter" had the most famous garage in the world, and since everybody knows what a "garage band" is, I named the group "Cooter's Garage Band." We'd play honky-tonk and country rock music on Saturdays, and on Sunday we'd mellow out with some real fine bluegrass. People kept flocking in. Folks would grab a cold drink and a barbecue sandwich and then sit out by the river in the shade of some cherry trees and just kick back with the music.

Our formula was real simple. Whenever a customer showed up, we'd say, "Thanks for droppin' by, and make yourself at home." As the word got around people started making trips down to Rappahannock County to check out "Cooter's Place." Alma would be a high-powered executive type during the week, and then come out and run the store on the weekends. Everybody starting calling her "Miz Alma."

Before we closed for the winter at Christmastime, we knew for certain that we had seen visitors from every state in the U.S.A., and from over twenty foreign countries. Just after we opened, a family came in heading back to D.C. from the Blue Ridge. They had two young African ladies with them as guests. Alma started to explain *The Dukes of Hazzard* to the girls. One of them retorted quickly, "Oh, yes. Yes. We have *The Dukes of Hazzard* in Botswana, of course."

So "Cooter's" was off to a good start, and it created new opportunities for me. I cut a CD with the Garage Band, with several of my own compositions on it. I figured that if I could pull off the singing bit, then maybe there was a songwriter in there somewhere, too. The band was playing several nights a week at clubs, resorts, and various Moose Lodges up and down the Valley. I was learning a new craft and loving every second of it.

Pretty soon the word really got around about "Cooter's Place." The Associated Press did a story that ran all over the country, as did the *Washington Post.* A lot of people would come out from the city just to get some fresh air and get a sense of what the world is like beyond the Beltway. A few of my former House colleagues dropped by, and I sensed from them just a tiny glint of envy as they headed back for the hallowed halls of Congress. Sometimes we win by losing.

It wasn't long before CNN and Fox News sent crews down to our little roadside stand. *Entertainment Weekly* did a piece, and we were even written up in *Condé Nast Traveler.* You know, Tahiti. Provence. Cooter's Place. Rio de Janeiro . . .

We live and learn, hopefully. Since autumn is glorious in the Blue Ridge Mountains, I had the idea of doing a Fall Festival, with lots of bluegrass bands, mountain crafts, and an antique car show. On top of that I rented a Ferris Wheel and a few other carnival rides. John Schneider came to headline the show. I had pictured a perfect fall day with blue skies above and brilliant leaves of brown and gold and red all about us. Well, that morning it snowed on the mountain, and a cold hard wind cut like a butcher knife down the river. A few hundred hardy souls, bundled up like Inuits, sat in plastic chairs and huddled against the elements. Nobody dared to get on the Ferris Wheel.

But diehard *Dukes* fans came from every direction, a dozen of them driving their own "General Lees," beautiful replicas of our 1969 Dodge Charger. Although we lost our shirts on the Fall Festival, we didn't lose hope that it was a good idea with some sort of future.

In our second year the buzz continued to grow and our weekend crowds grew even larger. We brought in other members of the cast and they couldn't believe the reception they got. When James Best rolled up to the store as Rosco P. Coltrane, he was greeted by the Rappahannock County High School Band and a red carpet laid across the rocky parking lot. When Catherine Bach visited, the line to meet her was well over four hours long. It stretched down the highway for a quarter of a mile. It was obvious to anybody who saw what was going on that folks loved "Cooter's Place" and that America had a deep and abiding affection for our crazy old television show. We had become a permanent part of Americana, just like Mickey Mouse or Babe Ruth.

The Little Girl Without Any Shoes

Mama died in February of 2000 at the age of eighty-one. She had outlived the last of her twelve brothers and sisters by thirty years. She outlived her husband of fifty-five years by a decade. She never forgot the days after she lost her parents and she had no shoes to wear to the new school she was to attend. She had a difficult life, but she faced it with a bottomless amount of humor and spirit. She was an inspiration to her family and to all who knew her. She countered the deep pain of her childhood and the difficulties of her marriage with a song or a poem for every occasion. She instilled and encouraged in my brothers and me every bit of talent and success we ever had. She had been dealt a tough hand, but she played it to win. And win she did. If one measures success by the good works she did, by the friends she made, and by the size of her great heart, she was the most successful person I ever knew. She never gave up on any of her boys. In fact, I don't think she ever gave up on anybody. With Mama, hope did indeed spring eternal. Hope and love and dreams of a better day.

It never mattered how hard things got for her. Down deep, no matter what, there was music in her soul. Whether she was peeling potatoes, shelling beans, making biscuits, hanging out the wash, or scrubbing an old fry pan, there was always a song in her heart. Her love of the muses sustained her through a thousand hardships, and she sustained us. I used to think that if fate had put her on a different path she would have been one of America's great actresses, a great singer, a famous playwright.

Then I realized that of course she was a great actress, she was a great singer, and she was a great writer. And we, her family and friends, were blessed to be in her exclusive audience. We were so lucky to be touched by her ever-flowing creative gifts, and blessed to share her gift of laughter and song and unconditional love. Move over, up there in the Angel Choir. Y'all make room for Ila V.

You don't need shoes to get into Heaven.

The Belly of the Whale

I think Alma and I are both possessed with a turbocharged energy pack. Neither one of us seems to have any middle gears. We're either in a low idle or we've got the hammer down and the pedal to the medal. I thought I was hyperactive until I met her. Her dynamism is something special to be around. I probably wouldn't hit a lick at a snake if it wasn't for Miz A. I'd just lay around under the porch with my basset hound, Junior, the only creature the Lord ever made who was lazier than me. But when Alma says, "Let's go," I put my helmet on, sharpen my cleats, and leap into the fray of the day.

It wasn't until a couple of years ago that I figured out that I had been playing "catch-up" ball for most of my life. When I was a kid, I had that feeling of being "less than" and not worthy of anything. That might have had something to do with the secretive abuse I went through, or it may have been simply that I felt different because I was different. At any rate, it wasn't until I dried out from twenty years of heavy addiction that I knew instinctively I had a lot of catching up to do. I was out of shape in every way, and I was years behind my potential. And so I went at it hard, studying and running and campaigning and writing and working my tail off.

So when "Cooter's" took off, me and Miz Alma took off with it. Suddenly Cooter's Garage Band was playing all over the Northeast, at festivals and fairs and concerts. I was also back to making personal appearances throughout the country, often taking the General Lee along for company. In 2002 we did a really smart thing and a really dumb thing. The smart thing was to open a second "Cooter's Place" in Gatlinburg, Tennessee, smack up against the Great Smoky Mountains National Park. Over 12 million visitors a year enjoy that park, and most of them drive right by "Cooter's" on their way. Another great location for all things Hazzard County. Working with April and Pearl Cornett, we renovated an old garage, which seemed just right for "Cooter." Yep, where there used to be a grease pit, there is now a big cutout of Daisy Duke.

That was a good move. But the next one wasn't. Whenever anyone asked me about whether or not I might make a comeback of some sort in politics, I had a stock answer. "When Jonah got out of the belly of the whale," I would say, "he didn't go back for his hat." I couldn't foresee any circumstances that would get me to throw my hat back in that ring. But I did anyway. The Seventh Congressional District of Virginia, where I now live, had been redistricted by 2002, and as is routine in the United States these days, it was created as a "safe seat" for the incumbent. And our little mountain county was put into it. We were now the tail end of a District which was centered in Richmond, two hours and a different world away from us. It was a newly carved District which had a freshman incumbent, a lawyer by the name of Eric Cantor. Eric's great claim to fame was that he was the only Jewish Republican in the House of Representatives. He had spent his first term parroting the talking points of the George Bush doctrine, and raking in enormous piles of special-interest money for his campaign treasury. It was of course just a coincidence that he voted 100 percent of the time with his deep-pocketed corporate contributors.

To me Eric Cantor was exhibit A about what is wrong with the American political system. It seemed to me that he was little more than a bagman and a bought vote, and that rather than representing his District in Washington, he was representing Washington to his District. So I was looking for someone to support in the race against him. But no race against him was planned. Here again a Congressional seat was being conceded without a fight. It reminded me of my first race against Pat Swindall, when I felt that without at least two names on the ballot, there might as well not be an election. Or a democracy.

A lot of people asked me to run. I began getting phone calls of support from across the District. I had a high profile and was known as somebody who loved a good fight. We knew that if I volunteered to run I would not be able to run a conventional campaign. We had a lot of commitments, concert dates, and appearances already scheduled, and two stores to run. We had just opened our Gatlinburg store and were on the road almost constantly. It was crazy to even consider it. But I convinced myself that not only was it the right thing to do, but it was something I had to do. Somebody had to "take one for the team." So I did it.

I look back now at what I said and what I wrote during that campaign and I seem like Nostradamus. Everything that I said was going to happen as a result of Cantor's support for Bush's policies happened. I was right. He was wrong. And it didn't make a dime's worth of difference. Again I didn't take any PAC money, so I was outspent almost twenty to one. Cantor and his cronies spared no expense in "sleazing" me with direct mail, lies, distortions, and mockery. On top of that, the *Richmond Times-Dispatch,* by far the largest and most influential news outlet in the District, served as an adjunct to his campaign from the get-go. They were not taking any chances with their investment.

I was even attacked for being associated with the General Lee. Suddenly I was being called a "racist" because the General has a Confederate Battle Flag painted on its roof. For a kid who grew up in Sugar Hill, shed a little blood fighting for equality, and was made an honorary Life Member of the NAACP, that accusation angered me as none other could have. These people would stoop to anything. And that is how they operate. Gutlessly. Political hacks believe that the ends justify the means.

The greatest reward I had from that "rebel flag" incident was that Andrew Young and John Lewis, two of our nation's greatest leaders of the Civil Rights Movement, both stood up for me and praised my commitment to the cause of equality. Those who were attacking me, including former Virginia Governor Douglas Wilder, refused to debate me.

Yes, I lost that race. I knew down deep that it didn't make any sense for me to get into it, that there are only twenty-four hours in a day and we were already working twenty of them. But I love the give-and-take in the arena of ideas, and perhaps down even deeper I still felt like I had some unfinished business on Capitol Hill. If compulsive politicking is one of my demons, then I'll just have to live with that one. But I am afraid that my third term in Congress will have to wait until my next life.

Isn't it frustrating that the folks who are not the lackeys of special interests simply can't afford to compete in races where millions of dollars are required? Only when we finance campaigns publicly will the public candidates have to answer to the public. Whoa now, there I go again, being Don Quixote. Enough with the sour grapes. . . .

A Really Big Show

Back in the 1950s and early '60s, Sunday night television belonged to Ed Sullivan, host of the last great variety show on the air. Sullivan, who was as stiff as the proverbial board, always opened the evening by promising that "Tonight, ladies and gentlemen, we have a really big show for you, a really big show!" And more often than not he delivered. An elephant act might be followed by an opera star, then a Borscht Belt comedian followed by twelve tumbling Chinamen, a ventriloquist, an impressionist, and then Steve and Eydie. And though Sullivan appeared to be devoid of any sort of talent, nobody else has ever succeeded like he did with that show.

Alma and I thought it was time for us to do a "really big show."

By 2001 the rekindling of interest in *The Dukes of Hazzard* was getting a lot of attention. New licensed products were being released almost monthly, we had done a second reunion movie, and the VHS sales of the show were hot. And we were doing the voices for our third video game. The General Lee had been named the most popular car in the history of television and film, leaving the Batmobile in the dust of Hazzard County.

So we put on our first DukesFest. Several members of the cast came, and about forty "General Lees" showed up. And several thousand people flocked down to the hills for the shindig. In 2002 it was even bigger, more cars and more people. By 2003, DukesFest and "Cooter's" had outgrown our little spot on the two-lane highway. We had at least ten thousand folks over the weekend and there was an enormous traffic jam. We were used to the traffic jams at "Cooter's," but our neighbors weren't happy about it. And some folks didn't like the music coming through the hills and hollers. We had maxed out. It was like what Yogi Berra said about a very popular restaurant: "Nobody goes there anymore; it's too crowded." Quiet, bucolic Rappahannock County was getting too crowded. At Christmas of 2003 we closed our little store in Virginia. And in 2004 we moved DukesFest to the famed Bristol Motor Speedway, where over twenty thousand people attended. Then in 2005 an estimated thirty-five thousand came to Bristol. That year we opened a "Cooter's Place" in Nashville and there was immediate interest to bring DukesFest 2006 to Music City.

DukesFest 2006 was the first time our whole cast had done a live show together. We had lost Sorrell Booke and Denver Pyle over the years, but the resurgence of our show was something that had brought our *Dukes* family closer together, in some ways even closer than we had been back in the years when we originally filmed. John Schneider, Tom Wopat, Catherine Bach, James Best, Sonny Shroyer, and Rick Hurst joined more than one hundred General Lees at the event. Jessi Colter, who was Mrs. Waylon Jennings, also joined us, along with our original *Dukes* stunt team. The Country Music Television network (CMT) was our title sponsor, and they did a great job helping us promote it.

The result was the largest event of its type ever held in Nashville. During two days in June an estimated eighty thousand fans came from all over Hazzard Nation to enjoy the music, the cars, the stars, and the spectacular stunt show. We had "rasslin'" with Jerry "The King" Lawler, a demolition derby, and the world's fastest lawnmower race. We had a parade of General Lees accompanied by a spectacular fireworks show. The highlight was when Schneider and Wopat, who are just two good ol' boys, sang "Just Two Good Ol' Boys" in front of tens of thousands of flashing cell phones. What's not to like?

Corey Eubanks, who had started as a stuntman on our show when he was nineteen, flew a General Lee over two hundred feet through the air. And I've got the pictures to prove it. CMT DukesFest was also by far the largest fan event for any film or television show ever. It was an amazing success, and again the entertainment industry was scratching their collective heads wondering why there was all this interest in our crazy old show.

The first question from the media to me was always "What in the world is going on here? What accounts for this resurgence of popularity?" By now, I could write a dissertation called "The Influence and the Cultural Ramifications of *The Dukes of Hazzard* on the Mores and Politics of Heartland America." Or something like that. But don't worry, I won't.

I will say what I have said before. That there are millions of people longing for the kind of entertainment they can watch with their kids and not be embarrassed or insulted by the content of what they see. Some might consider that quaint or reactionary or hopelessly old-fashioned. Many, if not most, of the executives who "greenlight," or produce film and television products, like to think of themselves as "on the cutting edge of popular culture," and they like to "push the envelope" and any number of other clichés they can spout to justify the barge load of garbage they concoct. They insist that they are merely responding to public tastes. But whether or not they want to assume the responsibility, these are the same people who greatly influence public tastes. The environments from which they come are almost exclusively urban, and though they could never understand it, they are provincials. The Hollywood community is a tiny sliver of an urban subculture that has long since lost touch with the

America of the factory worker, the farmer, the small businessman, and the little towns. Sure, they have the right to produce and disseminate any piece of crap they want to, but doesn't every right come with a responsibility to the culture? They would call that question naïve. And that is where the disconnect occurs.

EXHIBIT A: When an expensive big-screen version of *The Dukes of Hazzard* was made, it was a travesty. The producers mocked our show. Rather than being just good ol' boys, Bo and Luke were portrayed as foulmouthed, dope-smoking, excessively horny suburban punk types. Daisy was a tart who could have starred in a "hootchy-kootchy" show at a low-rent carnival. Uncle Jesse, whom our show portrayed as a mountain of virtue, was played as a lecherous, dirty-joke-telling pothead. And so on. Miscast and misbegotten, that feature film was voted "worst film of the year" by scores of film critics.

It is one thing to make a godawful film. It happens all day long in La La Land. But these folks then spent another $30 million marketing this meadow muffin to our audience of kids. They targeted those families who had trusted the values of our show for almost thirty years. They sold it to those kids who watch our reruns and our DVDs every day.

(By now you have probably figured out that I am not a prude. Or, to use my native tongue, "I ain't no goody-two-shoes." My all-time favorite television show is *The Sopranos.* Paulie Walnuts for Secretary of Defense!)

But I not only feel protective of our show, I feel protective of our audience of impressionable kids and trusting parents. So I raised hell about the movie. I went on a number of television talk shows, including the *Today* show, so I reached a lot of viewers with a simple message: "Don't take your kids to see this film thinking that it is a reflection of the values or the spirit of our still-popular television series."

I have been thanked for taking that stand by thousands of Americans. What I didn't say was that before the show started filming I had begged the producers in a long letter to understand that our show was a family show and was still extremely popular with a new generation of youngsters. I never got a response to my letter. But I can truthfully say that "I told them so."

After the ballyhooed opening, the feature film was quickly and mercifully gone from America's screens. We hoped that they would bury all prints of it somewhere out in the Mojave Desert, where only the coyotes could get a whiff of the stench. Meanwhile, when the Country Music Television network presented the original show in reruns, over 23 million people watched the first weekend. That would have been a gigantic opening for any theatrical release. I told them so.

This Is My Own, My Native Land

A really good character actor, Sam Melville, once gave me one of the finest compliments I ever heard. Sam was guest-starring in a *Dukes* episode when a young "Valley girl" starlet, hearing me talk, said, "You talk funny. Are you from the South or something?"

Sam smiled and said, "Honey, he's not just from the South. He *is* the South!"

I'd love to think that Sam had that right. He is gone now, but I thank him for it. Apparently there is something deeply imprinted in my DNA that has created in me a fierce love of my native Southland that is dedicated to her heritage, her reputation, and her prosperity. And though I am not blind to the faults of the old Confederacy, I find myself exasperated with the prejudice that the region faces. It is ironic but true that a region which is historically known for slavery, for Jim Crow, and for segregation is itself constantly characterized in a bigoted way by academics, politicians, and politically correct bozos of all persuasions. As one who has spent time in every major American city, I can confidently posit that race relations in the South are generally much further along than in any other part of the country.

Of course it goes without saying that the food, the music, the sports, the climate, and the literature are also better than anywhere else. Live theater is better in New York City. Lobster is better in Maine. Tex-Mex food is better in El Paso. But after that, it is all in the South. You may think those remarks arguable, but they are not arguable around here.

Because of my unabashed defense of the display of the Confederate Battle Flag, I've been asked to be on a few "talking head" shows to explain myself. Of course my attitude is that I am not the one who has any explaining to do. The people who have to defend themselves are the clueless generation that heaps insults upon the tens of millions of us who are descended from those who fought for the South.

To insist that the "Battle Flag" is a symbol of bigotry, racism, and white supremacy, tantamount to displaying the swastika, is a fallacy, a wrongheaded conclusion based neither on history nor upon any thoughtful social observation. It is an elitist "canard" and as such has been a very divisive wedge among well-meaning people.

Let me do just a bit of history. The "Battle Flag" is a St. Andrew's Cross. St. Andrew was said to have been crucified in a spread-eagled X position, as in Caravaggio's remarkable painting. It is the same Cross that is used on many flags, including the Union Jack, the national flag of Great Britain. Although the St. Andrew's cross was used in the second and third National Flags, the "Battle Flag" was never an official flag of the government of the Confederacy. Also, it is not now and never has been called "The Stars and Bars." That was another flag altogether, the first flag of the CSA government.

Because the Confederacy and her armed forces considered themselves quintessentially American, early flags of both sides were confusing to troops of both armies. In 1861 there were many instances when fire was mistakenly held because the enemy was thought friendly, and cases of "friendly fire" being poured on friendly troops. After First Manassas, the Southern Army adopted battle flags which looked less like Union flags.

Though to some the War Between the States is ancient history, it really wasn't that long ago, and its effects are still palpable, both socially and psychologically. Many of the older folks with whom I grew up had early memories of that crisis. My "Aunt Sally" was born a slave.

There are thousands of photographs of Union and Confederate "Reunions" at major battlefields well into the 1920s. The last survivor of the Civil War, Walter Williams of Texas, died at age 118 in 1959. I graduated high school that year.

General Lewis Armistead, whose courage gives me my middle name, walked at the head of Pickett's Charge directly into the Union guns at Gettysburg. He was himself "the High Tide of the Confederacy." And he died at the cannons of his best friend, Union General Winfield Scott Hancock. It seems to me that if folks are too lazy to learn this sort of basic American history, then they should keep their mouths shut about things they know nothing about. That particularly goes for the boneheaded KKK trash who run around in bedsheets desecrating the symbols of the Confederacy to spread their racist garbage. They also burn the Christian Cross and wave the American flag. But they don't reflect or represent Christianity and they don't represent America. And they don't represent the millions of descendants of the Confederacy any more than they represent those of us who sleep on bedsheets.

Prejudice is born of ignorance and fear. At its basis is the insecure need to feel superior to someone else. It applies everywhere there are people, not just to race but also to class. It is like a deeply rooted neurosis that can often be triggered by circumstances. Demagogues have played on this neurosis, and this fear, since time immemorial.

The Battle Flag is not going to go away. We of the South have a rich heritage, and for many of us, that flag is a part of it. My "white" ancestors were on the wrong side of history, and our defeat was total. After Appomattox the people of the South, black and white, had absolutely nothing. We had nothing left but pride, that dignity that no defeat can take away. There are those who wish to denigrate all things Southern, who wish to rewrite history, and who in their "political correctness" find Southern things to demonize because they might hurt someone's "feelings." Well, hey y'all, we got feelings, too. It seems to me that there can be no final healing until the sentiments of all sides are considered in a historical perspective. Slavery was evil and from a distance it can have no defense, no rationalization. But these were people of their time and place.

Symbols mean different things to different people at different times. If you have a dollar in your pocket, then you carry a picture of one of Virginia's biggest slave owners, Mr. Washington. He bought and sold human beings, but we named our capital after him, and there stands his monument.

When I fly the Battle Flag, I am honoring the effort and sacrifice of my ancestors, and not the cause of the planter aristocracy. And understand if you can that I am also honoring the victims of slavery and the noble struggle of their descendants for dignity.

And every time somebody takes down one of those old flags, you know what we do? We put two of them back up. That's why they ain't goin' away . . .

One time I overheard a black friend of mine at our old "Cooter's Place" in the Blue Ridge Mountains talking to a curious "Yankee." The lady was from Massachusetts and wanted to know if my buddy was bothered by the Rebel Flag. He said, "No, mam, it doesn't bother me a bit. I know these people and I know they aren't hateful. Don't think that black folks can't tell who is being hateful and who isn't. We are just like everybody else." That sort of said it all for me.

These Days

Time is precious, and like the sand in an hourglass it seems to go more quickly as it nears the end. To me the days come too quickly, but they come soft and welcoming like an old leather easy chair that wants you to stay put for awhile. Or a hammock in the morning mountain breeze by the dew-damped clover. Some mornings are rocking chair days, drinking good coffee on the front porch of the little farmhouse I use for an office and a library.

I think a lot these days about the people with whom I have shared my life. No one could have possibly been more blessed than I. My father and I never quite connected, but in his way he did right by me. And I've been lucky to have inherited his iron constitution. My mother, like most mothers, qualifies for Sainthood. From her I got not just the gift, but the dream to use it. From uncles and aunts and cousins, from in-laws and out-laws, came the spice of life. My brothers and I went off in our separate ways, but we are closer than ever these days and our family is stronger. Brother Buck passed on a few years back, but he lives in his beautiful children and grandchildren. Brothers Bubba and Bryan have found the serenity that is so elusive and that comes with hard-earned wisdom. My children, two beautiful ladies and a mountain of a lad, give me so much love that sometimes I feel like every day is Father's Day and Valentine's Day. And love also comes from my "other" kids and grandchildren, from Alma's crew. I have been blessed with the friendships that endure. Not only does "my cup runneth over," but so does my rain barrel and my catfish pond. I owe them all so much. For they did not laugh when I fell down.

These days I've been working with a world-class jazz pianist named Bill Harris. He plays beautifully and I sing the Great American Songbook. At least it's great until I sing it. And the Garage Band is still going strong. We'll have another album out soon.

I'm putting together a documentary film called *Hazzard Nation* about the DukesFest phenomenon and the continuing affection that folks have for us "good ol' boys." And I still perform *Ol' Diz,* a one-man show in which I portray the Hall of Fame pitcher Dizzy Dean, one of baseball and America's most colorful personalities. A musical version is in development. And I still write a bit, songs and stories. And I stay involved in politics. We did everything we could to get Jim Webb elected to the Senate from Virginia. Our country really needs stand-up, no-nonsense, straight-shooting leaders like Jim, who are independent and not indebted to special interests.

These days I try to spend an hour or so every morning in prayer and meditation. The sober old drunks were right. The Higher Power gets higher and more powerful every day. If there is one thing I am certain of, it is that the Creator wants us to be in touch. And He wants to help. I make sure to talk to Howard Powell the first thing every morning.

Our home here in the Blue Ridge is indeed enchanted. We walk the hills in gratitude for the blessings of home and family. And right at the top of my list of blessings is the joy of sharing my life with little Alma Joyce Viator of Small, North Carolina. To me, Alma is the morning and the evening star. In the words of Johnny Mercer, she is "my huckleberry friend."

One evening at the gloaming time I was in our high pasture, where nothing can be seen that is manmade. I just sat under a tree, feeling the breeze at twilight and hearing nothing except the rustling leaves. Then from far off, very faintly I heard an old familiar song wafting through the hollows. It was the distant sound of a train whistle and it came from many miles to the west, over the Blue Ridge in the Shenandoah Valley.

I was born to that sound. And even now when I hear a far-off train call, I can so quickly go back to the little boy I was, deep in a winter featherbed in a railroad shack, dreaming of a glorious destination, a place where everything would be alright. And then I would awake in the freezing room, to look through the smutted windows and the rusted screens to the morning and the train yard, and to pray that my turn would come to someday see where the tracks finally end. I have come to that place now and it is good. But it is not the end of the line. It is just a new beginning. I am just starting out.

To absent friends . . . Carpe Diem, Y'all.

Acknowledgments

My life has been blessed with many thousands of friends and I owe them all. But to acknowledge them properly would require a book the length of the *Lord of the Rings* trilogy and still there would surely be countless sins of omission. So to my friends, all of them, I say, "Thank you for believing in me when I didn't believe in myself." Just to have known y'all has given me all the riches one life can hold.

The intrepid North Carolina journalist Perry Deane Young helped me immeasurably with this idea many years ago. In the process, he taught me how to shape a book. His guidance was invaluable and lasting.

The late Ralph Dennis was a fountain of knowledge and writing advice. He instilled in me the imperative of relentlessly polishing a sentence until it is as lean as a greyhound. It is, unfortunately, a lesson I have yet to master. Rest in Peace, Hardman.

For many years, I have had the great fortune to share ideas and opinions with good and old friends like Neill Clark, David Olney, Bill Dial, Craig Nelson, Pete Thomas, and Ray Patrick. All are members in good standing of the Third Patrol.

It was David "Mudcat" Saunders who finally got this memoir jump-started by convincing me that it was high time to sit down and do it. Since Mudcat has written a book himself, and since Mudcat is the only man in the Blue Ridge Mountains who is lazier than me, I was shamed into beginning.

The serendipity of a God touched happenstance brought the wonderful Candice Fuhrman into our lives. And it just happened to turn out that she was a world-class literary agent. I'd rather be lucky than good, buckaroos . . .

Talk about luck! No first book could have been brought to reality in better hands than those of Shaye Areheart and the caring souls at Harmony Books. I certainly would not want the task of trying to edit the work of a writer whose prose shows arrant disrespect to every rule of punctuation, tense, and voice. But the long-suffering stalwarts at Harmony cut me the necessary slack. I proudly claim every grammatical abuse herein. It is true that I just fell off the proverbial turnip truck, but with Shaye's help, I landed on my feet.

My brother Steve and I had a lot of fun reminiscing about our barefoot days back on the Sugar Hill side of the tracks. He and my brother Bryan have had to put up with me longer than anyone else in these tales. They have done this with patience, understanding, and great humor.

I have family and friends all over the country. Their kindnesses have sustained me. But very special thanks must go to our "kids": Wes and Monica, Michelle and Jim, Rachel, Jeanne, Michael, and Walker. Because of them, and especially because of my amazing wife, Alma Viator, my cup runneth over and over.

About the Author

BEN JONES is an actor, writer, musician, businessman, and political pundit who lives on a farm in the Blue Ridge Mountains of Virginia with his beautiful wife, Alma Viator, and an assortment of rural critters. He has appeared in hundreds of films, television shows, and stage productions. After starring as "Cooter" on the international hit show *The Dukes of Hazzard,* he served two terms in the United States Congress before returning to the civilized world.